JEAN RHYS

AND THE NOVEL
AS WOMEN'S TEXT

JEAN
RHYS

AND THE NOVEL
AS WOMEN'S TEXT

NANCY R. HARRISON

The University of North Carolina Press

Chapel Hill and London

"Song" is reproduced from
The Complete Poems of John Wilmot,
Earl of Rochester,
edited by David M. Vieth. © 1968
Yale University Press.
Reprinted with permission.

The paper in this book meets the guidelines for
permanence and durability of the Committee on
Production Guidelines for Book Longevity of the
Council on Library Resources.

92 91 90 89 88 5 4 3 2 1

Library of Congress Cataloging-in-Publication Data
Harrison, Nancy Rebecca.
    Jean Rhys and the novel as women's text / by Nancy R. Harrison.
      p. cm.
    Bibliography: p.
    Includes index.
    ISBN 0-8078-1790-2 (alk. paper)
    1. Rhys, Jean—Criticism and interpretation. 2. Autobiographical
fiction, English—History and criticism. 3. Women in literature. 4. Self in
literature. I. Title.
PR6035.H96Z66 1988   87-30520
823'.912—dc 19   CIP

In loving memory of my mother,

Martha Guice Harrison, 1912–1984

CONTENTS

ACKNOWLEDGMENTS

THIS BOOK found its first incarnation in Austin, Texas; its second, in Tuscaloosa, Alabama. I would especially like to thank two people for their generous attention and for spirited and scrupulous readings of the book in that first stage of its being: Gayatri Chakravorty Spivak and James L. Kinneavy, both, at that time, of the University of Texas at Austin. Particular thanks are also due to Janice Haney-Peritz for her consistently responsive reading and sensitive support; to Angela Ingram for her friendship and for her immeasurable help in garnering books and other library resources; and to Karen Umminger of Bookwomen. I owe a special note of gratitude to Ann Lindsey for unfailing moral support when I needed it most. I would also like to acknowledge the continuing influence of Lois Marchino, a good friend and an early mentor. To Amanda Masterson, my thanks for her good judgment, good humor, and practical help at a crucial stage in the manuscript's revision. For persistent, energetic encouragement toward publication, my thanks to Jane Marcus.

To the English Department of the University of Alabama at Tuscaloosa, and especially to Chairperson Claudia Johnson, my gratitude for the released time that allowed the final form of the manuscript to take shape. For special attentiveness to the needs of my work and for their contributions to the project in which we are all engaged, my thanks to Elizabeth Meese and Alice Parker. For sharing many difficult times in this second shaping of the book—and, importantly, for helping me to bridge the gap between the first and second—I acknowledge a debt of gratitude to Bethsaida Fletcher for her unflagging support, encouragement, and care.

INTRODUCTION

I BEGAN THIS STUDY with a basic assumption derived in part intuitively and confirmed often enough to arouse my further interest in verifying its general application: more often than not, women's novels in this century seemed to be more directly autobiographical than are men's novels. I wondered why this might be, and what effect it might have on a woman's writing practice itself (not simply on the content of the novel), and on another woman's reading response to that practice. My immediate background was in critical and rhetorical theory within the framework of feminist theory; my compelling interest, the practical effect of writing on both writer and reader. In particular I wanted to satisfy my curiosity as to how we respond to our "rhetorical situation" in our aesthetic practices. The "rhetorical situation," as Lloyd Bitzer defined it almost twenty years ago in an influential essay, is "a complex of persons, events, objects and relations presenting an actual or potential exigence which can be completely or partially removed if discourse, introduced into the situation, can so constrain human decision or action as to bring about the significant modification of the exigence."[1] Bitzer seems to assume that a community of people tends to introduce rhetoric, "discourse," into a specific situation primarily to stabilize it; even more, to maintain the general cultural equilibrium implicit in the phrase "the status quo." This phrase predicates a maintenance of the dominant culture and its idiom through a reinvocation of its conventions and the terms in which it sees itself. In Bitzer's development of his definition of a situation that is perceived by the community as "real" and to which it responds to rid itself collectively of a "defect" or "obstacle,"[2] we see that the definition of the "rhetorical situation" for white Western European men becomes a description of one of the ways they maintain control over other groups within the society that their culture dominates. For women in such a society, the maintenance of "their" culture cannot be seen as a response to our "rhetorical situation," the exigencies of which are, as a matter of course, not the same. *Our* "situational context"[3] (to use another phrase that connotes a configuration similar to Bitzer's, but with a difference allowing some expansion in our thinking) is of a different nature. Our rhetorical context, the situational context in which we find ourselves, is made up of a different "complex of persons, events, objects and relations"; therefore the "actual or potential exigence" we discern is not, and cannot be, construed to correspond to that of the dominant culture. Their "rhetorical situation" has often explicitly, as well as inferentially, demanded our capitulation to their more pressing needs, the "exigencies" of their situational context. The status quo is precisely what does not answer or respond to the exigencies of our situation.

In a literary context, audience-oriented theories and analyses that concern themselves with reader response offer a route toward possible answers to my original question.[4] Indeed, the framework of inquiry that readership or reader-response theories emphasize is one into which I have settled myself, but without direct recourse to most of the specific formalizations of the concept. My reasons for eschewing their specific aid are twofold.

A radical split separates how women theorists and men in the same profession see the possibilities of the relationship between reader and writer.[5] This difference itself seems clearly to mark our realizations of what for each group constitutes its "rhetorical situation" and the "exigencies" it identifies there. What for most masculine critics (and readers perhaps?) is an "implied or 'intended' reader" (Wolfgang Iser), which or who is correspondent with the "implied author" (Wayne Booth), who "sets himself out with a different air depending on the needs of particular works"[6] would indeed seem to be a "fiction" when compared to the way a woman reader identifies herself in relation to what and who she reads. In an essay entitled "The Writer's Audience Is Always a Fiction," Walter Ong observes that, from the critic's point of view, such a reader "has to play the role in which the author has cast him, which seldom coincides with his role in the rest of actual life."[7] The masculine theorists who are working with these ideas are looking for "critical tools," as one of them has put it.[8] For the analyst who is a feminist (possibly and simply a woman), the audience for a woman writer's work, and their (her) response to it, is no more a "fiction" than is the woman herself—writer or reader. In particular, the effect of the woman's work is not merely an aesthetic one, wanting only critical tools to release its full implications. A woman's view of the reading-writing relationship is more practical and more political than that.

Jane Gallop brings many aspects of this view into focus in a response to a special issue of *Critical Inquiry*—"Writing and Sexual Difference."[9] Gallop cites editor Elizabeth Abel's endorsement of Gayatri Spivak's "unsettling" contribution to the issue, a translation of the short story "Draupadi" by Mahasveta Devi: "With this story the volume shifts from West to East, from criticism to fiction, from implicit to explicit political perspective."[10] "Yet what is perhaps most unsettling about this text," Gallop responds, "is not the shift from metaphor to fact but rather that the switch to an explicit political perspective corresponds to a switch from nonfiction to fiction." She points out that the epigraph, a quotation from Barbara Johnson's *The Critical Difference* that stresses literary concerns, and the final entry, "Draupadi," could be said to represent "the two allegiances between which 'this moment of feminist inquiry' is torn: the literary and the political."[11] The "critical difference" in feminist inquiry, Gallop suggests in her conclusion, is that "in her inheritance from both feminism and criticism," the feminist critic "lives the at once enabling and disabling tension of a difference within."[12] As Gallop explains it, the "difference within" identifies the literary enterprise with the father and with masculine norms; the fictive—and the feminist political—identifies it with the mother.

This tension can be seen as both "enabling and disabling" insofar as we understand "inquiry" to mean the making of theory and the formal reading and analysis of texts, particularly literary ones. My own position is that, if we look to our fiction itself for some of the answers to our formal inquiries, we rightly identify and place those answers as formal answers to formal inquiry, derived from an "explicitly political perspective." As people interested in literature, if we attempt to read our literature—women's fiction—as "common readers" first and foremost, keeping our later critical eye on that first reading, we can minimize, avoid, even eliminate (not merely ignore or only "resist," as Judith Fetterley helpfully suggests we do)[13] the disabling effects of the father-text of literary criticism. In reading a woman's novel and recognizing that it is a novel we can *call* a "woman's novel"—one that is gender specific and shows itself to be—we can find a realization that enables us without disabling us at the same time. Such a response is exemplified in this volume by the work of Jean Rhys and by the response she invites from us. This response is political, if I may use the word generally. Such a "politics" is what women writers and readers are making clear to one another, not in the dialogue with men that Kate Millett describes in *Sexual Politics*,[14] but in the dialogue among ourselves. We even say the word *political* in discussion of our literary inquiries, as instanced by Gallop's review of the issues sketched above. In theoretical literary discussion in the more pervasively masculine arena, the word is rarely used except in dialogue concerning or including Marxist criticism or theory, or, increasingly, feminist criticism. Discussion in conventional settings seems to be firmly couched within traditions so politically entrenched and taken for granted as to need no specific mention. Indeed, the transparency (conversely the opacity) of the politics is not even "semi-transparent," as Virginia Woolf's "envelope" of life would have it; rather, it is the informing and enveloping medium through which they conduct their academically "objective" (and, by implication, non-political) discussions.

In recognizing the connection between the subjective, particular instance and the political conduct of our own kinds of discussion, we only name what we, and they, already know. Literature is political. For women, at least, "literary" analysis can no longer pretend to find itself in opposition to "real life." Rejecting Walter Ong's idea that "the role in which the author has cast [the reader] . . . seldom coincides with [the reader's] role in the rest of actual life," the woman reader (or the feminist reader of either sex) recognizes that a novel we can *call* "a woman's novel" most particularly does have to do with "the rest of actual life." In a woman's novel we readily see our own concerns. It is "political" in this general sense of a move from the individual to the collective. Indeed, I see, as Gallop does, that the "critical difference" between male and female readings is to be found in some combination of the "literary" and the real or the actual, which is to say, the political. The tension that results need not be thought of, or experienced, as disabling. On the contrary, our fiction itself, and our responses to it, can be enabling to our other enterprises, as the response to "Draupadi" shows. Our response can be put to both pragmatic and theoretical use. Such a realization thrusts our literary analytical concerns not out into the cold, but into the embrace of a thoroughly *enabling* meeting of our reading and our politics.

"The shift from West to East, from criticism to fiction, from implicit to explicit political perspective" mirrors the move in which the "critical difference" in our inquiries becomes enabling, without the disabling dilution or constraint of the other half of our dual heritage.

For the shift is located precisely in that move from an emphasis on criticism to a centering in fiction. I see a move that not only shifts our attention to fiction itself but also reinforces our sense of where our fiction and our politics come from. Just as our fiction moves us into an explicitly political sphere, so the fiction itself emerges from an implicitly political situation—the experience of our individual lives. The move from what is implicit to what we can see, in our recognition of it, as explicit, and thereby (and not paradoxically) implicitly political, is what I hope to show in my exploration of the work of Jean Rhys. Virginia Woolf said it, as she first said so many other things for us: "I sometimes think only autobiography is literature—novels are what we peel off, and come at last to the core, which is only you or me."[15]

My inquiry begins in an exploratory mode. I make assumptions and assertions in order to set a course that might allow me to answer my original question: Is a woman's writing different from a man's? We seem to think so, but there has been little examination of how the writing practice itself enacts the theories that we, and European (especially French) women theorists, have posited. In the United States, description, especially thematic description (mythological, archetypal, and sociological categorization, for example), and discussion of the content of our novels have been extensive. In France, there has been little or no attendant examination of an *actual* woman's writing; suggestions remain hypothetical. Our response to the woman writer's presentation of her novel and of herself in that novel as it is revealed in her writing practice—what the French call *l'écriture*—has been all but missing. Here I offer not only an interpretation of Jean Rhys's work but also a description of what she does when she writes. The two exemplary novels, *Voyage in the Dark* and *Wide Sargasso Sea*, themselves reveal how the woman, Jean Rhys, writes. Each novel's structure itself makes overt display of the process in its correspondence with, and as it corresponds to, the fictive "actual life" of Rhys's heroine-narrator. The structure of the novel in each instance itself serves as illustration of what it is "about."

I also want to show how Rhys's reader responds to this writing practice—how we respond not only to the novel's thematic content, but also to how it is put together; moreover, how we can apply what we see and recognize in her work to our own lives. I would call her novels political in the most basic sense, as I also call them [auto]bio-graphical. By [auto]biography, I mean the principle of women's fic-tion in which the "author" steps, not down, but away from the cen-trist position of authority, effectively bracketing out her "self," the autobiographical "I," to share the writing of her text with her readers.

I had first asked, "How does a woman's novel differ from a man's?" The further questions I asked of myself and of the novels I read became the demand, "Show me." I looked for the woman's work that seemed to do that with the greatest force and precision. I found that quality in Rhys's novels. Following my own admonition concerning women's writing—that it is in a basic constitutive sense "autobio-graphical"—I have attempted to recapitulate as much as possible my own thinking in arriving at the conclusions offered here.

My presentation reflects my feeling of the way toward the goal I set myself, beginning with the questions I pose, and reaching the exem-plary illustration. I intend such an approach to be of some use to the reader, who I hope derives a use of her own from the itinerary I trace. At the outset, I do not attempt to posit a theory; I wanted the theory, if it was there, to present itself to me. Only after I have moved far enough into the process of my own exploration of what I am doing, and why, do I feel it appropriate to pose the example and to posit the theory. As the exploratory aspects of my discussion lead us to firmer ground, that offered by the concrete example of the writing of Jean Rhys, I hope the general reader, as well as the more theoretically versed reader, will be satisfied with my critical analysis and theoretical description of Rhys's work, and with the broader ap-plication that formulation implies.

I begin, then, on a note both overly assertive and rife with general-ized assumptions, using my own naiveté, both actual and assumed, as a method of immediate self-exposure. "Preconceived opinions, fore-gone determinations, are all I have at this hour to stand by: there I plant my foot," Jane Eyre says to Rochester in Charlotte Brontë's novel.[16] One and a quarter centuries later, the poet Adrienne Rich writes, "a woman. I choose to walk here. And to draw this circle."[17] I attempt to overstep both of those boundaries. But first I plant my own foot within the circle I know and choose, to show the reader the place from which I take my first steps. The discussion that follows will, I hope, warrant the initial posture of hesitancy *and* presumption.

AUTHOR'S NOTE

MORE FREQUENTLY than most writers, Jean Rhys used ellipses as an integral part of her text. Consequently, in quotations from her work, I distinguish between Rhys's use of ellipses and my own: ellipses without brackets are in Rhys's original text; bracketed ellipses indicate that material has been omitted. This usage has been observed *only* in the case of Rhys. Ellipses in any other instance are used conventionally.

JEAN RHYS

AND THE NOVEL AS WOMEN'S TEXT

CHAPTER ONE.

TO BE OUR OWN

AUDIENCE: THE

THEATER OF THE

WOMAN'S TEXT

ET US SUPPOSE that the woman's novel acts out her
life, that it is in this sense dramatic—not lyrical (merely
self-expressive), as women's novels are often said to
be; nor abstract (merely a vehicle for philosophical exploration), as
men's novels often are.[1] Further, let us assume that if a woman's
novel acts out her life, it is also autobiographical, as it is gestural and
performative. We can find one explanation of this aspect of the woman's novel by examining some of our concepts of audience.

The relationship between reader and writer, between the writer's
book and the reader's response to that book, is usually considered to
be different in kind as well as in degree from that of a theater audience viewing a play. The response of the theater audience is public;
that of the reader, private. A play is written with a public audience
in mind. The experience will be shared with other members of the
audience, spontaneously, at any given moment. Reactions and response are expected to be immediate, or else one could not "follow"
the performance. The theatrical performance and its text are thus
drawn in broader strokes to elicit this response. The reader, in contrast, is always aware that she can turn back to a previously read
page, to savor ideas or phrasing or her response to them, or for
clarification. This security, as well as more complex responsibility, is
not offered to or expected of the playgoer.

We might assume that a playgoer has an easier task and an easier
path to enjoyment of the play before her; it is a mediated event. The
relationship is not one to one, as it is in the meeting of reader and

writer, or perhaps one should say of reader and *book*. This meeting between book and reader is one of the most private, most intimate of acts. Playgoing, in contrast, is public and communal: the actors, the stage, the production, the theater, the rest of the audience, the sharing of the experience—all intervene between playwright and audience, between a possible text of the play and the audience.

The book is another matter. Printed and bound, the author's name announced on the title page, it is *written*. One sees its lines, feels its weight; one feels a kind of directness. A book is, paradoxically one feels, like another person speaking directly to you, as in a conversation. It is not, we think, play-acting, although it may be fiction. Even if it is "mere" entertainment—a mystery, a spy thriller, or even a gothic romance—the reading of it is our own act, under our control to some extent. The playgoer is in a position of less control. She agrees to submit for the duration of a performance, to "give herself up" to it, at least superficially, by her mere presence in the theater; or she can walk out. There are no other options.

Thus there seems to be a radical difference between the theater audience and the audience of readers. Traditionally, this has perhaps been the case. In another context, Paul Hernadi observes, "Perhaps because our public reaction to performed plays is more observable and less idiosyncratic than our private reaction to printed or written texts, drama criticism has always been very concerned with the effects of works on an audience."[2] Yet my suggestion is that, in considering a woman's novel—what it is, what it has been, what it might be—one of the most fruitful ways for us to look at it, to "view" it, in fact, is to consider first its audience and that audience's responses to the writer's presentation. The presentation of a novel is just that: something actualized and presented, a *performance*, which is finally (or first of all) a gesture that another woman can recognize.[3]

This gestural, performative presentation, I will argue, can be called dramatic in its invocation of an audience whose response is attuned to a sense of community. Here is a community of women in which interaction with one another is the basis for, and a reflection of, a need for mutuality of response and recognition. Regardless of the writer's intention, the novels that are received in this way (Doris Lessing's *The Golden Notebook*, for example) are the women's novels that I am talking about. The intersection of the private and the public is where we may look for the woman writer's audience. That audience consists of those readers who respond to the gesture of such a book, the acting out on the page(s) by one woman of a woman's life they can recognize, another woman's life made public and disclosed privately, between the covers of a book.

This intersection between public and private allows for the audience response usually accorded to the mediated, staged performance. It is also the impulse of the woman writer who "stages" a life (usually her own) so that it is perceived as such—as a performance shaping that life on the page. This gesture is unavailable to white Western European men at this time in their history. The woman's staged performance achieves what can be perceived as a definite, though not always definable, feminine "style" of writing. Furthermore, it has led to innovation in the novel in this century.

Similar novelistic performances are, of course, encouraged by the rhetorical situations of other communities of people. I venture, however, that the women in any of these communities, by virtue of a plurality of impetus, will still have an aesthetic advantage over the men. And while there is (always has been) a male avant-garde, this position itself is predicated upon reaction to male predecessors and contemporaries. Women writers, in contrast, are moving from a position based not in reaction but in a consciousness that had not, previously, engendered continuous, recognized and recognizable formal patterns of representation. Making formal patterns of our own is an innovation that is not defined by its relationship to what has come before. It is not the masculinist avant-garde, not an advance guard for an already established "army" of writers.

The "self"-consciousness of the woman writer *is* different from the self-consciousness associated with male novelists in this century. When we think of the history of the novel as it has developed in Western European and American culture, that "narrative perspective [which] had become so intensely subjective," "we think," David H. Miles writes, "of Proust's private remembrances, Joyce's interior monologues, Kafka's narrated monologues."[4] The interiority of male subjectivity is met by the interiority of the (male) reader's response. A man's life is different from a woman's, and it shows. The performative aspect of the woman's novel, the feminine gesture that distances for perspective and *at the same time* invites the reader to personal participation, allows the drama of women's writing to surface in form as well as in content. For the woman reader, the woman's novel in-

vokes an audience whose response is communal, though private—
"communal" because it is perceived by each reader as private and
personal; as we say, "the personal is political." The juncture of private
and public is the locus of the reading of a woman's novel by a woman
reader. In woman's writing, female subjectivity and the female autobiographical impulse is rendered in a context different from a man's,
with a different result. It doesn't seek to exclude or to appropriate
what it finds to be different from itself. As Virginia Woolf observed
in *A Room of One's Own*:

> Anonymity runs in [women's] blood. . . . They are not even now
> as concerned about the health of their fame as men are, and,
> speaking generally, will pass a tombstone or a signpost without
> feeling an irresistible desire to cut their names on it, as Alf, Bert
> or Chas. must do in obedience to their instinct, which murmurs
> if it sees a fine woman go by, or even a dog, Ce chien est à moi.
> And, of course, it may not be a dog . . . it may be a piece of land
> or a man with curly black hair. It is one of the great advantages
> of being a woman that one can pass even a very fine negress
> without wishing to make an Englishwoman of her.[5]

One place where this difference is visibly registered is in the feminine audience's response to another woman's writing. Moreover, the
relationship between the work produced by the subject—the writer—
and her audience makes for that response. A seemingly communal
response is called up in the solitary woman reader by her private
response to the performance and the gesture of another woman's
work. In seeing ourselves for the first time as a community, as a
group of people with common interests, the "simple" gesture of producing a written work has become for us the gesture of spectacle and
performance. Our voices are becoming "visible," as well as merely
and traditionally (no matter how actively) whispering behind the
throne or the closed door.

"FLYING, STEALING"—the double meaning of the
French verb *voler* as used by some French feminist theorists suggests
the impetus and emphasis of our use of "their" (men's) language
for our own purposes, especially in our literature.[6] More modestly,
American feminist critics acknowledge that "the language of literature is a language dedicated to unearthing the patterns of and form-

ing connections in our world."[7] Yet "our world," for feminists and most other women readers and writers, is indeed the *feminine* world. It is the world of women, which was obscured until we learned men's codes well enough to body forth our own constructions, our own literary language to display our own patterns and to form our own connections. Our "rhetorical problem," as one male "feminist" critic has put it, is "telling the truth and at the same time" being "heard."[8]

The aesthetics of literary feminism is a joint enterprise: there would be no patterns in the aesthetic sense without our artists' displaying those patterns, the same patterns we see in our own lives and recognize upon formal presentation. Likewise, the connections are those that we form in response to that recognition. The enterprise, then, urges autobiography and founds itself in the autobiographical impulse. We may, in a second step, bracket out the *autos*, the hard-edged "self," the "I" (which, when deprived of community, is merely an abstraction) when we consider the result of the active participation involved in this "autobiographical act." The joint or collective enterprise might more reasonably be called *biographical* in the largest sense, and we might more accurately refer to women's novel writing and reading as "[auto]biographical."

In this display of our lives, the display of the self implicit in the act of a-woman-writing, a woman displaying herself, making a "spectacle" of herself, there remains the essential affirmation to be found in our reading of a woman writer. We would seem to have "gotten the message" and are turning it to our own use, reclaiming the aesthetic and creating our own morality of aesthetics. The dramatic use of our difficult—even, as some would consider, our untenable—position allows us to hail one another, figuratively, across a (no matter how crowded) room and begin to speak to one another, to make *connections*.

WOMEN'S FICTION of 1820–70, those years called the "feminine fifties," contains not the "hidden feminism" that some readers would like to find but an "unspectacular feminism."[9] What I suggest we can see in women's novels today, in contrast, is certainly "spectacular," in the sense of a "public show," and the reader is indeed "present at a performance or incident," rather than being a mere onlooker. The spectator in this case is a participant; she is part of the show. The audience is a select group, self-chosen by active participation; onlookers may become involved when they see them-selves in the mirror of another woman's work. A self-educating male reader, if he works hard to learn the patterns and the language (as women have done for centuries), can perhaps become a part of this audience, although the extent of his participation may be self-limiting.

In any event, participation for any reader—woman or man—be-gins in the privacy found between the covers of a book. From this private entry onto the public scene, the individual reader may pro-ceed as cautiously as she likes. But for the woman reading another woman's book, the essential conversation has begun; a bargain has been struck.

A "woman's novel," a "feminine novel," a "woman's text" exhibits certain qualities or characteristics. The "woman's novel," the "femi-nine novel," the "woman's text" is (1) *written by a woman and recognizes itself as a novel by a woman*; it recognizes its status as marginal, as a woman's novel in a man's world. Furthermore, it is (2) *written for an audience of women* and thereby refuses to acknowledge/play along with the rules of male novelists/male critics/male readers and resists (some-times even ignores) the possibility of a reading by a male reader/critic/writer.

The woman novelist and her novel are not "good sports" in a "sportsman's world"; the woman's novel is female specific, not male specific. It is likely to be deviant in terms of traditional masculine values, since the historical norm has been male, but it is not devi-ous—that is a man's word, used in an attempt to shame women (and "others") into conformity. Not being a good sport simply means that a writer is not responding to the male reader's expectations or needs and has not assumed them as her own. Her novel is speaking, rather, to what she acknowledges as the woman-in-herself. If a woman writ-ing seems to be a good sport, she may intend irony in the extreme. If she *is* a good sport, she isn't a feminine/feminist writer. For me, such a good sport's novel is not a "woman's text" or a "feminine novel." It *is* a novel written by a woman, but it is also what can be called a "male novel," a man's novel, a novel for the masculinist reader. A question arises here: How is a "feminine novel" different from many marginal novels written by men? A single criterion may suffice: Such a novel is not written by a woman. The first gesture or signal for a feminine novel's audience is the mere fact of female authorship.

I apply the appellation "feminist" to any woman's novel that fulfills the two criteria mentioned earlier, whether the writer of that novel would claim such an appellation, or the intention suggested by it, herself. It is, finally, the audience's perception of the performance of her novel that concerns us. In fairness, we must note that it is not the writer's intention, even an implied intention, that we want to emphasize, but that of her audience. What is significant is not the intention of the writer as she may interpret it outside the book itself, but the *gestural significance of her text* for its readers. The way the text displays itself may, in turn, reveal an "intention" of the writer that she herself would never claim, although she cannot dismiss it.

WE CAN find a definition, or at least a description, of the "gestural significance" of a woman's text in our culture if we look to the audience for that text. We look to the women who make up the readership, the constituency, of the "woman's text." Any number of readers, one by one, makes up this audience. Again, as with the writer, the first criterion is that the audience is constituted of women: the reader is a woman. I would like to say that this audience includes all women, but I cannot say that. I hope the possibility of that inclusion exists, however. Aside from "being a woman," the reader is characterized by an active interest in reading as a way of knowing the world and as an occupation that aids her in her ordering of the world. If not a "feminist," the reader is nevertheless interested in her own sex, in the likenesses and differences she shares, or doesn't share, with other women. Her interest in other women is likely to be, if not first, at least high on her agenda. She is alert to what other women have to say. Other women are important to her. She recognizes their voices and their demeanor as part of her own. In short, she sees herself as part of a community of women, whatever other allegiances she may hold. She listens to other women; she *looks* at other women and sees and hears them. This includes close attention to their work.

These are the readers who are likely to recognize the gesture and, having recognized its interpellative quality, attend to it and thereby give the gesture its significance. The gesture and its attendant significance are present to these readers in *"the way the text displays itself."* Seemingly arbitrary though such a designation of our audience may be, this self-chosen audience can represent for us one aspect of the rhetorical situation in which women who write novels and women who read novels find themselves.

Why is the "woman" reader different from the "man" reader? Why is this audience of women, this reader, any different from the typical or usual male (masculinist) reader? Annette Kolodny offers us a setting in which we might stage this difference, an analysis of Susan Keating Glaspell's story, "A Jury of Her Peers." The story, of a woman accused (and guilty) of murdering her husband, is "a fictive rendering of the dilemma of the woman writer,"[10] as well as a lesson in how women readers read a woman writer.

It is useful to set Kolodny's analysis of Glaspell's story alongside Jacques Lacan's analysis of Poe's "The Purloined Letter" and Jacques Derrida's analysis of Lacan's analysis.[11] One can see an interesting progression of ideas, from woman as a kind of interpretive currency passed from man to man (Lacan), to exposure of this male-authored interpretive strategy (Derrida), to exclusion, even outwitting, of the male "authors" of our experience by the women on the scene. As Kolodny points out, Glaspell's story does not

> necessarily exclude the male as reader . . . in a way [it is] directed specifically at educating him to become a better reader . . . [it does] . . . nonetheless, insist that, however inadvertently, he is a *different kind* of reader and that, where women are concerned, he is often an inadequate reader. . . . [It] is the survival of the *woman as text* . . . that is at stake; and the competence of her reading audience alone determines the outcome. Thus, [it] examine[s] the difficulty inherent in deciphering other highly specialized realms of meaning—in this case, women's conceptual and symbolic worlds. And further, the intended emphasis . . . is the inaccessibility of female meaning to male interpretation.[12]

"Reading" is to be taken in two senses: "reading" of the situation by the people around the central character, and "reading" of the story presenting the paradigm. For it is in their act of reading as a receptive, capable audience—not as societally accepted or formally schooled interpreters (as male readers are often considered to be)—that the women in Glaspell's story find a value that strengthens them. Their reading reaffirms their sense of their lives and offers validation, through active participation in the text, of the life of another woman.

Any concept of woman as text—whether sapping (as is often the case when the book is male authored) or strengthening (as another woman's book may be)—is of crucial, instructive, and *practical* concern to women in ways that use and "interpretation" of "woman as text" cannot be for the male "author" or interpreter. Women have a practical interest that goes beyond the pragmatic in reading the text of another woman. Our reading is formalized in the case of a text bound between the covers of a book, but the strategies and "clues" are not learned in a classroom or encased between those covers. They are learned in the living of each woman's life. The woman reader brings her own life, and the lives of other women she has known, to the life of another woman as it is rendered in the book she holds in her hands.

In another essay on the interpretive strategies of the feminist critic, Kolodny remarks:

> All the feminist is asserting, then, is her own equivalent right to liberate new (and perhaps different) significances from these same texts [texts that have been presented through the filter of aesthetic criteria other than her own]; and, at the same time, her right to choose which features of a text she takes as relevant because she is, after all, asking new and different questions of it. In the process, she claims neither definitiveness nor structural completeness for her different readings and reading systems, but only their usefulness in recognizing the particular achievements of woman-as-author and their applicability in conscientiously decoding woman-as-sign.[13]

Kolodny's plea is for a pluralism of interpretive strategies, but her emphasis is on the necessity for including a familiarity with "female" codes and their decoding. I address my remarks to, and venture an emphasis on, an audience of women. Without such an emphasis as part of an attempt to stabilize our own conduct of meanings and interpretations, our codes are likely to go under in a new wave of "mere" pluralism.

I am specifically interested in certain texts—those that are women authored, women decoded, and patently concerned with "woman-as-sign." One of my contentions is that, consciously or unconsciously, the woman writer whose book is centered in the consciousness of a woman will offer signals that the woman reader alone, in her psychosexual predicament, will be able to recognize as a *reader* first of all, whether she is in the interpreting business or not. Most women readers are not professional literary critics, and it is only as reader first, critic second that a woman recognizes the qualities constituting the "woman's novel," the implicitly "feminine novel," the "woman's text."

The woman writer who chooses a male protagonist and writes from a fictitious male consciousness is another matter. Such novels, whether prompted by psychological, political, or aesthetic motives, are not the ultimate objects of my study. Neither is the audience for them, although in many instances their audience and the audience for the woman's novel as I describe it certainly overlap. These audiences are not the same, however. Their motivations are different, and their responses to the woman's novel are likely to be demonstrably different from their response to other kinds of novels.

In reading a woman's novel, the reader—like the theater-goer—is able to relax (the seat at least is comfortable) and to identify with the narrative consciousness as well as with the protagonist, who may not be the same, of course, although frequently in women's novels they are accomplices. Without noticing it, perhaps, a woman experiences fewer levels of displacement when reading a woman's novel. In reading a man's novel she has to say, "Well, yes, it *is* about a human being. I'm a human being. Let's see how this man (a human being) works out his life." With a woman's novel she is likely to say, "Oh yes," simply, feeling that there are no inappropriate or self-contradicting equations to go through. For example, when an argument with the author occurs, she might say, "No, I'm not like that. *She* (one of the characters) is not like that. That's not what's going on." But, as a good (i.e., trained, obedient) reader of the male novel, she says, "Oh well, let the author have his way—maybe it will come right in the end." If a woman reader says "No" to a woman writer, she is likely at least to admonish herself to take another look. Then she makes another decision, usually a quick one, and knows that for her the author is either right or wrong. Men we have been trained to take on faith.

Let us return to the gesture and its significance, to the way the text displays itself. As I have already indirectly suggested, the mere fact or display of a woman writing a book, even today, is a signal. That is, however, not enough. A woman writing about another woman is yet another signal: "Our lives are important. This is a story of somebody like me." This is nothing new: the outstanding writers of the nineteenth century (Jane Austen, the Brontës, George Eliot), not to mention the writers of the "feminine fifties," certainly wrote about women and offered their heroines' lives as both instruction and entertainment. The fact of female authorship or a female protagonist can be boiled down to the category of statistics, which can carry symbolic, if arbitrary, meaning for us. Our response to such statistics may be initial or reflexive, nourishing for only a short time and having only a superficial effect on the reader. Reading a list of titles with their authors' names alongside offers the same effect; this effect is not minimal, however, even if it is short lived, and it *is* cumulative. However, it is in women's reading of contemporary novels about women, written by women, not in merely acknowledging another woman's achievement, that we begin to get some view of *how we are reading*, and why we read that way.

LITERATURE DESIGNED primarily for an audience of women readers would, as Adrienne Rich says, be accompanied by "a radical critique of literature, feminist in its impulses," that "would take the work first of all as a clue to how we live, how we have been living, how we have been led to imagine ourselves, how our language has trapped as well as liberated us . . . and how we can begin to see— and therefore live—afresh."[14]

Let us think for a moment of how we imagine ourselves and how we might lead one another to imagine ourselves. How can our language continue to "liberate" us? What we hope to do as readers, I think, is to imagine ourselves, to see ourselves, and to live accordingly. We hope to use our reading, not as an indulgence in utopian fantasies, but as a way to accomplish this imagining, this "seeing" and living, right now, and in the future. Reading, I suggest, is an integral part of this imagining and, most pertinently, of our living. Reading for us is not an exercise, but a practical sharing of ideas and a philosophical stance toward the world and each other. As a culture, a community, we have a lot of catching up to do—not with male culture but with ourselves, individually and collectively. Our thinking and our reading are as much a theater of action for our community as is the formal political arena. We are underprepared politically because our sense of community, while not amorphous, lacks centralizing images and consciously recognized patterns of communication. "Submerged" for as many centuries as the community of women has been, our signals have been "wrapped," "slant,"[15] serving as a backdrop for the world of men and for the dominant modalities of masculine culture.

Growing out of this underground culture, our modes of mutual recognition and codes of interaction have not been formalized. Only in the nineteenth century did women gain full access to the public line of communication that is the novel. Only in the twentieth century has formal experimentation with the novel encouraged a large enough body of readers to attend to a woman writer who embodies overtly in her text the previously "hidden" clues and signals familiar to the community of women at large. The avid reader, the educated reader, the feminist reader, the curious or interested reader, the concerned reader, the woman reader who is looking for something is going to find it, perhaps for the first time in history. No longer is the woman reader in isolation, for the enterprise is based in a collective recognition, in the admission of ourselves to ourselves. We allow entry to ourselves and to one another, and we admit what those selves are and remain true to them.

W H E N I S A Y that I want to emphasize the audience, I do not mean I want to de-emphasize the author. On the contrary, I emphasize the interaction between writer and audience—between what the writer does in her book and how she does it—and how the audience, the readers, perceive her presentation and what we ultimately make of it. In examining this interaction we may discover how we are reading and why we read that way, how the woman's text encourages us to read her text the way we do, and why the text offers us the opportunity for a particular kind of reading.

I N D I S C U S S I N G the novelist Dorothy Richardson, Elaine Showalter makes an observation that is especially relevant to the discussion of how we read:

> The most troublesome problem has been isolating the qualities, if there are any, that make the writing female in an absolute sense. It is one thing to show that fiction before 1910 differed from fiction after 1910, and to label the differences metaphorically "male" and "female" (or "masculine" and "androgynous" or "bisexual"). It is another thing altogether to talk about fe-

male style when you mean female content. And it is the hardest of all to prove that there are inherent sexual qualities to prose apart from its content, which was the crucial point Richardson wished to make.[16]

Nowhere is the problem more acute than in the distinction between style and content. As Showalter observes, indeed, "It is another thing altogether to talk about female style when you mean female content." As to proving "that there are inherent sexual qualities to prose apart from its content," we can observe, along with Virginia Woolf, that "the nerves that feed the brain would seem to differ in men and women."[17] There are differences; we know it, we feel it, but there is no point in attempting to assign origins to those differences. As women, we know (as men do) that for reasons of history and culture alone we view the world differently, we live in the world differently, we experience ourselves and each other differently. What matters is not our differences from men, but our similarities to other women. In the forms of our novels we can find at least one of our means of recognizing one another, of recognizing ourselves in one another.

In the contemporary context, I suggest we look for something in the form or structure that offers the gesture the woman reader recognizes, and that, like all good form, enhances its content. Form is closely allied with the presentation of woman-as-text. Her form is multiple, no longer a matter of covert meanings, not a split personality. Rather, it is a presentation of a multiplicity of selves that the twentieth-century woman explores, accepts, and welcomes, in contradistinction to the more pressing split (into two) that was the more usual presentation and life situation of the nineteenth-century woman writer. An experimenter such as Dorothy Richardson tried to evade this "doubleness" by an unending presentation of "things as they are" *for a woman,* an unfolding that has no end as she presents it. Richardson's twelve-volume set of novels called *Pilgrimage,* which required thirty years to complete, presents a heroine whose life parallels the author's. This was a useful gesture in itself, but without the violently self-displaying tactics of such practitioners as James Joyce (to whom she is compared, as a female "counterpart" in the "history of the novel"), her experiment failed. Indeed, Richardson's novel and her reputation didn't "go anywhere." A woman writing and reading today would not find herself at such a dead end. Another model for a spectacular display was in the making elsewhere: it was a direct response to, as well as an outgrowth of, an established nineteenth-century tradition of women's writing.

Recent studies coherently and persuasively describe the patterns extant in the important nineteenth-century novels.[18] The main bequest of that legacy, the "female schizophrenia of authorship,"[19] is already only one identifying characteristic of early twentieth-century novels. Indeed, this characteristic is celebrated and transformed in the pioneering work of writers such as Gertrude Stein, Virginia Woolf, and Jean Rhys. Currently, the hallmark of the most striking contemporary women writers is forthrightness, a clarity of experiment openly relating to their lives, an open plot rather than one to be deciphered. The methods of nineteenth-century writers—"simultaneously conforming to and subverting patriarchal literary standards"[20]—need no longer be central to our imaginative formulations.

According to Sandra Gilbert and Susan Gubar, our nineteenth-century writers produced "literary works that are in some sense palimpsestic, works whose surface designs conceal or obscure deeper, less accessible (and less socially acceptable) levels of meaning."[21] All too often we in this century still employ these methods, both on the page and off. We are still exhorted to "work within the system," disguising our own confirmations and aims. Some of us have always excelled at it, and perhaps more are doing so. The reading method best suited for such writing seems to be a method such as Showalter suggests—one revealing the "other plot," the "hidden plot," one allowing us to "see meaning in what has previously been empty space." On the other hand, perhaps we are walking naked in public; perhaps we have nothing, or very little, left to hide. Perhaps *that* is the other plot, and indeed it may be anonymous. Perhaps that is the best-kept secret of all.

Feminist critics now choose to fix their eye on the "other plot," which, for us, "stands out in bold relief." The difficulty is in keeping one's eye on the object of one's choosing. It is, finally, a matter of choice and coordination, conditioned and developed, not a matter of innate ability. The trouble with this process lies in its difficulty, in the squint of concentration involved, even in the choosing itself. What of the novel whose plot is revealed, the text walking naked in public, while announcing its shape and form for any who care to look upon it? This is the novel of our present, of our coming-to-be-the-present, and perhaps of our future; its readers are those who look at it and, in their looking, see themselves as well as the woman who presents her book to their gaze.

What was the "other plot" in the nineteenth century? "Is there any *one* other plot?" Gilbert and Gubar ask. "What, in other words, [had] women . . . to hide? . . . what literary women have hidden or disguised is *what each writer knows is in some sense her own story* . . . in Carolyn Kizer's bitter words, 'the private life of one half of humanity' . . . the one plot that seems to be concealed in most of the nineteenth-century literature by women . . . is in some sense *a story of the woman writer's quest for her own story.*"[22]

This is what the hidden plot was. The plot is the same today; however, it is no longer hidden. It *is* the plot. The empty space has somehow taken precedence over the filled space, which indeed is, for us now, the "anonymous background." The "quest" is no longer concealed. The striptease is over. We may play in gardens of our own making; we have our own tales. Our patterns and modes of communication are only now forming as we talk in the places where we make our art and tell our tales. We do have a body of literature, small but growing, that one could call our "avant-garde." I prefer not to use that term, however, because the concept is militaristic while our endeavor is not. All patterns and modes of behavior, cultural or political, need extremes to set the mark, to help establish the broad outlines of emergent forms. Novels indicative of this ironic or parodic "call to arms" include *The Female Man, Les Guérillères,* and *The Lesbian Body (Le Corps Lesbien).*

The original quest is over. The plot is no longer hidden; neither is it any longer a lone vigil. The woman's novel of the twentieth (and, I would venture, of the twenty-first) century, is *a display of her own story revealed and explored,* presented to other women for their perusal. The nineteenth-century writer did seem to seek to "unify herself by coming to terms with her own fragmentation,"[23] but as this century progresses, no longer does the woman writing find that she is "broken in *two* / By sheer definition," as the poet May Sarton describes it.[24] Nor is the wholeness that the woman writer presents to us a healing of the "female schizophrenia of authorship" that represents a kind of doubleness. She recognizes that she is many "selves"—not the reactive model of the split or broken two. She now presents unashamedly all the selves that make up her wholeness.[25]

In the nineteenth and early twentieth centuries, reaction and anger generate the polarities of angel and monster that women's novels present. But the monster has been absorbed or released. "Doubleness" is no longer the basis for the plot structure, hidden or otherwise, of our story. With the absorption of the monster (or, more specifically, of the angel *into* the monster), camouflage is no longer the business of today's artist; she is more likely to display than to disguise herself. Rather than presenting a "drama of enclosure and escape,"[26] twentieth-century writers are more likely to "frame" their space for us to examine closely, to frame themselves in an open space so that their lives are on view to us. Their frame may be a window—literal or figurative, as in Virginia Woolf's *To the Lighthouse*—which is open to our view. Or the scene may open out onto, or even begin, "in the open."

In a discussion of Edith Wharton's *The House of Mirth*, Myra Jehlen observes that the protagonist, Lily Bart, is presented to us as standing in the open, alone, at Grand Central Station.[27] The male character who sees her lets us know that this is a striking and characteristic oddity: "She stood apart from the crowd, letting it drift by her to the platform or the street, and wearing an air of irresolution which might, as he surmised, be the mask of a very definite purpose."[28] He further observes, "it was characteristic of her that she always roused speculation, that her simplest acts seemed the result of far-reaching intentions."[29]

Given that Wharton's book was published in 1905, Lily Bart might well wear "an air of irresolution" as she "stood apart from the crowd"; likewise, this air of irresolution might very well be the "mask of a very definite purpose." A product of the nineteenth century, Lily, like her creator, has made that first move. She is out in the open, and she may be uncertain, but at least the initial terms, the "frame" of the drama, have been set. She is—openly—a "woman alone," standing "apart from the crowd." We *see* her, first and foremost. We look at her; we cannot take our eyes off her. She stirs our curiosity. Like the male observer, having seen her we are drawn to speculate about her. Wharton has presented her so to our view.

Lily Bart may be punished for what is finally only an attempted escape. But she has taken that first step and her author has taken the step with her. This woman and her life are open to our view, and the scene is set so that we are made to know this: we are asked to *see* it in our reading of that first page of Wharton's novel. Similarly, in Ibsen's drama, *A Doll's House*, Nora takes her step out of the house, closing the door firmly behind her, at the *end* of the play. We see her leaving. We don't see her arriving. The male author could help her get beyond the door. What she did afterward is a "woman's story."

I N *The Madwoman in the Attic*, Gilbert and Gubar present a parable. The woman artist, in the person of Mary Shelley, enters the cavern of her own mind, the sybil's cave. "The body of her precursor's art, and thus the body of her own art, lies in pieces around her, dismembered, dis-remembered, disintegrated. How can she remember it and become a member of it, join it and rejoin it, integrate it and in doing so achieve her own integrity, her own selfhood?"[30] My initial response to that question is snappish; I feel peeved. They imply that they are speaking not only of the nineteenth-century woman artist, but of a continuing and perhaps immutable condition of women's lives. For women now, the answer is, I would say, "by tending her own garden," not by exploring "caves" (a man's symbol of womanhood). It is by attending to her self (her many selves)—by becoming a member of the collective enterprise through *recognition*, which is a *re-knowing*. We achieve a re-knowing by encountering ourselves in one another, presenting and recognizing those selves. Such an ambition is not easy to realize, especially through the overlying grids of race, class, religion, culture, philosophy, politics. But one way to achieve this recognition of ourselves in one another is by our writing and reading. To solve the problem they present in the parable of the cave, Gilbert and Gubar suggest that "if we can piece together their fragments the parts will form a whole that tells the story of the career of a single woman artist, a 'mother of us all,' . . . a woman whom patriarchal poetics dismembered and whom we have tried to remember."[31] Perhaps, as June Arnold, of Daughters Publishers, Inc., suggested, the new women's novel can be seen as a "spiral" in which we see "experience weaving in upon itself, commenting on itself, *inclusive*, not ending in final victory/defeat but ending with the sense that the community continues. A spiral sliced to present a vision which reveals a whole. . . ."[32] To remember we must recognize, and to do so we must display ourselves to one another. We must step out of the male mirror and into our own "frame" to stage our lives, presenting them to one another and recognizing all our selves.

This is the collective enterprise we engage in knowingly, offering [auto]biography for our own history. We do this not with birth images—cave as womb from which we are birthing ourselves—but with novels whose reading can be applied to adult people in the real world, not women metaphorized into baby and mother ceaselessly wandering the area of womb or uterus. We may even bypass the womb, that sacred place, and look directly at one another, as one adult to another—not as mother to child, not even as mothering woman to another woman in need of mothering, not even as ourselves mothering ourselves. We have no need for overdetermined metaphorical trappings (Plato's cave, Freud's womb) even if we are incidentally reappropriating them. Rather, we now stage our own life.

Although I use the theatrical metaphor, life as theater and book as stage, the theater remains real and common property. Men have appropriated this metaphor only generally, not specifically. It is our theater, our stage with its own gesture, its own signal, our recognition of our lives in one another. Such presentation and recognition give us full cognizance of our adult status, woman to woman, woman as writer performing for a fully participating audience. In making this analogy I invoke not formal phenomenology but pragmatism. Mine is a practical view, one emphasizing the usefulness of reading and writing in our lives—to recognize, to reknow, in short, to remember our selves. In re-membering we effect that wholeness of self that is visible in the mirror of other women's lives. Our remembering is finally a present knowing, a cognition of ourselves. Without such knowledge and "membership" we have no art—or politics—at all.

CHAPTER TWO.

READING AS SEEING:

A SPECTACULAR VIEW

OF OUR SELVES

Deeply did I feel myself privileged in having a place before that stage; I longed to see a being of whose powers I had heard reports which made me conceive peculiar anticipations. I wondered if she would justify her renown: with strange curiosity, with feelings severe and austere, yet of riveted interest, I waited. She was a study of such nature as had not encountered my eyes yet: a great and new planet she was: but in what shape? I waited her rising.
  —"Vashti," Charlotte Brontë, *Villette* (1862)

She stepped out against the white wall, a woman-shaped hole, a black cardboard cut-out; with a crooked, charming smile she clapped her hand to her mouth, either taking something out or putting something in—see? . . . Come up close and you'll see that her eyes are silver, most unnatural. It came to me that we had been watching this woman perform for half an hour and had not given one thought to what might be happening around us or to us or behind us.
  —"Jael," Joanna Russ, *The Female Man* (1975)

A DISPLAYING TEXT gives us the signal to attend, to be alert to the performance that unfolds when we give that attention to the text of another woman. The signal is a gesture, and gesture is a matter of movement, of form rather than content alone. Content speaks, but it cannot hail the reader. In order to be seen a novel needs to make the gesture, to signal to us. Form itself "bodies" forth a "message." It stands, it takes a stance; it signals as a gesture signals for attention of a certain kind.

The reader notes the gesture: this is not only a woman writing, it is a woman making something. It is as if something moves, as if one can see it in space like the hailing signal of the hand, uplifted, a wave, fingers and palm together in a certain movement, a pose that moves, a stance that one recognizes. "I'd know her anywhere," one says of a friend, "that walk, the set of the shoulders, the lift of the chin." Her silhouette is kinetic, dynamic, inseparable from her movements, inseparable from the space she now inhabits, now displaces in motion.

This is not the "writing of the body" that some French feminist theorists recommend, but it is not thoroughly dissimilar, either.[1] What is important is that a voice goes with the picture. A woman's text is not "silent." It speaks as it displays; it speaks *in order* to display. That is how it is like a play, a dramatization, and its actors (all of whom are the author) are conscious of their audience. The audience is listening as well as watching, but the eye is the initial organ of perception. And, the eye having been caught, it is the voice that enables the pictures to move, the voice that fuels the movement in space on which the reader's "eye" continues to be fixed, the voice that propels the movement that "makes" the story and unfolds the drama. Imagining the voice allows the *tableau vivant* of the woman's novel to take kinetic shape in the theater of voice and movement that the writer and the reader have established together. The writer stages the performance; the audience supports and encourages it.

THE DIFFERENCE between acting in films and on the stage, John Gielgud remarked, is the presence of the audience in the theater.[2] Gielgud said that as a stage actor he has tried to be a "vessel for the play," that learning to relax, to "support" the play, and not to "show off" is the hardest part of acting for the stage. These remarks have some usefulness for us, particularly if we put them alongside Joanna Russ's *envoi* to her "little daughter-book" (an extension of Chaucer's *envoi* to his "litel bok")[3] and consider the implications for our metaphor of book as stage and the reader-writer relationship as that of the theater audience to a play.

In one sense, a play has two audiences: the initial or primary audience, consisting of the actors and other technicians who interpret and stage the play, and the secondary audience, the people gathered in the theater to view the play. The playwright is only one of the people responsible for the collective effort resulting in the presentation viewed by the theater audience. The novelist, in contrast, herself produces the novel that is presented to the audience of readers. Who or what serves as a "vessel for the play"? Who learns to "relax," to "support" the play and not to "show off"? Text? Author? Characters? Audience?

If we look to Joanna Russ's admonition to her "little daughter-book," we see how these analogies may serve us. "Go little book," she writes, "behave yourself in people's living rooms. . . . Do not scream when you are ignored, for that will alarm people . . . do not fume. . . . Live merrily, little daughter-book. . . . recite yourself to all who will listen; stay hopeful and wise. . . . Do not complain. . . . do not mutter angrily to yourself. . . . Do not get glum. . . . Do not curse your fate. *Do not reach up from readers' laps and punch the readers' noses."*[4] She speaks to her book as if it were a person, an actor, an agent capable of so much self-directed activity as to need a warning *not* "to reach up . . . and punch the readers' noses." Where does the virtue of the kind that Gielgud suggests, the virtue of active passivity, reside? In the book? Is the book in the position of actor, on a stage? (I've already suggested that the book itself is the stage.) Is it in the writer, the author herself? (No; she let the book "go," sent it out into the world alone.) Is it in the production, the achieved presentation of the text itself—text as opposed to book—if we see the text as the interwoven and moving pattern of the words on the page as the reader perceives them, and the book as the stage, the concrete place of presentation for the text? The active passivity Gielgud suggests lies perhaps in the text, if it can be seen as active, moving, participating in the "show" of the narrative (or the narrative of the show) on the stage of the novel, the concrete book.

The book is the frame, the arch of the proscenium, the window into which the audience—the reader—may direct her view for the "showing off" of the text, which has become the actor(s), moving and on full view. Meanwhile the original actor, the writer, recedes into the background, withdrawing in the essential artistic and aesthetic modesty crucial for effective performance.

For such a novel the audience is, at least metaphorically, like the audience for the drama: stage actor and writer are each initial audiences; reader and theater-going audience are secondary but ultimate. They are of the utmost importance, for without the buoyancy of the interaction between actor and audience, between writer and reader, the dynamism achieved by mutuality of need and intent, a performance could not be said to take place. Certainly it would lack the effectiveness that allows us to recognize aesthetic satisfaction or achievement.

The play of the text, then, and not the author herself, is to be "supported." This support, however, needs the text offered by the author, who, *as her text*, allows herself to "relax" and not to "show off" and allows her book to be the "vessel for the play." She herself is no longer actor, as Gielgud of course intends the actor vessel to be, but the book is the theater, the place of staging for the play that is acted out by the text. The showing off is accomplished by the play itself, play between book and reader; the reader supports the action of the text, furnishing a part of the dynamics of book meeting reader, especially when a woman's book is in the hands of a woman reader. It is then that the text is enabled to assume a voice and begin to "speak."

What has been missing in the previous paragraphs is the matter of *voice*, specifically, a voice speaking. The actor's voice is central to the performance, to the movement and shape of the text. In the staged performance that is the book, there is no movement without the voice. The action stops, freezes, enacts nothing. It would be at best a photograph, a "still," or that old-fashioned amusement, a *tableau vivant*. By definition, a *tableau vivant* is constituted by live but motionless and silent figures, a literal "still life." But always one knows that the figures *could* move.

What if the figures, the characters, began to move? That would be to break the rules of the game, to go against the form of the art itself; *that* is the pleasure of the *tableau vivant*. But what if the figures began to move, and in moving, began to speak? Rather than trying to say *why* they might speak, or speculating on the voice with which they might speak, let us consider where such a voice comes from, *whose* voice it is (besides the author's, besides the characters'). Where does it come from? The woman in the man's text has been the object of the eye-object dialectic, the *tableau vivant*, where the titillation comes from knowing that she *can* move and speak but the rules of the game require that she cannot. The "voice" of the contemporary woman's text is making the woman (and women) "move."

Several such *tableaux vivants* appear in Edith Wharton's *The House of Mirth*. Wharton describes those *tableaux vivants* that precede one presented by the protagonist, Lily Bart, and distinguishes Lily's presentation from the others. In doing so, Wharton gives us a pictorial, as well as an expository, representation of the woman-in-the-text. Although this woman is as yet silent, a "voice" begins to make itself felt in the "predominance of personality" that Wharton stresses. In Wharton's description of Lily Bart as artist of the *tableau vivant*, we are presented with the woman's body, her figure in space, the "flesh-and-blood" woman expressing herself in an art form that, typically, had been all self-effacement and lack of self-expression.

Our male observer, Selden, gives us another insight into the contrast between women's and men's watching of women. We must remember that Edith Wharton allows him to speak. Her voice speaks on the page; her eyes see through his, as ours do.

> Indeed, so skillfully had the personality of the actors been subdued to the scenes they figured in that even the least imaginative of the audience must have felt a thrill of contrast when the curtain suddenly parted on a picture which was simply and undisguisedly the portrait of Miss Bart.
>
> Here there could be no mistaking the predominance of personality—the unanimous "Oh!" of the spectators was a tribute, not to the brush-work of Reynolds' "Mrs. Lloyd" but to the flesh-and-blood loveliness of Lily Bart. She had shown her artistic intelligence in selecting a type so like her own that she could embody the person represented without ceasing to be herself. It was as though she had stepped, not out of, but into, Reynolds' canvas, banishing the phantom of his dead beauty by the beams of her living grace. The impulse to show herself in a splendid setting—she had thought for a moment of representing Tiepolo's *Cleopatra*—had yielded to the truer instinct of trusting to her unassisted beauty. . . . Its expression was now so vivid that for the first time he seemed to see before him the real Lily Bart. . . . Lily had not an instant's doubt as to the meaning of the murmur greeting her appearance. No other *tableau* had been received with that precise note of approval; it had obviously been called forth by herself and not by the picture she impersonated.[5]

Lily Bart's "artistic intelligence" is not very different from that of Lucy Snowe in Charlotte Brontë's *Villette*. In a visit to the Brussels museum, Lucy rejects Rubens's *Cleopatra*, a picture of "portentous size, set up in the best light, having a cordon of protection stretched before it, and a cushioned bench duly set in front for the accommodation of worshipping connoisseurs," a picture which, in short, "seemed to consider itself the queen of the collection."[6] This production "represented a woman, considerably larger," Lucy remarks sardonically, "than the life," and is so at variance with her own perceptions that she cannot for a moment take it seriously: "Pots and pans—perhaps I ought to say vases and goblets—were rolled here and there on the foreground; a perfect rubbish of flowers was mixed amongst them, and an absurd and disorderly mass of curtain upholstery smothered the couch and cumbered the floor."[7] Through Lucy, Brontë offers us a corrective description that attempts to wrench the picture back into some semblance of a woman's "real" life. Lucy rejects this unrealistic and obscured representation of a woman, just as Lily Bart rejects a view of yet another male painter's *Cleopatra*, because it is inadequate to represent her self.

Later in *Villette*, Brontë contrasts the same unrealistic representation of a woman that Lucy had earlier rejected with the actress Vashti's dramatic presentation of herself/her character.

"Where was the artist of the Cleopatra?" Brontë writes. "Place now the Cleopatra, or any other slug, before [Vashti] as an obstacle, and see her cut through the pulpy mass as the scimitar of Saladin clove the down cushion. Let Peter Paul Rubens wake from the dead, let him rise out of his cerements, and bring into this presence all the army of his fat women."[8] We might imagine from this impassioned prose that Vashti (and Brontë, and her Lucy) would make short work of this overfed army, which has nothing to do with them and which, in their view (her view in each case), fails abysmally as artistic representation. The representation itself is overfed, encumbered and encumbering, aesthetically as well as pragmatically wrong. The accurate representation of a woman—as Lucy's indignation and as Vashti's "scimitar"-like performance show—is unencumbering and *like herself*, as demonstrated by Lily Bart's artistic intelligence, her instinct in "selecting a type so like her own that she could embody the person represented without ceasing to be herself."[9]

Two writers, Brontë in 1862 and Wharton in 1905, thus described a woman's artistic sensibility, telling us what we might expect from a woman's art. In both cases a woman's art is a blend of the "real" (the real "self") with the representation (the "picture"). The representation offers the exposure, the display, the revelation of the woman in "real life." As Brontë writes, true to her time, but thrilled by the "immorality" to which she is witness:

> It was a marvellous sight: a mighty revelation.
> It was a spectacle, low, horrible, immoral.[10]

From the modern perspective, Gilbert and Gubar offer us several observations in their discussion of Brontë's *Villette* which are pertinent here: "Unlike the false artists who abound in *Villette*, Vashti uses her art not to manipulate others, but to represent herself. Her art, in other words, is confessional, unfinished—*not a product, but an act*; not an object meant to contain or coerce, but a personal utterance.... By transcending the distinctions between *private and public*, between *person and artist*, between *artist and art*, Vashti calls into question, therefore, the closed forms of male culture."[11] Calling into question "the closed forms of male culture" is not, however, central to the act we are examining. Vashti's concern, as presented by Brontë, is with her own act, not in reference to, or in reaction against, male culture. The act, the performance and presentation of the actress Vashti, is self-referring, which is where its effect lies, where its power for Lucy (and for Brontë) resides. It is another character, Dr. John, who assesses Vashti's act in terms of the male culture. Simple or reflexive response is initial (as Lucy's is, and as Brontë presents it); comparison may follow and may even be partial explanation for what is recognized as new but, more importantly, as "ours." In opening out the closed forms of male culture in which we have been contained, women make connections. We do not escape in an aura of "transcendence"; we literally work with what we've got. A woman's art is *"not a product, but an act."* This act itself, "unfinished, confessional," can be equated with a *"personal utterance."* Acting is speaking and speaking is acting. Together the two offer the performance of a woman's text. To act, to speak, the woman must first find a voice. To find a voice she must, indeed, define her own body in space, lay claim to her own boundaries and her own arena of performance.

WHILE BRONTË and Wharton were publishing their novels in England (1853) and in the United States (1905), what was happening in the lives of some other people in the Western world?

Alice James (Henry and William's sister), age nineteen, is sitting in her father's library in Cambridge, Massachusetts. The year is 1868, the year when she will have her first "breakdown." She describes her life at that time: "As I used to sit immovable reading in the library with waves of violent inclination suddenly invading my muscles taking some one of their myriad forms such as throwing myself out of the window, or knocking off the head of the benignant pater as he sat with his silver locks, writing at his table, it used to seem to me that the only difference between me and the insane was that I had not only all the horrors and suffering of insanity but the duties of doctor, nurse and strait-jacket imposed upon me, too."[12] Alice's description is from a diary entry written two and half years before her death in 1892.

In Paris, in 1885–86, the thirty-year-old Sigmund Freud, five years after receiving his M.D. degree, is studying with Charcot, the famous clinician and teacher. Photographs of Charcot's female patients at the Salpêtrière were published in 1876–78 in two volumes with the artistically scientific title *Iconographie photographique de la Salpêtrière (Service de M Charcot)*.[13]

Stephen Heath describes Charcot's work:

> In Charcot's clinical teaching practice at the Salpêtrière, the Tuesday lessons attended by Freud, attention was paid to the realisation of a photographic record of the cases presented, a veritable iconography of hysteria: "we saw," write the compilers of the record, "from M Charcot's example how considerable were the benefits to be had from representations of this kind."
>
> Charcot's cases included men and children, [but] the photographs are of women, plates interspersed within the text of the clinical details; often a portrait of the particular woman as she is at rest, the "normal physiognomy," much like any other late nineteenth century portrait photograph, then the stages of the "attack" so dear to Charcot in his endeavor to bring hysteria into the order of medicine, to define a clinical *picture*, the *"tableau clinique"*: very occasionally . . . nurses intrude, by the side of the patient, fixing the camera, determinedly posing; now and then an effect of "beauty," a young girl composed on her bed

. . . something of Millais' *Ophelia*, "terminal stage of the attack,"
no trace of disturbance, in her "the delirium sometimes takes
on a religious character"—the *aura* of hysteria, part of the picture. The interest for Charcot, and for the compilers, is in the
stages, the step by step unfolding of the attack. Where others
had seen only disorder, merely the random, Charcot saw order,
a repeated pattern which the photographs must serve to give:
hence the series of plates for a single patient, an attempt at duration, a movement in time . . . a sixteen year old girl in the
throes of the period of delirium: the various "passionate attitudes" are shown in sequence and named—attitudes of "threat,"
"appeal," "amorous supplication," "eroticism," "ecstasy," "halluci-
nations of hearing." The effect is of a kind of cinema: the spac-
ing of gestures in a succession of images, the holding of those
same gestures to the clarity of a narrative meaning: one can
imagine the Salpêtrière *Iconographie* as a catalogue of gestural
signs for the use of performers in silent films—and such an
imagination would not be too far from the spectacle of the les-
sons, which all the contemporary pictures and prints pick up:
the excited audience, the master, the young woman in a series
of pathetic scenes according to script (there is a certain contro-
versy over the demonstrations and the repetitions of the stages
of the attack: hypnotized by the master's zealous assistants, with
pressure applied to their "hysterogenic zones," was there any
other part for these woman?).[14]

"What is missing in the photographs," Heath goes on to observe, "is
the voice, an absence signalled, as it were, in the naming of the 'hallu-
cinations of hearing' plate. . . . The text restores a little of the voice,
almost nothing: when a patient cries 'Mummy!', Charcot comments,
'You see how hysterics shout. Much ado about nothing. Epilepsy
which is much more serious is much quieter.'"[15]

Charcot's female patients are caught in these photographic frames;
their gestures are fixed in them. By presenting these fixed gestures
in succession Charcot attempts to give a kind of "narrative meaning"
to each case in the series and an overall meaning to the species of
patient called the "hysteric," who is, by visual definition at least, a
woman. As Heath points out, Charcot had men and children as patients, as well as women, but the photographic presentation was re-

stricted to women. If a voice is allowed to the woman it is edited and minimal—the "Mummy!" for example. The woman's voice is mentioned in the text accompanying the photographs as an occasion for Charcot to comment on the noise of the hysteric, her "shouting," which is meaningless (only the succession of photographs is to carry meaning). The really "serious" case, an epileptic, for instance, is much "quieter." But even here the woman is edited out. She is not an epileptic in Charcot's words; she is lost in the designation of her disease—"epilepsy." Charcot seems to suggest that the silent presentation, the series of photographs, the artificial "life" given by a succession of *tableaux vivants*, typical postures and poses, would allow a practitioner to recognize an afflicted woman far better than her own version of her condition, or any verbalization on her part at all.

Apparently many women tried to conform to such expectations of immobility before they were ever diagnosed as "hysterical." Recall Alice James's feeling that she had not only the "duties of doctor and nurse" imposed upon her if she was to keep herself "immovable," but that of a "strait-jacket" as well. She continues in the same diary entry: "Conceive of never being without the sense that if you let yourself go for a moment your mechanism will fall into pie and that at some given moment you must abandon it all, let the dykes break and the flood sweep in, acknowledging yourself abjectly impotent before the immutable laws. When all one's moral and natural stock in trade is a temperament forbidding the abandonment of an inch or the relaxation of a muscle, 'tis a never-ending fight."[16] Although Alice was diagnosed and treated for her nervous illness, she ultimately chose to make an art of invalidism, achieving her early death at the age of forty-three.

"WHAT IS MISSING in the photographs" Stephen Heath writes in 1978, "is the voice."

"What is wanted," says Freud, writing for publication in 1905, "is . . . an elucidation of the commonest cases [of hysteria] and of their most frequent and typical symptoms." To this end, he presents "Fragment of an Analysis of a Case of Hysteria."[17] "Dora" (the fictitious name for the young woman whose case Freud recounts) was a more independent young woman than Alice James. Freud first saw Dora when she was sixteen. Her most persistent symptom was *tussis nervosa*, a nervous cough; his statement of her attitude toward treatment two years later was this:

> When, at the age of eighteen, she came to me for treatment, she was again coughing in a characteristic manner. . . . The most troublesome symptom during the first half of an attack of this kind, at all events in the last few years, used to be *a complete loss of voice*. The diagnosis that this was once more a nervous complaint had been established long since; but the various methods of treatment which are usual, including hydrotherapy and the local application of electricity, had produced no result. . . . Moreover, she had always been against calling in medical advice, though she had no personal objection to her family doctor. Every proposal to consult a new physician aroused her resistance, and it was only her father's authority which induced her to come to me at all.[18]

Freud's general description of the girl is as follows:

> Dora was by that time in the first bloom of youth—a girl of intelligent and engaging looks. But she was a source of heavy trials for her parents. Low spirits and an alteration in her character had now become the main features of her illness. She was clearly satisfied neither with herself nor with her family; her attitude towards her father was unfriendly, and she was on very bad terms with her mother, who was bent upon drawing her into taking a share in the work of the house. She tried to avoid social intercourse, and employed herself—so far as she was allowed to by the fatigue and lack of concentration of which she complained—with attending lectures for women and with carrying on more or less serious studies. One day her parents were thrown into a state of great alarm by finding upon the girl's writing-desk, or inside it, a letter in which she took leave of them because, as she said, she could not longer endure her life. Her father, indeed, being a man of some perspicacity, guessed that the girl had no serious suicidal intentions. But he was none the less very much shaken; and when one day, after a slight passage of words between him and his daughter, she had a first attack of loss of consciousness—an event which was subsequently

covered by an amnesia—it was determined, in spite of her reluctance, that she should come to me for treatment.[19]

Alice James's treatment also began in her middle teens; she too had thought of suicide. It was her father who determined, but more actively than Dora's father did, Alice's attitude toward an attempt on her life. In a letter to his youngest son, Robertson, the elder Henry James describes an interchange. "One day a long time ago," he writes,

> [she] asked me whether I thought that suicide, to which at times she felt very strongly tempted, was a sin. I told her that I thought it was not a sin except where it was wanton. . . . I told her that so far as I was concerned she had my full permission to end her life whenever she pleased; only I hoped that if ever she felt like doing that sort of justice to her circumstances, she would do it in a perfectly gentle way in order not to distress her friends. She then remarked that she was very thankful to me, but she felt that now she could perceive it to be her *right* to dispose of her own body when life had become intolerable, she could never do it. . . . [20]

One could draw many more parallels between the two young women; indeed, this scenario for the hysterical young woman of the Victorian age was acted out in upper-middle-class houses throughout the United States and Western Europe. Dora and Alice James are two typical "cases." Both found that, as Alice put it, if they were to keep themselves "immovable," to persist in their "moral and natural stock in trade," they must assume the "duties of doctor, nurse and straitjacket" to keep to the normal course of events in their lives. Lest they forget that, as women, they are (like children) to be "seen and not heard," M. Charcot's *Iconographie photographique*, his *tableaux cliniques*, can be seen figuratively, as well as literally in the case of his patients at the Salpêtrière, to "put them in their place." Their place is that of image, a series of staged gestures and poses to which their own unwilling bodies submit them (as Alice writes): "So, with the rest, you abandon the pit of your stomach, the palms of your hands, the soles of your feet, and refuse to keep them sane when you find in turn one moral impression after another producing despair in the one, terror in the other, anxiety in the third and so on until life becomes one long flight from remote suggestion and complicated eluding of the multifold traps set for your undoing."[21] Meanwhile Charcot's colleagues, nurses, and assistants—with students such as Freud looking on—assist the patients in their "routine," help put them through their paces to furnish material for his *tableaux cliniques*, his iconographical representations of hysterical women.

It is chilling to contemplate the use of women to *represent themselves*, but not as themselves, in a *tableau clinique* that is not far removed, in its implications, from the *tableaux vivants* with which people amused themselves at social gatherings. In both cases the female figure represents something preconceived, something other than herself. She represents something already known. Her images are merely a replication of that which is already "proved." She serves to confirm the status quo, to give an image to others' knowledge, others' desires.

No wonder a young Victorian woman who could salvage a selfhood so unendingly beleaguered felt she had to play doctor, nurse, and straitjacket to herself. Such was the iconography of her culture. But the battle with herself, the battle to remain silent and immovable, to mimic in life the images presented to her, was a "never-ending fight" that she sometimes lost. It is not surprising that women's literature of this time should "enact a drama of enclosure and escape";[22] nor that Freud's work in this time should leave a legacy in which even the iconoclastic French psychoanalyst Jacques Lacan portrays "woman" as the place where men (as little boys) first see only a lack (of the penis), and later (as men) see a place on which to "hang" their imaginings: women become the place of metaphor for men. Women are reduced to images, to symbols—indeed, to icons.[23]

Male proprietorship of the gaze—of seeing and of determining what is to be seen and in what way—was already being challenged in the nineteenth century. Edith Wharton's novel, *The House of Mirth* (1905), Susan Glaspell's "A Jury of Her Peers" (1917), and Charlotte Perkins Gilman's "The Yellow Wallpaper" (1892) all refute male proprietorship of the gaze, as did Charlotte Brontë's *Villette* (1853) several decades earlier. In her discussion of *Villette* in the feminist classic *Sexual Politics*, Kate Millett writes: "*Lucy watches women . . .*" (the emphasis is my own). She then describes the first of the women Lucy watches—Ginevra Fanshaw.[24] The next paragraph begins, "*The other women Lucy watches . . .*" (and she enumerates them—Madame Beck and Mrs. Bretton, and Paulina Mary). Then Millett observes, "*Lucy has watched men look at women,* has studied the image of woman in her culture." Millett goes on to say, "There is probably nothing so subversive in the book as that afternoon in the Brussels museum when she scrutinizes the two faces of women whom the male has fashioned, one for his entertainment, one for her instruction: Rubens' Cleopatra and the Academician's four pictures of the virtuous female."[25] Further, Millett writes:

> The disparity in the contradiction of images represented by the two pictures explains the techniques of *Villette* better than any other moment in the novel. It is a division in the culture which Brontë is retorting to by splitting her people in half and dividing Lucy's own responses into a fluctuating negative and positive. The other dichotomy is between her newness, her revolutionary spirit, and the residue of the old ways which infects her soul. This inner conflict is complemented by an exterior one between her ambitions and desires and the near impossibility of their fulfillment.[26]

With these remarks Millett returns us to the argument that Gilbert and Gubar pursue, to that perception of the disease and anxiety felt by the woman and the woman artist in the nineteenth century, the woman "broken in two / By sheer definition."

I point again, however, to the pairing of images in *Villette* that I have already emphasized: not the two images of woman presented to her by man, but the implicit image of a woman that Brontë emphasizes by Lucy's rejection of Rubens's *Cleopatra*, set alongside the image of a woman presented *by a woman* in Vashti's performance. Vashti's image, Lucy realizes, is not an "image" at all, but the *woman herself.* Here we have not a woman broken in two, not a woman split in half, but a woman looking at another woman and seeing "a great and new planet" whose "rising" she awaited, "a study of such nature as had not encountered [her] eyes yet."[27] A century later Joanna Russ writes, "it came to me that we had been watching this woman perform for half an hour and had given not one thought to what might be happening around us or to us or behind us."[28]

It is plain, then, that to "step out of the picture" of the masculine conception, our first step is simply to look at one another and *see,* to watch one another, as Millett makes clear Lucy is doing in *Villette.*

Hard on the heels of that first step is the second, which is to be conscious of what we are doing and what that doing implies. In seeing with our own eyes, we have begun to act, and in such action we will perceive our differences from other women as well as our likenesses. In stepping out of the picture, the images into which we had been fixed, we find ourselves "in action." In that action we begin to find our voices as well.

"DORA" LOSES HER VOICE; Alice James remains immovable; Charcot's patients are presented: " 'the delirium sometimes takes on a religious character' . . .—the *aura* of hysteria, part of the picture." Three centuries earlier, the sculptor Bernini, in his *Ecstasy of St. Teresa*, fixed St. Teresa forever in his shaping of her "ecstasy." Her words were disallowed, her own attempt to fix her own experience of ecstasy disallowed—shoved off the page—in favor of her shape in space, molded by the male eye into sculpture, that purest form of fixing in space for the gaze of the eye.[29]

"Riding high above the complex," Robert M. Adams reminds us, "is a scroll bearing an amazingly audacious motto spoken to Teresa in one of her visions by the Lord Himself: *'Nisi coelum creassem ob te solam crearem'* ('If I hadn't already created Heaven, I would create it for you alone.') Very few women can have received so courtly a compliment from so high an authority; it is a compliment that Bernini in his chapel—which catches in a single ecstatic instant death, life, love, violence, and surrender to make of them a world—does not hesitate to repeat."[30] Bernini used "Teresa's own poems and autobiography," but these "poems and autobiography" are appropriated into Bernini's scheme of representation in marble, the better to catch the life. Even if the words engraved on the scroll are those reported by St. Teresa herself—indeed, it is *her* audacity thus to report them—they were *spoken* by the Lord Himself. It is His voice cast into stone, she and Adams tell us, not Teresa's—this "amazingly audacious motto"— the whole given to us by Bernini. St. Teresa is edited out in the process, just as Charcot edited the voices of his hysterical patients, the image to speak for the woman, or rather to remind us that the woman does not speak for herself except in her silence. She, Teresa, and the Alices and Doras who came after her are silent, contained, fixed, created by men and displaying the *jouissance*, the joy in play that the male eye feels when it looks upon the image. The display of women in joy becomes the occasion for his *jouissance*, and he calls it theirs, calls *his*, hers: the *Ecstasy of St. Teresa*.

But what if the image began to move, the picture began to speak? What if Alice James had begun to move, following one of her "violent inclinations," and had indeed knocked off "the head of the benignant pater"? What if Dora had chosen to speak rather than to "lose" her voice? What if the scroll "riding high above" were ripped off its metaphorical hinges and St. Teresa's marble lips, so ecstatically parted, began to move? What "mighty revelation," to quote Charlotte Brontë, might we expect? What "spectacle"? I venture that the spectacle was then and is now merely the *ordinary*, the spectacle of the "common woman," as the poet Judy Grahn calls her.[31]

IN AN ESSAY entitled "The 'Uncanny'" (1919) Freud points us to a kind of explanation for the phenomenon that "specularizes" the "common woman" and that made her movement in her own space so distracting and "unnatural" until this century: "The subject of the 'uncanny' is . . . undoubtedly related to what is frightening—to what arouses dread and horror; equally certainly, too, the word is not always used in a clearly definable sense, so that it tends to coincide with what excites fear in general. Yet we may expect that a special core of feeling is present which justifies the use of a special conceptual term. One is curious to know what this common core is which allows us to distinguish as 'uncanny' certain things which lie within the field of what is frightening."[32]

The "uncanny," for Freud, is "that class of the frightening which leads back to what is known of old and long familiar. How this is possible," he writes, "in what circumstances the familiar can become uncanny and frightening, I shall show in what follows."[33] What follows, as one might expect, is Freud's attribution of the essential fears of the Oedipal situation, the fear of castration for little boys in particular, as the constituting factors of that "common core . . . which allows us to distinguish as uncanny certain things which lie within the field of what is frightening." Freud uses a story by E. T. A. Hoffmann, "The Sand-Man," to illustrate what he considers to be the underlying basis for the aesthetic effect of the story. As Freud points out, the story contains the original of Olympia, the doll that appears in the first act of Offenbach's opera, *Tales of Hoffmann*. "But I cannot think," he writes,

> —and I hope most readers of the story will agree with me—that the theme of the doll Olympia, who is to all appearances a living being, is by any means the only, or indeed the most important, element that must be held responsible for the quite unparalleled atmosphere of uncanniness evoked by the story. Nor is this atmosphere heightened by the fact that the author himself treats the episode of Olympia with a faint touch of satire and uses it to poke fun at the young man's idealization of his mistress. The main theme of the story is, on the contrary, something different, something which gives it its name, and which is always re-introduced at critical moments: it is the theme of the "Sand-Man" who tears out children's eyes.[34]

Having one's eyes torn out, for the male child at least, according to Freud, is tantamount to and symbolic of castration by the father. The maker of the doll Olympia, Professor Spalanzani (who models the "perfect" young woman, the protagonist Nathanael's "idealized mistress") and the itinerant optician, Coppola, who furnishes the doll with eyes (figuratively the "eyes" of the beholder, Nathanael) both function as "father figures." Thus Freud felt himself enabled to assign the conflict of the Oedipal situation acted out in this story of high romanticism the central place in "our" response to it. He sees the doll Olympia as a mere prop pointing up the conflict that finally drives the young man mad. The doll, on the other hand, is literally torn apart by the two "fathers"—Coppola and her putative father, Spalanzani, who furnished her mechanism, her "clock-work":

> Nathanael rushed in, impelled by some nameless dread. The Professor was grasping a female figure by the shoulders, the Italian Coppola held her by the feet; and they were pulling and dragging each other backwards and forwards, fighting furiously to get possession of her.
>
> Nathanael recoiled with horror on recognizing that the figure was Olimpia [*sic*]. Boiling with rage, he was about to tear his beloved from the grasp of the madmen, when Coppola by an extraordinary exertion of strength twisted the figure out of the

Professor's hand and gave him such a terrible blow with her, that Spalanzani reeled backwards and fell over the table among the phials and retorts. . . . But Coppola threw the figure across his shoulder, and, laughing shrilly and horribly, ran hastily down the stairs, the figure's ugly feet hanging down and banging and rattling like wood against the steps.

Nathanael was stupefied [so am I, but I'm not surprised; recall Alice James's "So, with the rest, you abandon the pit of your stomach, the palms of your hands, the soles of your feet"]—he had seen only too distinctly that in Olimpia's [*sic*] pallid waxed face there were no eyes, merely black holes in their stead; she was an inanimate puppet. Spalanzani was rolling on the floor; the pieces of glass had cut his head and breast and arm; the blood was escaping from him in streams. But he gathered his strength together by an effort.

"After him—after him! What do you stand staring there for? Coppelius—Coppelius—he's stolen my best automaton—at which I've worked for twenty years—my life work—the clock-work—speech—movement—mine—your eyes—stolen your eyes—damn him—curse him—after him—fetch me back Olimpia—there are the eyes." And now Nathanael saw a pair of bloody eyes lying on the floor staring at him; Spalanzani seized them with his uninjured hand and threw them at him, so that they hit his breast.

Then madness dug her burning talons into Nathanael and swept down into his heart, rending his mind and thoughts to shreds.[35]

Olympia is a doll made up of clockwork, seen and having her "seeing" only in the eyes of the beholder, the male romantic, the male "lover." She is possessed by her "creators"—her fathers—the optician (the "Sand-Man") and the professor, who "worked" on her for twenty years, "her speech—her movement—all" his. Movement, speech, minimal as they are, are given to her; they are her repertoire. But her eyes are never her own. They are the locus as well as the objects of dispute and conflict for the men involved in her "life." The lack of eyes emphasizes Olympia's lack of life.

Freud may dismiss her "place" in the story as the focal point, following, as always, the story of his own concerns, the concerns of men.

But for a woman reading, the figure of the doll Olympia is central; she ("it"—but one cannot really call her "it" because her constraints, her confirmation and limitations are so recognizable that even for a woman reading now, almost two centuries later, too much is familiar), *she* is too familiar. One sees too much of oneself in "the doll" to dismiss the *reality of the presentation*.

Freud, however, does just this. In the early portion of his discussion he writes of an earlier investigation of the subject:

> When we proceed to review the things, persons, impressions, events and situations which are able to arouse in us a feeling of the uncanny in a particularly forcible and definite form, the first requirement is obviously to select a suitable example to start on. Jentsch has taken as a very good instance "doubts whether an apparently animate being is really alive; or conversely, whether a lifeless object might not be in fact animate"; and he refers in this connection to the impression made by waxwork figures, ingeniously constructed dolls and automata. To these he adds the uncanny effect of epileptic fits, and of manifestations of insanity, because these incite in the spectator the impression of automatic, mechanical processes at work behind the ordinary appearance of mental activity.[36]

I recall my own experiences at "formal" dances in the culture of American high schools of the mid- and late 1950s. The description of Olympia's first appearance in society is not very different from that of the middle- or upper-middle-class American female adolescent in a similar situation:

> Olimpia [*sic*] was richly and tastefully dressed. One could not but admire her figure and the regular beauty of her features ["the prettiest girl in class"; "The Most Beautiful" heralded in the school yearbook]. Yet the striking inward curve of her back, as well as the wasplike smallness of her waist, appeared to be the result of too-tight lacing [Marilyn Monroe; the "merry widow" bra], and there was something stiff and measured in her gait and bearing that made an unfavorable impression upon many [the stiff tulle, the scratching lace, the "stiletto" heels]. It was ascribed to the constraint imposed upon her by the company [she's "stuck-up; she's unsure of herself; it's her first dance"].[37]

I will not belabor the persona, now or then, but the presentation is unmistakable. A woman recognizes herself, or rather, the image of herself used—even by herself—and presented publicly as a *doll*, an automaton, and presented as such with some sardonic smirking by Hoffmann himself (as Freud points out), readying his readers for the more pertinent conflicts and personae to take center stage.

I am "stuck," willfully, with Freud's "doubts whether an apparently animate being is really alive; or conversely, whether a lifeless object might not be in fact animate." With Freud's inclusion of the "uncanny" effect of epileptic fits and "manifestations of insanity," we return to Charcot's *tableaux cliniques* as well as to Edith Wharton's (and society's) *tableaux vivants* and to Alice James's and Dora's attempts to play the doll, to keep to the "uncanny" experience of attempting to demonstrate, to themselves and others, that an "apparently animate being" *is* "really alive" (or vice versa). As Alice pointed out, proving you're alive by pretending to be animate, albeit constrained, is futile: "Conceive of never being without the sense that if you let yourself go for a moment your *mechanism* will fall into pie and that at some given moment you must abandon it all" (my emphasis). This is the woman pretending to be the doll—the "Olympia complex," more relevant for the woman and the girl child than is the "Oedipal complex." And the "immutable laws" are those of the fathers: the providers of "eyes," the makers of, the tinkerers with, the mechanism.

In working through the "Olympia complex" the doll begins to move, the woman begins to speak. The effect, even to herself, may at first be "uncanny," that combination of the *unexpected* and the unbridled in the atmosphere of the contained familiar. Frightening it may be at first, but after one has seen it, by watching other women, the "horror" of it, the spectacle itself, becomes one of freedom of movement. One feels comfort in the familiar, the comfort of moving in one's own element. For, after all, one is moving one's own limbs, one's own hands and lips and eyes and mouth, one's own body in a familiar and comfortable space. One is seeing *oneself with one's own eyes*—no longer the "pallid waxed face" in which "there [are] no eyes." One might say, in such a situation, that one is "all eyes."

> "*Lucy watches women . . . Lucy watches . . . other women.*" This is Lucy Snowe as Brontë presents her to us in 1853, as Millett points

out for us. In 1975 Joanna Russ can write, "She stepped out against the white wall, a woman-shaped hole, a black cardboard cut-out . . . *see? . . . come up close and you'll see . . . her eyes . . .* most unnatural."[38] The lesson is simple: to regain our own voices, to gain our voices, we use our eyes. We see. We see one another. The gesture of the text, then, occurs in the context of "watching other women"; to signal our desire to speak and be heard, we must move, we must make the gesture. To hear we must attend to that gesture; and to attend to that gesture we must first *see*. To see, along with Lucy Snowe, we must observe; we must *watch* one another. Like Russ's protagonist(s) in *The Female Man*, we must be able to find ourselves watching the performance of another woman so intently that we give "not one thought to what might be happening around us or to us or behind us." We must be, in fact as well as in aspiration, "our own audience."

If the effect is "uncanny," we might contemplate again what that word means. The literal translation of the German word *unheimlich* is "unhomely," "unhome-like"—something unfamiliar, something one is not used to experiencing in ordinary circumstances. The etymology, both German and English, is intriguing: an exploration of both words—*uncanny, unheimlich*—leads us back to familiar and not unexpected surroundings, both that which is so close, so familiar that we dare not contemplate it, and that which is "otherworldly," including the religious, the spiritual, the mystical. As Freud points out in his tracing of the German etymology and usage of the word *heimlich*, it "is a word the meaning of which develops in the direction of ambivalence, until it finally coincides with its opposite, *unheimlich. Unheimlich* is in some way or other a sub-species of *heimlich*."[39] In English, too, this is the case, and with regard to the "Olympia complex" the discovery is the same.

For our purposes, we can see as "uncanny" the notion of the allegedly unusual, the allegedly unexpected, the doll "coming to life," the woman "coming to life" and expressing that life, freeing herself from mechanisms and models not her own, from restraints which, however familiar and habitual, have always felt strange to *her*. "Uncanny" is the restrained woman finally following her "violent inclinations," which after all are only ordinary movements previously restrained by habit and custom.

On the other hand, the truly uncanny thing is that women were ever stilled, "killed" into life, "into a 'perfect' image" of themselves, to start with (as well as, or *rather* than, into "art").[40] In letting loose the spectacle of ourselves, as we see it with our own eyes—no matter how "low," "horrible," or even "immoral" we may for a moment feel it to be—we discover that this "spectacle" we are making of ourselves is, actually, that which is merely familiar to us: our lives, our bodies, the informal acts of our living—the ordinary, the commonplace, the homely. The "mighty revelation" is that we are looking at ourselves and it doesn't feel bad. It is not "immoral"; it is, finally, not even "uncanny." What is uncanny is that it took us so long to look at one another without the mediation of the male eye. The uncanny thing is the strength of will that it took to hold the pose for so long.

Having retrieved "our own eyes" in the nineteenth century, we began using them, and the woman's text began to emerge. In the twentieth century we have begun to make a spectacle of the commonplace, the ordinariness of the "common woman." The spectacular itself—uncanny phenomenon—becomes the commonplace, and the ordinary, more and more spectacular. This spectacular framing of our lives can be seen in the presentation of our lives, in the [auto]-biography that is our present and growing story. We include our "I's" in order to exclude them, so that we may speak and be heard, so that we may "tell the truth" and still be heard.

CHAPTER THREE.

THE DISPLAYING TEXT:

THE WOMAN'S NOVEL

AS [AUTO]BIOGRAPHY

THE SPECTACLE presented in the woman's novel, in that fictional act that I call [auto]biography, is not that "transcendental representation" of the "actual features" of the woman's life or consciousness, in which the "finite, individual self is transmuted into an infinite, aesthetic self."[1] The woman's novel, her [auto]biography, does not posit a mirror-imaging of the world through the "passive instrument" of the "symbolic hero" (or heroine).[2] Neither is the woman's novel a romanticizing device for her readers, or for the writer herself. The writer is not assumed to be a mirror image for her audience and her novel is not held up as a mirror of their lives. Reading a woman's novel is not so philosophically narcissistic an enterprise. Rather, we glimpse a being *not unlike* ourselves; a being who is in a basic way *like us*. In this being's movement, her *making* of something, we are taken by what we see and give ourselves up to further observation of the being whose similarity to us has forcefully "caught our eye"; our eye is caught by her vigorous immersion in her task, the action of her text.

Thus it is the product of the writer's work, her presentation of it, that concerns us. Her work is given to our view, and if the text contains and makes visible the signal or gesture we recognize, the writer's intentions no longer pertain as a matter of the first order. The book is in our hands; the initial gesture is fixed in our gaze. The novel's beauty or usefulness is, indeed, in the beholder's eyes, yours and mine. Our response becomes the measure of such a novel. We do not look into a mirror. We see with our own eyes not a universal, idealistic, or infinite self; rather, we see an object of another woman's making, and it is the *making* that we see in process, the making that presents itself to us in the shape of the woman's text.

INTIMATELY CONNECTED with the form of any text is the question of genre. At the outset I will restate that the mark of the twentieth-century "woman's novel," as I describe it, is a mixing of genres: the novel—the fictional narrative—and autobiography. "Narrative" has received much attention in the last several decades; similarly, "autobiography" is at present under scrutiny.[3]

In *The Autobiographical Act: The Changing Situation of a Literary Genre*, Elizabeth Bruss writes:

> If our task is to capture living generic distinctions, and not simply to "herd books into groups" [a reference to an epigraph from Virginia Woolf], then we must seek for any further specifications—on the relationship between autobiographer and audience, for example—in the context where they emerge and within the literary community which animates them. Definitions of what is appropriate to the autobiographical act are never absolute: they must be created and sustained. The rules I have sketched simply reflect major distinctions which have survived and which continue to be observed.[4]

Her task, as she outlines it, is not to point to the "absolute"; rather, definitions and distinctions appropriate to the autobiographical act must be "created and sustained." "Created and sustained" by whom? We are given no answer to this question. The prescription, the exhortation, remains modestly non-specific, non-attributable, a passive imperative. The ghost of an immutable law seems to float somewhere in the vicinity of this emanating statement.

In an essay entitled "Women's Autobiography and the Male Tradition," Estelle Jelinek makes a comparison basic to her discussion and relevant to ours:

> Recent reviews of two autobiographical works, one Buckminster Fuller's *Synergetics* (1975), the other Kate Millett's *Flying* (1974), demonstrate the continuation of this bias ["social bias against the condition or the delineation of their (women's) lives" that "seems to predominate over critical objectivity"] to our

present decade. O. B. Hardison, Jr., critiquing Fuller's work, writes,

> It is alternately brilliant and obscure, opaque and shot through with moments of poetry. What becomes clear with patience is that the virtues and the liabilities are one. . . . Primary dissociation occurs in language. Words carry with themselves a vast clutter of attitudes, myths, errors, and sloppy approximations that have nothing to do with what we recognize, on reflection, as reality. Hence Fuller's style. It is not an accident. It is as carefully and self-consciously formed as the style of James Joyce, and its purpose is similar to the purpose of poetry: to tell the truth, neither more nor less, as far as possible. Properly understood it is not English but an artificial language with—let it be admitted—all of the liabilities associated with the first version of any complex invention.

With hardly a change of wording, this review could have been describing *Flying*, but typical of the ruthless attacks on that work are Louise Montague Athern's remarks, which annihilate the intention and style of *Flying* in one devastating condemnation.

> . . . a book? No. It is the personal outpouring of a disturbed lady—albeit genius—whose eclectic life is of more interest to her than to the reader. There is no story line, no plot, no continuity. Her writing is a frantic stringing together of words without any thought for the ordinary arrangement of noun and verb. It is hard reading. . . . It is utter confusion.[5]

Jelinek's point is that women are "reviewed" differently from men. And indeed that is often a valid accusation. More important is that the *difference* in response to what is, or can be, "expected" of a woman is founded in the anticipation of conformity. The male (masculinist) writer, on the other hand, is praised for nonconformity, for expanding a genre as it exists, particularly if the "stretching" can be found to originate in an acceptable progenitor (Joyce in the case of Fuller's book).[6] Jelinek further observes:

> More significant are discrepancies between the critical canon and women's autobiographies on matters relating to their form and content. Despite the fact that women's life studies are excluded from the evidence from which the characteristics of the

genre are drawn, it is assumed that they will either conform to them or else be disqualified as autobiographies. One may reasonably question whether including women's autobiographies in critical studies might force modifications in their definitions and theories. Or we might find that different criteria are needed to evaluate women's autobiographies, which may constitute, if not a subgenre, then an autobiographical tradition different from the male tradition.[7]

(Note here, by way of comparison, that Bruss's examples of the mutability and yet the maintenance of autobiography are four, all men: John Bunyan, James Boswell, Thomas De Quincey, and Vladimir Nabokov.)[8]

I suggest that women writers are likely to be subjected by "objective" critics and reviewers to an especially rigorous examination of their credentials, including their adherence to the genre they are attempting, as their professional readers (critics, reviewers, academicians) define it. Such definitions of genre and the evaluation of a writer's "generic credentials" are likely to obey the "immutable laws" that we might call "shadow genres." "Shadow genres," the ghosts of the law, are with us yet. And women's writing is more likely than men's to be subjected to this sub-law, to this "sub-genre" of the "immutable laws" to which Alice James responded with such vehemence.

In response to the *shadow* of the law, rather than to the law itself, the woman's novel stretches the genre of the novel. Just as Jelinek suspects that women's autobiography "may force modifications in . . . definitions and theories,"[9] so I suspect that the mixing of two traditional genres, the novel (prose fiction of an extended length) and autobiography, may modify our expectations of the novel.

Some of this law-breaking is deliberate; much of it is not. Most of us recognize that we ourselves have broken the icon, stepped out of their frame and into ours, only after we have committed the act. But having stepped forward, we cannot step backward. The act begins in innocence; after we have seen its effects, we take the law into our own hands.

A woman is making something. That is what we see in a woman's novel: this display is framed for our attention. The writer frames the space and gives it the contours that allow us to fix our gaze on the performance of her text. An implicit, finally explicit and mutual, recognition of our proprietorship of the womanly gaze occurs in this context—the context of women watching other women in the act of making their texts.

Our literature helps us in "deciphering other highly specialized realms of meaning—in this case, women's conceptual and symbolic worlds."[10] The concepts and the symbols themselves are continuous, and the architectural (archi-textual?) meanings of our literature, the shapes that it regularly and characteristically assumes, represent a continuum of concepts and symbols. Moreover, I suggest that an established, formal recognition of the aesthetic shapes these concepts assume can be of practical as well as theoretical help to us.

We have our own patterns of perception, be they constituted by history or by sexual or gender difference. Recognition and codification of these patterns for our own purposes, in life and in art, work in tandem. The sooner we establish a common frame of reference—artistic, theoretical, and practical—the sooner any of our enterprises will flourish. It is a matter of establishing and maintaining communication in its most basic, communal sense. In recognizing one another in our aesthetic constructs, in coming to reknow one another, we come to reknow ourselves as well. Thereby, we gain knowledge on two fronts and of (our) many selves. If we look at the woman's novel in this context, we can see it operating in the interest of the constitution of a community while, concomitantly, it strengthens each of us.

IF THE woman's novel promotes formation of a community of readers and if that community, in turn, offers the novelist commonly held patterns of perception and recognition through which she develops the form of her novel, then we are talking about a distinct reading and writing community. As I observed earlier, this is a joint enterprise: no patterns in the aesthetic sense could exist without our artists' formalization of them. The artistic enterprise is in this sense "autobiographical"; at the same time, the collective endeavor might more reasonably be called "biographical" in that it is a collective "writing" of what is common to both reader and writer, despite the individual differences of their contextually specific life stories. Thus we might more accurately refer to women's novel writing and reading as [auto]biographical. If the woman's novel can be said to work toward the constitution of community, as, at the same time, it emerges from that community, so the acknowledged community, in developing its own conventions, encourages the development and assertiveness of any individual woman's sense of "self."

A "displaying text," then, is the formalization of the mutual act of display and anticipated and anticipatory recognition. The form of the display, the novel's prominent pattern or structure, can itself be considered an allegorical presentation of the woman's gaze—the woman reader's, the woman writer's—and the novel the point at which they meet. The form of the displaying text makes visible this meeting of their gaze, makes the "invisible" visible; it allows the structure of the text to "speak," to carry the author's voice as well as our own.

The textual voice of the woman's novel can be seen to move in that place where the writer's gaze meets the reader's, in their mutual focus. The meeting of their "eyes" is also the meeting of the "I's" of reader and writer, as well as the blending of their voices. Here the "individual" I of the masculine literary tradition brackets itself out for the duration of the meeting, the reading of the novel. This aesthetic generosity allows the meeting to reinforce the sense of community and relation to others that the woman's novel attempts to achieve.

We might return to the metaphor of theater. We can mark the place of meeting as the stage of the theater displayed by the frame, the arch of the proscenium: voice, text, reader, and writer are joined at just this point. The relationships and the process that are melded into a single image on this stage characterize what I am calling the "displaying text" of the woman's novel. Such a rendering allows us a visual representation of the theater of the text of the novel. It is a metaphor dependent precisely on our visual apprehension of the space, the context, in which we live, and write, our lives. As Adrienne Rich writes, "*I choose to walk here. And to draw this circle.*"[11] So we place ourselves unequivocally in our novels by a paradoxical inscription of ourselves in the scene, the place, of our lives, in order to expand and share both the inscription and the living.

IN AN ESSAY called "Women's Autobiography in France: For a Dialectics of Identification," Nancy K. Miller asks, "To the extent that autobiography, as Diane Johnson has put it, 'requires some strategy of self-dramatization,' and 'contains, as in fiction, a crisis and a denouement,' what conventions . . . govern the production of a female self as *theater*: that which literally is given to be seen? How does a woman writer perform on the stage of her text? What, in a word, is a one-woman show?"[12] I began my inquiry with nearly identical questions. Although Miller's approach to the relation between women's autobiography and women's fiction diverges from my own, her essay serves a complementary purpose.

Miller proposes

> a dialectical practice of reading which would privilege *neither* the autobiography *nor* the fiction, but take the two writings together in their status as text. . . . [N]ot to perform an expanded reading, not, in this instance, to read the fiction *with* the autobiography is to remain a prisoner of a canon that bars women from their own texts. . . . [A woman writer's] textual "I" is not bound by *genre*. . . . The historical truth of a woman writer's life lies in the reader's grasp of her intratext: the body of her writing and not the writing of her body.[13]

I am in perfect agreement with Miller's thesis concerning thorough critical reading of a woman writer. It is the woman writer's inscription of self, not a textual rendering of her biology or body, that is of primary importance. At the same time, I stress the "common reader's" meeting with a text, a novel *or* a professed autobiography. Such a meeting is likely to take place between (or on the stage of) a single volume and the reader. Such a reader may have neither the opportunity nor the motivation for reading the whole text of a given writer—a circumstance that, in Miller's terms, seems to preclude an involvement with, or a reading of, the "intratext" of the writer, the "body of her work."

The trace of the autobiography, the *autobiographical self*, will appear in the writer's fiction. If the choice were between autobiography and fiction, fiction offers us a more intimate connection with other women than does the typically more decorous and constrained facticity of autobiography. In speculating on useful readings of *any* woman's novel, particularly perhaps those of women who have written fiction exclusively, I must proceed as if the fictional text is all there is. I suggest that it is enough.

My concern is the meeting of reader and writer, which, in my view, is most fully accomplished through the medium of fiction; that is, in the theater of a woman's fictional text. The aesthetic experience of an individual novel, as opposed to the critical study that concerns itself with the whole of a woman's work, is bounded by the single stage of one novel's performance, which is framed for the individual text's display. The meeting is singular; the performance, discrete. However, the practical aesthetic advantage of the fictional text is its capacity for textual theatrics.

The textual voice of the woman's novel blends speech and sight, reader and writer, to *show* us those things that have been left "unsaid," literally unspoken, in all likelihood, within traditional modes of masculine discourse. But in the theater of the woman's novel the "unsaid things" are marked all the more clearly to allow us to say "I *see*." What we see are our own patterns of response, recognition, and building. In the realm of fiction we remain in the realm of what we have been taught to think opposes itself to "fiction": the context of our common life.

Indeed, the woman writer's textual "I" is not bound by the literary contexts and borders of genre. By shedding one kind of "generic" identification—the autobiographical "I"—for the meeting on the stage of another woman's text, we find ourselves engaged in a fundamental conversation. In reading a woman's novel we commit ourselves not only to a dialectics of identification, but also to the conversation that will expand into an articulation of our differences.

CHAPTER FOUR.

THE FUNDAMENTAL

CONVERSATION

Perhaps we must now put our toes to the ground again and get back to the spoken word, only from a different angle.
—Virginia Woolf in a letter
to George Rylands (1934)

"FEMINIST DISCOURSE has always picked up the terms of anti-feminist discourse and been determined by it," write Elaine Marks and Isabelle de Courtivron about the critical debate with men throughout the course of French (and, by extension, Western European) history.[1] For most of that history and even more recently no debate was possible. In this century, on the contrary, our most energizing fiction writers have "picked up the terms of anti-feminist discourse" and *used* them. In the first third of the century, those who accomplished this did so not from a position of apparent strength but out of necessity, from a position of relative "weakness."[2]

Many theorists writing in the 1960s and 1970s project (perhaps inadvertently) a sense of the pallor of the language available for use in women's creative endeavors. Frustration is often implicit in their own descriptions of the perceivable state of women's previous language practice. Suppressed anger is probably the filter for such an effect, as it is the fuel for the feeling of urgency infusing their writing. The exigencies of the situation seem to demand an alert stance, and, above all, energetic action.

Recognizing this need, Xavière Gauthier, for example, asks, "how can women speak 'otherwise,' unless, perhaps, we can *make audible* that which agitates within us, suffers silently in the *holes of discourse*, in the unsaid, or in the non-sense."[3] She quotes the novelist Monique Wittig, who points to "the *intervals* that your masters have not been able to *fill* with their words of proprietors and possessors, this can be found in the *gaps*, in all that which is not a continuation of their discourse."[4] "Blank pages, gaps, borders, spaces and silence, holes in discourse," Gauthier concludes her essay, "If the reader feels disoriented in this new space, one which is obscure and silent, it proves perhaps, that it is women's space."[5]

More recently, writers offer commentary with an air of parodic cynicism that they intend to undermine, even as they simulate its cadence. Nancy Miller suggests, "perhaps we shall not have a poetics of women's literature until we have more weak readers."[6] Miller cites the "repressed content" of the novels of women writers, a content she identifies as "an impulse to power," an egoistic desire rather than an erotic one (as Freud would suggest), an impulse that would "revise the social grammar in which women are never defined as subjects." "I am talking, of course," Miller says, "about the power of the weak."[7]

In a similar vein, Xavière Gauthier suggests, "perhaps if we had left these pages blank, we would have had a better understanding of what feminine writing is all about."[8]

> In fact, what surprises us is the fact that men and women seem to speak approximately the same language; in other words, women find "their" place within the linear, grammatical, linguistic system that orders the symbolic, the superego, the law. . . . And we can marvel . . . at the fact that women are alienated enough to be able to speak "the language of Man." "*If there is a madman, then it's definitely the Woman.*"[9]

She assesses our situation in this way:

> Women are, in fact, caught in a very real contradiction. Throughout the course of history, they have been mute, and it is doubtless by virtue of this mutism that men have been able to speak and write. As long as women remain silent, they will be outside the historical process. But if they begin to speak and write *as men do*, they will enter history subdued and alienated; it is a history that, logically speaking, their speech should disrupt.[10]

As Shirley and Edwin Ardener's diagram of the relationship between the dominant (men's) and the muted (women's) cultures of a society shows us,[11] the muted culture is not "mute"—not silent, dumb, or without speech—but muted. It is a culture that is subdued in its sounds, not lacking in them. Like a musical instrument, its "resonance" has been affected, even deadened, but *without any effect on the vibrations of the instrument* (as the *OED* describes the effect). As a metaphor, the latter phrase echoes the pathos of Gauthier's "that which agitates within us, suffers silently in the holes of discourse." It is not the *power* to speak that is absent, but the felt authority to effect release of the resonance of our speech. Such a release we may effect for ourselves.

As Elaine Showalter points out, by using the word "muted" Ardener

> suggests problems both of language and of power. . . . Another way of putting this would be to say that all language is the language of the dominant order, and women, if they speak at all, must speak *through* it. How then, Ardener asks, "does the symbolic weight of that other mass of persons express itself?" In his view, women's beliefs find expression through ritual and art, expressions which can be deciphered by the ethnographer, either female or male, who is willing to make the effort to perceive beyond the *screens* of the dominant culture.[12]

Thus, as Showalter describes it, Ardener's view suggests that we may take the word "muted" to mean "screened." We can also use Showalter's other phrasing of the situation: "all language is the language of the dominant order, and women, if they speak at all, must speak through it." Not with it, by means of it, but *through* it, so that the full resonance of our speech shows through the "gaps, [the] spaces . . . the holes in the discourse." The skeleton of our initial discourse is revealed by these gaps; they provide a window into the larger space that aids the formalization of our own "archi-textual" principles, our own principles of articulation.[13]

The first step in identifying and examining a woman's writing, a woman's novelistic discourse, is thus to look for (and at) these gaps, the spaces and the holes in (male) discourse. It is there that the woman is shaping the "other" language. The woman writing displays the possibilties of her language in the shape of her text precisely by filling the gaps; her *writing*, even more than her language, is to be found, as Wittig reminds us, "in all that which is not a continuation of their discourse." Our discourse, then, is literally to be found in a space of our own. We might call this a sculpting in space if we did not already have the word "writing" to indicate such an activity. At the same time we call making our text(s) a "weaving"; our texts are written in a context, woven into and out of a context, that includes men's language as a dominant idiom. But that dominance does not by any means predominate in the place(s) of *writing* as their spoken language dominates "public" *speech*. Such domination occurs "privately," too, when the public language is brought to bear upon the private language practice of men and women together, as Jean Rhys's novels reveal.

We might most simply refer to the practice of a woman's text, considering practice to be not only the "exercise of an art or skill," but a demonstration of the *usual* or *conventional* conduct of a woman's text. "Conventional" is a key word here, referring to the conventions of a body of texts as they are determined by the community from which they emerge and for which they are written. Recognition of a conventional practice defines that writing as the presentation of a formal practice or activity whose *resonance* is heard and understood, its value as a way of knowing accepted as given, a part of that community's epistemology.

In this respect, we can view 1949, when Simone de Beauvoir's *The Second Sex* was first published, as a date that signals a public recognition of ourselves as a collectivity and also marks the shift from a nineteenth-century to a twentieth-century sensibility. Similarly, the emergence of Jean Rhys's writing practice is implicated in forces of "history" on a larger scale: the two World Wars and the ideological, political, and social shifts that generated and attended them. Middle-class women perforce came out of their houses and into the public sphere; working-class women found a new valuation and voice, and economic improvement. Having moved into the public sphere by means of historical circumstance, women found themselves able to see and to speak to one another in ways unavailable to them before; they became able to see themselves actively, publicly, and collectively. A woman writing in this way, making visible what was formerly "invisible," illustrates for us that we are—indeed, must be—our own audience.

The writer who most forcibly brought home to me this necessity is Jean Rhys, a woman of my grandmother's generation, a woman whose language is used in such a way that her *writing* strikes us as particularly "modern." The note of modernity can perhaps be attributed to the crucial time in which Rhys came to adulthood and wrote her first four novels (published between 1928 and 1939). She spent her life between the two World Wars primarily in two national capitals (Paris and London) in a period of ideological upheaval and economic depression (revolution and the establishment of the socialist state in the USSR; the Spanish Civil War and the rise of fascism in Germany and Italy). Similarly, it was a time of intellectual and psychological innovation (e.g., Freud, Jung)—a time that can now be said to have been the laboratory for the fundamental crises of the society we live in today. With virtually no specific reference to external or political events, Rhys nevertheless catches the tone of what have become familiar aspects of our lives. Her writing seems our contemporary, even if the woman is not. Jean Rhys has extraordinary current appeal for many readers. I wondered how she was able to achieve so much in the seemingly little space she gave herself; her novels are short, and they portray a woman who is victimized or down and out, psychologically as well as economically or socially. How was she able to produce novels that speak to us now with such appeal and force? The answer seems to be that Jean Rhys was, for reasons to be enumerated, unself-consciously, and perhaps "thoughtlessly," her *own* audience. These reasons partake of the stereotypically feminine—the narcissism, vanity, and peculiarly inverted egoism of the underclass. Rhys was "her own audience" in an undisguisedly self-centered way that is morally suspect in our society. We will discover, I think, that her writing is in the strictest sense highly moral. It is true that she wrote *for her self*; in the most specific way possible, her writing was written *for a woman*. And in this writing she both disrupts the framework of masculine discourse and fills in the gaps in that discourse to expose her own language—our language—and theirs. In this process of exposure she places the "silent" speech, the "unsaid things," center stage. Her writing speaks out loud what is left unsaid, showing us, allowing us to hear, the full resonance of our speech through the gaps, the spaces, the "holes" in masculine discourse.

AN EXPATRIATE COLONIAL, Jean Rhys was born Ella Gwendolen Rees Williams in 1890 in Dominica, an island in the West Indies.[14] Rhys left Dominica in 1907, when she was sixteen; she spent a year in England and the following nine years on the Continent, mostly in Paris. She returned to England in 1927 and lived there for the rest of her life, making occasional trips to France. Interest in Rhys has steadily increased since the publication of *Wide Sargasso Sea* in 1966. In the mid-1960s Francis Wyndham, an early admirer, remarked that Rhys's books were "ahead of their age, both in spirit and in style."[15] In 1974, when Rhys was eighty-four years old, she was called "quite simply, the best living English novelist."[16] After Rhys's death in 1979, V. S. Pritchett appraised her work and its appeal for "the later generation who came to see her point":

> [Rhys] became—what she was to remain all her life—an early example not of the Bohemian but of the displaced person. At that level, she turned to her first secret writing of a diary; for years it was her *capital*.
>
> And here one has a clue to her curious position as a writer later on and her original quality. She was not a feminist. She was simply feminine and took the rough with the smooth, without foresight. . . . Her eye is as sharp as a needle, herself—indifferent? In one of her novels she mentions a discovery: that there is more than one way of looking at things. Her position as a displaced person was that there was no position. That was what caught the attention of the later generation who came to see her point. Displacement had become a norm.[17]

Indeed, this is one way of reading her work and assessing it; it is also a way to account for her appeal to men. On the other hand, most male critics take pains to demonstrate the success of her "craft," which is readily noted, along with the appeal of the position from which she writes. Albert Alvarez, for example, characterizes Rhys's vantage as a "position of weakness: as though orphaned."[18] This sentimental view of the position from which Rhys writes, the same position as that assumed by her heroine-narrators, is usually counterbalanced by male critical response to the "lucid, exact, and swift . . . [the] exceptionally clean" qualities of her style.[19] Alvarez calls her style "youthful, light, clear, alert, casual and disabused"; a style that "simply" tells the "truth." He sees a "purity" in her novels.[20] Pritchett sees the source of this stylistic "purity" in Rhys's possible "indifference," her "cold detachment as an artist." She is not "swamped by feeling," he suggests; "she watches it in others."[21] "[W]hat a stoic thing she makes the act of writing appear," Naipaul comments with evident admiration.[22]

For the woman reader, none of these explanations seems sufficient. The clarity, exactness, and lucidity conjured up by such descriptions of Rhys's style may point us in the right direction, but my
perception of the source of the effect of her work is at extreme variance with a view of these qualities as the result of "indifference,"
"detachment," or "stoicism."

Rhys would have agreed that she was a "displaced" person. She
had no place in the "official" world and its societies as she knew
them: as a woman with no reliable protector and no money, a Creole
and a colonial who was separated by her mind-set from other Creoles
and from colonials as well. But as for her "detachment," we have her
word, and the evidence of it in her work, that she recorded "what
he *said* and what [she] *felt*."[23] In other words, she recorded what he
said, and what she *wanted to say* but didn't. If her (and her heroine-
narrator's) inability to speak out loud, to say what she felt in conversation with "him" or "them" is considered a deliberately chosen position, then one may call her "artistry" "cold," her "detachment" "indifferent."

The masculinist tradition, perhaps, *sees* the Rhys heroine clearly.
What readers in this tradition see, apparently, is "needle-sharp."
They attribute this acuity to Rhys's "eye"; they note her "discovery"
that there is "more than one way of looking at things." What they
perhaps fail to see, as well as to hear, is that there are only *two* positions: up and down, that of the oppressed (or the "repressed," as
some feminist critics prefer) and of the oppressor. Or, rejecting this
vocabulary (as Rhys herself does), we are left with the salient distinctions in our society: sex and/or gender marking. All other distinctions aside (and Rhys does not, finally, put them aside; nor will I as
my discussion develops), there are women and there are men.

The upshot is that a "displaced" person, as presented by Rhys,
does not feel that there is "no position." Rather, there are essentially
and emphatically only two positions: people with a place—both
women and men, especially those whose place is "at the top"—and
people with no place, who are likely to be "at the bottom." The result,
as she announces in *Good Morning, Midnight*, is "What they call an
impasse."[24]

Rhys demonstrates the displacement of "Woman" (of women) in
her conversations, her dialogue, with "Man" (with men). In the writing of her books, she can be said to have fulfilled one of her ideas of

a "book": "Before I could read, almost a baby, I imagined that God, this strange thing or person I heard about, was a book. Sometimes it was a large book standing upright and half open and I could see the print inside but it made no sense to me. Other times the book was smaller and inside were sharp flashing things. The smaller book was, I am sure now, my mother's needle book and the sharp flashing things were her needles with the sun on them."[25] The "large book" can be considered to represent or to belong to the father, the earthly as well as the heavenly father—symbolically in either case. Her mother's "small" book, an earthly, commonplace needle book, made sense to her, containing useful things for sewing, for drawing material together: "her [mother's] needles with the sun on them," shining and illuminating, *known*, unlike the large book whose "print" she could see but which nevertheless made no sense to her. If, as a writer, her "eye is as sharp as a needle," she seems to have chosen for this fulfillment the "smaller book," which had inside it "sharp flashing things." Rhys chose the material "mother-book" as her model for knowing the world.

At the same time, the "book"—"God"—is compounded of both these images. Rhys's symbolic for God, who "made" the world, her world, contains both "books." Rhys's own writing practice traces the relationship between the two books in her own model for the presentation of the dialogue that is God—the book.

If the woman's novel itself makes a gesture to which the woman reader responds, if this gesture is a signal for the woman reader's attention, then it is the writing *practice* to which we attend as much as the content, the plot or story the novelist presents. If Rhys's craft is as exact as her critics (male and female) agree that it is, we might especially attend to this aspect of her work. Since thematic concerns and stylistic presentation are especially bonded in Rhys's work, we are even more encouraged to look at the implications of her techniques.

The display of Rhys's text is achieved in her explicit presentation of language(s) or idioms: her language, our language, men's language. For the moment, we can consider the basic or framing text to be the common text of our language as it is structured and practiced by men for their own purposes. Rhys reveals not only the woman's story, the *place* of the woman's language, but also the clash of male and female idioms, the stunning impasse implicit in a language use that is both the instrument of the ascendant, dominating idiom (the manipulation of which comes to seem indifference for, or toward, both men and women) and the paradigm for other repressions, a model for sustained control.

What Rhys does is present the doll moving, the silenced woman speaking, the woman as automaton brought to life through her actions on and use of *the language given to her by men*. This larger context—the language text we share unevenly, asymmetrically, with men —is the initial and given body of material upon which we work in the particular purposive use of language that we call "writing."

In the long history of this unevenly shared use of language within the mainstream novelistic tradition, Rhys may be the first practitioner of a woman's writing who allows women's language to reveal itself through overt dialogue with the language and discourse of men. Others before her—Jane Austen, Charlotte Brontë, George Eliot in *The Mill on the Floss* and *Middlemarch*, Charlotte Perkins Gilman, Susan Glaspell, Kate Chopin[26]—had articulated women's difference from men in plots and characterization, in what are usually called the "central concerns" of a writer, or of her novels. Others exploited difference in what, given the literary conventions of their eras, can be seen as idiosyncratic language or writing practices. Emily Brontë in the mid-nineteenth century, for example, and later Dorothy Richardson and May Sinclair attempted to mold a prose to reflect a woman's consciousness.[27] Gertrude Stein formed her own language-in-writing in a fashion and to a degree that is idiosyncratic in the extreme.[28] Virginia Woolf attempted a more global rendering of consciousness that is "womanly" in the most basic sense; her womanly, indeed, feminist, concerns appear most overtly in her essays *A Room of One's Own* and *Three Guineas*, and in her experiments with the essay-novel form.

According to one's perspective, these endeavors either remain embedded in the context of male structures or they emerge most forcefully when they are construed as marginal to the dominant societal framework. They are "marginal" in the sense of constituting a powerful evocation of their heroine's, or the writer's, marginality. The language practice itself, in its broad appeal, remains firmly centered in male discursive practice—except for the opposite extreme, which leads to idiosyncrasy rather than to a direct, collective appeal to its audience. Virginia Woolf's booklength essays and the essay-novel are an exception, in that they engage the dominant framework, but they do so, at least insofar as our initial or superficial perception of them, *as exposition* rather than as novelistic formulation.[29]

Rhys's work brings this marginality out of the closet and places it center stage in books that we clearly recognize as novels. Her plots, the protagonists and their stories as she presents them, are stereotypical: "Woman" as victim, classless except as she is attached to a man, powerless, marginal in her own life and integral in her marginality to the moneyed male culture that dominates life, a woman used in all the ways that a woman might be used. In the early novels a Rhys protagonist sees herself as "mannequin" or "doll." She is—and comes to know she is—mask and symbol as well as flesh and blood woman misused. At the same time, through Rhys's writing, the "grinning mask," the doll, talks back. She is moved, pawnlike, by fate, by men, and by money, which are the same in her world. But by means of the dialogue that Rhys frames, "she" (writer and heroine-narrator) takes them on at the level where they are at once the most powerful and the most vulnerable: at the level of their language. Her *writing* of their language reveals their weakness, their strengths—and her own. She seizes a place for herself from within their own most basic structuring device: the language they, and we, use.

In her actual life, Rhys may or may not have been able to "talk back" to men, but the evidence is strong that the insights and experiences of her heroine-narrators are close to her own. And in her writing the fundamental conversation is taken up. Rhys's writing presents a continuing dialogue with the dominant language, and at the same time makes explicit the place of a woman's own language. This place is one Rhys makes out of the stuff of the other language, within the context of which she is forced to live as well as to speak. In writing, the speaking of the language is transformed. Rhys *writes* what her characters may not, do not, *say out loud*; she writes the "unsaid things."[30] The "hidden" plot, the "other plot" in nineteenth-century fiction, has become dominant; it is central to Rhys's novels and to Rhys's writing practice. Rhys displays the meeting of male and female language practices at the historical moment at which, and of which, she writes.

The Rhys heroine may be "torn apart" psychologically by men as the doll Olympia is torn apart by men in Hoffmann's "The Sand-Man." But the feminine practice of writing, of writing "books," retrieves the voice as well as the eyes, the essence of the life of the doll, the victimized and passive woman. In her unfinished autobiography, *Smile Please*, Rhys relates a scene from her own childhood that is reminiscent of a scene remembered by Hoffmann's Nathanael. Each recollection is central to its story, but with a difference.

Rhys's nurse found the little girl's reading annoying and improper and tried to frighten her into stopping:

> My nurse, who was called Meta, didn't like me much anyway, and complete with a book it was too much. One day she found me crouched on the staircase reading a bowdlerized version of *The Arabian Nights* in very small print.
>
> She said, "If all you read so much, you know what will happen to you? Your eyes will drop out and they will look at you from the page."
>
> "If my eyes dropped out I wouldn't see," I argued.
>
> She said, "They drop out except the little black points you see with."
>
> I half believed her and imagined my pupils like heads of black pins and all the rest gone. But I went on reading.[31]

In Hoffmann's tale, the nurse tells the child a frightening story in which the Sand-man causes children's eyes to "jump out of their heads all bloody; and he puts them into a bag and takes them to the half-moon as food for his little ones; and they sit there in the nest and have hooked beaks like owls and they pick naughty little boys' and girls' eyes out with them."[32]

As Freud points out concerning "The Sand-Man," the loss of the boy-child's eyes amounts to castration, and the fear of such a happening is the fear of castration within the framework of the Oedipal complex. In Rhys's case, the incident with the nurse is directly connected to the act of reading; neither nurse nor child suggests or imagines that the child's actual *sight* could be taken from her. We can take such a construction straightforwardly, despite whatever psycho-analytical constructions we put on Rhys's own description of the origin of her ideas of books. Books can be construed as both God as itself and God as unacknowledgedly mother's, or, as God-as-itself, God-as-father, and God-as-mother. The two books of "father" and "mother" provide the dichotomous base for the over-arching image or view of God-as-book. The father-book can easily be seen as phallic; the other, vaginal. What the child "saw"—in either case—was a "book," and the activity that was reading was pursued fearlessly, for "the little black points you see with" remain with you, the essence of the activity is not lost, the essential organ and ability remain. Unlike the doll Olympia or her lover Nathanael in Hoffmann's tale, Rhys had and kept "her own eyes" and made full use of them.

Rhys herself can help us if we are not overly insistent on using the Freudian lexicon or if we prefer, for example, newer psychological constructions that posit the power of the mother in a daughter's development in particular.[33] Rhys preferred the Catholic catechism to the Anglican, she tells us, because it was "more forthright." She relates a repeated incident that was a source of evident pleasure and "confirmation" for her. It occurred at the Catholic convent to which Rhys (an Anglican) was sent and in which she was one of a minority; "coloured" girls constituted the majority of the students:

> "Who made you?" it asked, and my chief memory of the catechism was a little girl who persisted obstinately in saying, "My mother!"
>
> "No, dear, that's not the answer. Now think—who made you?"
>
> "My mother," the stolid girl replied. At last, the nun, exasperated, banished her from the class.[34]

We have opposed here two "books"—her mother's and God, the father's, the dialogue between the two making up God itself. Again, mother as maker rather than God, the father as maker, seems to be Rhys's chosen model. Her own place in the dialogue is clear, and her own books display for us the dialogue between the two.

Initially the "fundamental conversation" is the dialogue between a woman's language and men's, between her idiom and theirs. The other, perhaps more urgently fundamental, conversation consists in the woman reader's recognition of the authenticity of the dialogue and her concomitant recognition of her own language in Rhys's rendering of it. The form of Rhys's novels insists on the centrality of her own language, of a woman's language in contradistinction to that of men. This insistence is achieved by the aesthetic practice of rendering women's *speech* (or non-speech) into a woman's *writing*. It is this quality, I suggest, to which we respond in Rhys's work. As a woman, the reader recognizes the dialogue, and the fundamental conversation, of which she too is a part. Like Rhys in *Wide Sargasso Sea*, Rhys's own response to Charlotte Brontë's *Jane Eyre*, we read ourselves into her text and continue the conversation. We place ourselves through our own language into a weave of our own making, a context of our own.

THE FEMININE NOVEL that Rhys presents is cast in the mold of an obsessive autobiography—five novels in which seemingly "only the name of the heroine is changed": *Quartet* [called *Postures* in the original English edition] (1928), *After Leaving Mr Mackenzie* (1930), *Voyage in the Dark* (1934), *Good Morning, Midnight* (1939), and *Wide Sargasso Sea* (1966). This last novel, published more than a quarter-century later, is the retelling of *Jane Eyre* from Bertha Rochester's point of view, or more precisely, the insertion of "Bertha's" story into the weave of Brontë's text.

Although published third, *Voyage in the Dark* presents the first leg of the life journey undertaken by the young woman who is Rhys's continuing protagonist. It is also her most instructive and compelling novel for initial examination. *Quartet* is second chronologically in the narrative of the heroine's life. *After Leaving Mr Mackenzie* is third in the narrative chronology; its third-person presentation carries the heroine's story forward, or downward, if one accepts the view that her career, like Rhys's, followed "every rung of that long and dismal ladder by which the respectable citizen descends toward degradation."[35] *Good Morning, Midnight* completes the explicit chronology of the apparent narrative presented in the first four novels and demonstrates a variation—more thematic than technical—on the basic concerns Rhys reveals in *Voyage*. It was the last of Rhys's novels before she became "silent" for almost three decades. *Wide Sargasso Sea* expands the context of Rhys's presentation technically, thematically, and autobiographically.

Let us examine Albert Alvarez's description of Jean Rhys's work and life:

> Miss Rhys's apparently autobiographical heroines have been, in their time, chorus girl, mannequin, artist's model, even a part-time prostitute. In other words, they are in the Muse business, the stunning, vulnerable girls who, when Miss Rhys began writing, more usually inspired books than wrote them. At the beginning of "Voyage in the Dark" the 19-year-old virgin chorus girl is reading "Nana"; at the end she like Nana, is on the game, but

chillingly and without any of Zola's unearned polemic. This makes the world Miss Rhys creates seem strangely unprecedented. . . . She makes you realize that almost every other novel, however apparently anarchic, is rooted finally in the respectable world. The authors come to their subjects from a position of strength and with certain intellectual presuppositions, however cunningly suppressed. She, in contrast, has a marvelous artistic intelligence—no detail is superfluous and her poise never falters as she walks her wicked emotional tightrope—yet is absolutely nonintellectual: no axe to grind, no ideas to tout.

She also writes from a position of weakness: as though orphaned, her women . . . "too vulnerable ever to make a success of a career of chance."[36]

We note that Alvarez's assessment is rooted in an identification with the respectable, the precedented, the "fathered." This identification is unlike Brontë's Lucy Snowe or Rhys and her heroines, who identify with their own state as orphans—morally, aesthetically—politically, in the broadest sense. The "wicked emotional tightrope" Jean Rhys walks, her "strangely unprecedented" world, is a spectacle preeminently disreputable, dizzyingly "nonintellectual"—above all, not *respectable*. A "Muse" turned creator, the world turned upside down: all this achieved through a "position of weakness," which is, of course, "orphaned"—not "fathered."

The "poise," the tightrope walking, may be the impression the male reader (the masculinist reader of either sex?) is most likely to receive. V. S. Naipaul perceives that "balancing" act as her real achievement, something that is "less of a 'statement,' more balanced and effective, lighter and truer."[37] What the woman reader, or the feminist reader of either sex, is likely to read are the spaces beneath and around that tightrope, the language that inhabits "empty" space. Rather than walking a "wicked emotional tightrope" over the abysses of the language differences between women and men, Rhys fills in the spaces and spells them out.

The world Rhys presents to the reader is not a demimonde within the framework of social and economic structures and hierarchies. Nor is it a demimonde in its "literal meaning," as Elgin Mellown describes the world of the Rhys heroine: "theirs is only a partial existence. They know that they are alive because they suffer and because money passes through their hands. The respectable world views such women as commodities to be bought and hostages who must pay their way."[38] Rhys's "unprecedented" world is a world of women's speech, of women talking back, saying what they *want* to say, in the interstices of the "real" dialogue. It is this presentation, integral to the basic technical achievement of the novels, for which Rhys sets the precedent. It matters not if what her heroine-narrators want to say is unsuitable for today's more "liberated" woman: the recording of a woman's *unspoken* response within the set framework of masculine speech or discourse is the point.

"Rhys's achievement is very grand," Naipaul said in 1972. However, he continues, "Her books may serve current causes, but she is above causes. What she has written about she has endured, over a long life, and what a stoic thing she makes the act of writing appear."[39] Alvarez remarked that Rhys is "too pure an artist to allow herself the luxury of self-pity."[40] As I have already suggested, there is nothing "stoic" about the act of *writing* in Jean Rhys's novels. If a reader identifies Rhys with her heroines so closely that the reader believes Rhys's work to be straight autobiography, as we often define "autobiography,"[41] then, yes, her narrative style would be a remarkable achievement, one attesting to her ultimate moral fiber. As the writer of her own life, she would have wrenched a kind of artistic success out of the jaws of calamity (not to mention the jaws of imprudence).

But this is not the case. Rhys is writing fiction, no matter how autobiographical much of her material may be. In fact, for her first four novels, Rhys extrapolated from a ten-year period (1919–29) in a life eighty-nine years long. Her short stories continue this [auto]biographical stance. As Elizabeth Vreeland reemphasizes, "The chief character in almost all her work is a woman who seems to follow in her creator's path step by step: from a West Indian childhood, through the ordeal of life in the provincial theater in pre-World War I England, to an elderly solitude in the English countryside."[42] However, Rhys's editor late in her career, Diana Athill, points out the difference between Rhys's fiction and her life:

> What Jean Rhys used to say about the relationship between
> her life and her novels only confirms what is understood by
> most writers and students of writing, but perhaps it is worth re-

calling here. All her writing, she used to say, started out from something that had happened, and her first concern was to get it down as accurately as possible. But "I like shape very much"— and again, "a novel has to have a shape, and life doesn't have any." If the novel was going to work, then it would soon start to have its own shape (her feeling seemed to be that the novel had it, rather than that she imposed it). Then she would be compelled to leave out things that had happened, or to put things in; to increase this or diminish that—all this to suit the shape and nature of the work of art which was forming out of the original experience.[43]

What Rhys seizes out of the context of her material is her own use of the language of men. She takes the unprecedented further step of speaking her own language in the interstices of the "dominant" language. She makes herself heard through the medium of the novel, in her practice of the writing of their language and hers, languages that we recognize.

V. S. Naipaul, discussing "the Jean Rhys tone" in *Good Morning, Midnight*, writes that "the middle-aged narrator will say something like this" (the narrator does in fact say precisely "this" [*Midnight*, pp. 25–26]):

> Well, let's argue this out, Mr. Blank. You, who represent Society, have the right to pay me 400 francs a month. That's my market value, for I am an inefficient member of Society, slow in the uptake, uncertain, slightly damaged in the fray, there's no denying it. So you have the right to pay me 400 francs a month, to lodge me in a small, dark room, to clothe me shabbily, to harass me with worry and monotony and unsatisfied longings till you get me to the point when I blush at a look, cry at a word. . . . But I wish you a lot of trouble, Mr. Blank, and just to start off with, your damned shop's going bust.[44]

Naipaul is right when he says this captures Rhys's "tone." The tone of her early novels is that of the heroine "talking back" (but without tangible effect) to the man or men controlling her life, to "Mr. Blank." It is more difficult to pin down the "truth" of what she may or may not have expressed, that formulation which is "more balanced and effective, lighter and truer" than a "statement."[45] But the *tone* is right. And, one agrees, it is not a matter of making statements. What matters is Rhys's initiation of a dialogue, her mapping of the terrain upon which we may *begin* to argue. In *Wide Sargasso Sea* Rhys delineates and expands the possibilities inherent in that dialogue and in that terrain once we recognize it as our own.

BEFORE MOVING to a specific analysis of Rhys's novels, I want to make some general comments concerning Rhys's approach and technique, especially regarding the apparent subjectivity of her presentation. The emphatic subjectivity of the first-person narration in *Voyage in the Dark*, for example, allows a more marked response to the display of the world that Rhys's heroine-narrator inhabits than would be allowed by the allegedly more seductive narrative world of third-person narration. Rhys's writing specifically and consistently "opposes" her language to "his," effectively replacing it as the focus of our interest, especially as this focus is expanded in *Wide Sargasso Sea*. This is the stylistic reward of her books, for Rhys and for her readers—the clarification of her opposition to the language and the system it effectively represents. A subjective experience *within* the language context, the essential context of *Voyage in the Dark*, as I read it, suggests ways of "reading" the language subjectively that are by no means limited. Rather, such a limitation allows the reader to see the slippages in the language context (its blanks, silences, gaps and holes) as we experience them, which can only be subjectively. Through the inexperience and subjectivity of the naive heroine-narrator of *Voyage in the Dark*, Anna Morgan, we see these blanks and gaps more clearly than in the more aesthetically distanced presentation of *Good Morning, Midnight*.

Of course, a reader sees the heroine-narrator's subjective naiveté, but "the aesthetic value of both *Voyage in the Dark* and *Good Morning, Midnight* is raised [in comparison with Rhys's first two novels] because the first person point of view is the technical correlative of Jean Rhys's understanding of life."[46] This recognition by Rhys herself, the "solution to [her] narrative problem," as Elgin Mellown has characterized it, came first in *Voyage*; it shows the strength of a first impression somehow adhering to the naive narrator's point of view. It is a perspective that is rawer, more subjective than that of the next-composed novel, *Good Morning, Midnight*.

Mellown suggests that there is more "action" in *Voyage in the Dark*, although *Good Morning, Midnight* is "actually the most accomplished of the four novels [prior to *Wide Sargasso Sea*] in terms of *character* development."[47] What Mellown calls "action" I would call a demonstration, perhaps, of the concerns to which Rhys returns in *Wide Sargasso Sea*:[48] the overriding importance of subjective context, especially as we see it in language, and its seemingly inevitable clash with an *other* context which is, or attempts to prove that it is, dominant. Character development is not the emphasis or the point of *Voyage in the Dark*; the novel is, rather, a demonstration of point of view. The world of language that we inhabit is perceivable only from a delimited point of view, one defined by its (and our) limitations. Those limits are what the heroine-narrator draws for us, repeatedly, until they are indelible. The more limited the point of view and the more subjective (or naive) the narrator, the more clearly the lines are drawn. And one can understand that expression—"the lines are drawn"—to mean both the outlines of the structure that she and Rhys present to our view and the lines of opposition that we seemingly cannot cross. These lines can be construed both as borders, with the suggestion of separate countries—legal and political entities—and as battle lines.

Rhys's world in her first four novels is one of oppositions. The borders represented by these oppositions are the lines we cannot cross, as is demonstrated pervasively in our structures of speech and in the context of our language practice. This impasse is what is on display in the Jean Rhys novel, notably in the technical accomplishment of *Voyage in the Dark*.

Voyage in the Dark presents Rhys as she was when she was young and impressionable. The writer herself, however, was nearing middle age as she prepared the presentation of this young "self." In *Smile Please* Rhys says that the diary upon which the novel was based was written in white heat at the close of the affair that was obviously the model for the one described in *Voyage*.[49] As Rhys told Elizabeth Vreeland, "I wrote the makings of *Voyage in the Dark* long, long ago. I wrote it in several exercise books and then I put it away for years."[50] The connection between the childhood scenes in *Voyage* and reuse of similar material in *Wide Sargasso Sea* suggests a basic vision in the earlier novel that is absent from the other three early novels.

Wide Sargasso Sea represents a coming full circle—as well as an expansion of Rhys's ideas of language, context, and point of view—

when it is examined in relation to *Voyage*. A more direct relationship can be established between *Voyage* and *Wide Sargasso Sea* than between *Wide Sargasso Sea* and the other early novels. This relation suggests that technically, as well as emotionally and thematically, Rhys was more nearly displaying her "subject" in *Voyage* than she was in the other three early novels. The word *subject* itself suggests another usage: we can identify the constitution of the self of the writer, herself as subject, with the process and production of her work. In *Wide Sargasso Sea* the context is expanded but the paradigm remains: our life is lived within the context of our language. The context of our language is a model of the context of our life, of our life in the society in which we live. As far as writers are concerned, this remark is a truism. But the display of the outlines of a woman's language or idiom is formally presented here—metaphorically, thematically, and technically—for the first time.

The aesthetic patterning that Rhys establishes shows itself almost diagrammatically. In the actual story of *Voyage in the Dark*, Anna and the other characters say out loud much less than they think about saying. These unspoken words (of the heroine-narrator in particular) furnish the other half of the dialogue we are used to hearing, the conventional conversational patterns that oil the wheels of our society's power structure. Putting "thoughts" into other characters' minds is not something Rhys (or her narrator) often does in this carefully constructed introduction to her semi-autobiographical heroine-narrator; that comes later in the heroine's story, in a particularly refined form in *Wide Sargasso Sea*. What we *hear* as we read is the whole dialogue, even though the "actual" dialogue (the one that the characters engage in aloud) carries the conventional conversation along. Their conversation also advances the narrative as it is traditionally conceived.

Of significance is the style of the heroine-narrator's internal dialogue, which appears alongside the "spoken" dialogue, her half of the dialogue that is presented to the other characters. This internal and unspoken dialogue is, textually (i.e., according to typographical conventions), presented as standard dialogue would be—with quotation marks, the speaker noted, and so on: "I thought," the narrator "says," and Rhys writes, "I thought, 'Now then, you mustn't laugh . . .'"; "I imagined myself saying, very calmly,'. . .'"; and even more explicitly, "I didn't answer. I was thinking, '. . .'" The "internal dialogue" is always dialogue; it is *not* internal monologue, not even when the heroine is "talking to herself." She is, always, self-consciously, addressing someone, even if it is nominally herself, even if it is the reader or whoever may be listening.

The unspoken dialogue—the "real" dialogue—abuts the *spoken* dialogue within the conventional framework of scenes. Both kinds of dialogue are truncated yet juxtaposed, sometimes with an explicit regularity that is especially revealing—as in Chapter Nine of Part I of *Voyage.* Sometimes the two levels of dialogue are interwoven in less overt counterpoint, with a new level or a new irony or comment added, or even a new or ambiguous addressee—"you," as in "You can laugh now . . ." (p. 20). The "you" shifts the subject, displaces it, becomes a stand-in for "one" rather than for the narrator herself. The "you" becomes representative of the heroine-narrator's capitulation to the world, to the demands of a context other than her own. In *Voyage in the Dark* this shift is to "his" context, his world. It signals a displacement of context as well as a displacement of the "subject."

These separate conversations, marked by "I said, '. . .'"; "he said, '. . .'"; and so on; or "I thought about saying, '. . .'"; "I imagined myself saying, '. . .'" are also marked by the textual verification of the truth—*for the narrator*—of what she, or he, didn't say. One is guided by this deployment more than one realizes, especially because the narrator, the "I," is so abject. Her humiliation is so rawly presented that we may be led by our complicity with her victimization. I suggest that, aesthetically at least, this victimization is a ruse. If we do identify with the heroine-narrator's victimization, and if at the same time we feel some complicity in her humiliation, that is because we identify with or understand the two *idioms*—of the oppressor and the oppressed. But the structure of both idioms is perceivable in the heroine-narrator's use of *her own* language. We are led, more than we at first realize, by her words—Anna's as well as Rhys's. Instrumental in the heroine's "humiliation" is the use of language as power, as the controlling mechanism to keep the heroine "in her place," to show her—and us—that place over and over until she has "learned" it, and so have we. That place is her place in masculine discourse, which is paradigmatic of her position in the society that language use reflects. Rhys shows us the conversation, the dialogue, between the powerful and the powerless. She displays the use of language as the tool of repression. Language is thus a context as seemingly inescapable as the society in which one is raised or tries to live. Rhys has achieved that metalinguistic state of "transparency," as it is sometimes called, which we recognize as literary art in her use of the fixing quality of language (the ultimate "fix" being writing) to display the ruse and danger implicit in any language use. The ultimate, most dangerous use of all can be writing itself, as Rhys's presentation of the man's narrative in *Wide Sargasso Sea* makes plain. Writing, we feel, becomes an immutable and incontestable witness to any human situation; it acts in our society in ways that no number of spoken "actions" can. "Sticks and stones may break my bones, but words can never hurt me," our children chant. Spoken words may not be able to hurt us, we like to think, but written ones certainly can.

Rhys shows us how spoken words, particularly *as* and *how* and *to whom* and *by whom* they are spoken (or not spoken when they might be) can hurt us; more, how they can control our lives. At the same time, she acknowledges the preeminence of the *written* word as the ultimate controlling mechanism in our language use. She acknowledges the paralegal aspect of "the written word" even in situations that seem external to society's organized legal system, but that, thereby, are more viciously prevalent in the seemingly immutable laws of our society. Furthermore, Rhys herself resorts to the written word in presenting her "story," her life in part, in a series of novels. Rhys knows the power of writing and occupies that place of power for the duration of the novel. The reader gives Rhys and her heroine-narrator's words, spoken and unspoken, but all *written*, a "hearing."

CHAPTER FIVE.

GETTING BACK TO

THE SPOKEN WORD:

VOYAGE IN THE DARK

*To play with mimesis is . . . for a woman to try to recover
the place of her exploitation by language, without allowing
herself to be simply reduced to it. It is to resubmit herself . . .
to ideas—notably about her—elaborated in and through a
masculine logic, but to "bring out" by an effect of playful
repetition what was to remain hidden: the recovery of a possible operation of the feminine in language. It is also to
unveil the fact that if women mime so well they are not simply reabsorbed in this function.* They also remain
elsewhere. . . .

    —Luce Irigaray (1968); quoted and translated
      by Nancy K. Miller (1981)

"**G**LASSY CLEAR yet somehow distorted, as though
she were looking up at things from the bottom
of a deep pool" is how Rhys's creation of the
"strangely unprecedented" world of her novels seems to Albert Alvarez to have been achieved.[1] Francis Wyndham also sees a "glassy ob-
jectivity to be among [Rhys's] most extraordinary distinctions."[2] Indeed, Rhys's creation of her world does seem "glassy clear" and
simultaneously "somehow distorted." What is fixed clearly on the
page is the use of a language whose authenticity is undeniable; yet,
since it is "unprecedented," it seems, especially to the male reader,
"somehow distorted." This writing practice, this use of "his" language
and "hers," will strike a note of apparent authenticity or even objec-
tivity (what masculine commentators on Rhys usually call "truth")

while seeming strange, even distorted as a view of the world. Alvarez's cue for this metaphor is perhaps given to him by Rhys, who frequently uses drowning imagery in her books, as in this passage:

> [. . .] I didn't care anymore.
>
> It was like letting go and falling back into water and seeing yourself grinning up through the water, your face like a mask, and seeing the bubbles coming up as if you were trying to speak from under the water. And how do you know what it's like to try to speak from under water when you're drowned?[3]

Rhys is talking about trying to speak "from under water." Alvarez, of course, sees her view of the heroine-narrator as Rhys renders it, from the outside (a "face like a mask," "grinning up through the water"). He is allowed to imagine that while *being seen* she is *seeing* the world above, through this mask. What concerns Rhys, though, is trying to *speak* from such a position to that world above.

Rhys's narrator knows that trying to speak is the crux, and that the grinning mask, which itself signifies "being under water," suppressed by seemingly unbreakable social and linguistic conventions, is not a configuration through which one *can* speak. More specifically, being suppressed by the conventions of masculine discourse and control is not a configuration through which a woman can speak. What Rhys's novels are about is just this: the attempt to speak and, in speaking, to be heard. Her resolution of this problem was to write; in writing, she achieved that "glassy clear" presentation that to a masculine reader appears "somehow distorted," *despite his perception of its clarity.*

Alvarez's phrases could be taken as a nearly concrete description of a distorting mirror, which is indeed the figurative looking-glass we find the male narrator in *Wide Sargasso Sea* looking into when he contemplates the woman's point of view. Furthermore, the clarity of the text is to be found, in part, in its movement, rather than in a linguistic fixing-in-amber, which a phrase like "glassy clear" suggests. For the feminine reader of this woman's text, which is a primer on the writing of a woman's difference from men, the clarity is a clarity of focus. Rhys's novel is a seeing of the attempt to speak which, although frustrated in the lives of the heroine-narrators, is achieved in Rhys's record of their attempts.

"I imagined myself saying, '. . .'" Anna "says" in *Voyage in the Dark.*

We *read* what she "didn't say" or only "imagined herself saying," and, in effect, *it has been said*. It stands out all the more for its being marked as *not* being "said."

What prompts our basic response to Rhys's novels is our recognition of the dialogue in which the heroine-narrator of the novels is engaged and which engages us as we read. This multileveled conversation is directed toward us, toward her male partners, and toward the world. The heroine's world is constituted of these male partners and those in deliberate or helpless collusion with them: herself some of the time, as well as other women. The context of words and of speech, especially speech that communicates, that is *heard* by others, especially by men, and that therefore exerts force or power in the world she describes, is invoked in the initial sections of *Voyage in the Dark*. Rhys also shows us the place of *writing* in the speech-language-communication context that is the metaphor for the context of the woman's life she presents to us.

A clue to Rhys's attitude toward writing appears in an early scene from *Voyage in the Dark*. The eighteen-year-old heroine-narrator, Anna Morgan, is an actress in an English provincial touring company. She is sharing a room in a local boardinghouse with Maudie, another chorus girl from the company.

> I was lying on the sofa, reading *Nana*. It was a paper-covered book with a coloured picture of a stout, dark woman brandishing a wine-glass. She was sitting on the knee of a bald-headed man in evening dress. The print was very small, and the endless procession of words gave me a curious feeling—sad, excited and frightened. It wasn't what I was reading, it was the look of the dark, blurred words going on endlessly that gave me that feeling. [. . .]
>
> "I'll get dressed," Maudie said, "and then we'd better go out and get some air. We'll go to the theatre and see if there are any letters. That's a dirty book, isn't it?"
>
> "Bits of it are all right," I said.
>
> Maudie said, "I know; it's about a tart. I think it's disgusting. I bet you a man writing a book about a tart tells a lot of lies one way and another. Besides, all books are like that—just somebody stuffing you up."
>
> Maudie [. . .] was twenty-eight years old and all sorts of things

had happened to her. She used to tell me about them when we
came back from the theatre at night. "You've only got to learn
how to swank a bit, then you're all right," she would say. [. . .]
    "Swank's the word," she would say. (p. 9)

Rhys introduces here the importance of words—especially in their
seemingly trivial forms and usages, as talismans, for example. We are
given the emotionally affecting context of what makes Anna "sad,
excited [. . .] frightened." It wasn't "*what* [she] was reading, it was
the look of *the dark, blurred words going on endlessly*" (my emphasis), a
phrase and an image reminiscent of the "print" inside the "large
book" that was God and that the child Rhys "could see but [that]
made no sense [to her]."[4]

    Rhys is writing just such a book—"a book about a tart"—and when
Maudie asks her about the book she's reading, Maudie assumes it's a
"dirty book." The narrator's laconic opinion is, "Bits of it are all
right." As we look at Rhys's novels, we can perhaps see which "bits" of
her books *are* "all right." Especially in this early scene, we are given to
believe that for once we are not being told "a lot of lies one way and
another" because this book, about a "tart," is being told us by a
woman, by the "tart" herself.

    One version of the problematical conversation is demonstrated by
Maudie. Anna and Maudie allow themselves to be picked up by two
men, whom they take back to the sitting room of their boardinghouse:

"Make yourselves at home, you blokes," Maudie said. "And
allow me to introduce Miss Anna Morgan and Miss Maudie
Beardon, now appearing in *The Blue Waltz*. What about opening
the port? I'll get you a corkscrew, Mr What's-your-name. What
is your name, by the way?"
    The tall man didn't answer. He stared over her shoulder, his
eyes round and opaque. The other one coughed.
    Maudie said in cockney, "I was speaking to you, 'Orace. You
'eard. You ain't got clorf ears. I asked what your name was."
    "Jones," the tall man said. "Jones is my name."
    "Go on," Maudie said.
    He looked annoyed.
    "That's rather funny," the other one said, starting to laugh.
    "What's funny?" I said.

> "You see, Jones is his name."
> "Oh, is it?" I said.
> He stopped laughing. "And my name's Jeffries."
> "Is it really?" I said. "Jeffries, is it?"
> "Jones and Jeffries," Maudie said. "That's not hard to remember."
> I hated them both. You pick up people and then they are rude to you. This business of picking up people and then they always imagine they can be rude to you. (pp. 11–12)

Aside from participating in the banalities attendant upon beginning a conversation with people one doesn't know, and in this case in an already compromised situation, Maudie properly introduces herself and Anna. She tenders the most basic of credentials, a name, signaling that the men have not yet thus identified themselves. At the same time she acknowledges the men's privilege of anonymity, which she bluffly disdains for herself and her charge. After Maudie has proffered these credentials and a direct request for reciprocation, the men do not speak. Trying another idiom or dialect, Maudie repeats her question in "cockney," a maneuver that allows her to reprimand Mr. What's-your-name in the guise of humor: "I was speaking to you, 'Orace." She chooses a name in the idiom, misnaming him so that he is forced to speak for himself, to her, to emphasize that she is *speaking* and expects an answer.

When the man says, "Jones is my name," Maudie of course thinks he is still resisting her request. The other man finds this exposure of Mr. What's-your-name "funny," since he knows their basic anonymity ('Orace, Jones) in the situation itself signals their lack of need for a name. The men in such a situation need not identify themselves. Their purpose, their identity as far as the women are concerned, is beyond question; yet Maudie, a "tart" who might as well be nameless, insists on such an exposure, insists that the men make explicit what is acknowledged but unspoken—that is to say, their relative positions. She has, however, momentarily, turned the tables on the men, naming herself and demanding a reciprocal exchange of identities. "'Jones and Jeffries,' Maudie said. 'That's not hard to remember,'" consigning them to a burlesque billing, putting them in the place where she and Anna already find themselves.

The young Anna understandably remarks, "You pick up people

and then they are rude to you. This business of picking up people and then they always imagine they can be rude to you." This fragment of a sentence, whose subject is lengthily explicit but for which no predication can or need follow, states the case: the rudeness is conventional, expected; it is static, a given. Significantly it is fought against, ironized, by the more experienced Maudie at the level of language, in a defensive attack that uses speech strategies. The subject of the young Anna's predication-lacking sentence is a statement of context.

When the man Jeffries begins to talk, his attention on Anna, he "spoke very quickly, but with each word separated from the other," listening to "everything I said with a polite and attentive expression [. . .] then he looked away and smiled as if he had sized me up" (p. 12). It is not farfetched to hear the sound of a cash register, or coins being counted out, in this description of the man's measured speech.

Maudie is still trying to right the balance: the verbal exchange is as important as the financial or sexual exchange in their encounter. "Tell us about yourselves for a change," she says. "Tell us how old you are and what you do for a living. Just for a change" (p. 13). When Jeffries says, "I work in the City. I work very hard," Maudie conflates the systems of exchange—the sexual (implicit in their meeting), the social or class exchange, and the financial: "You mean somebody else works hard for you. [. . .] And what does Daniel-in-the-lions'-den do? [She yet refuses "Jones" the name he himself would not declare originally.] But it's no use asking him. He won't tell us. Cheer up, Daniel, d'you know the one about the snake-charmer?" (p. 13). "What I'd like to know is this," Maudie says later to Anna when they are alone, "why they think they've got the right to insult you for nothing at all?" Maudie thus voices what Anna had thought more explicitly, *but not said*—and not as a question, but as a statement of context (p. 14).

"Name-calling" or giving nicknames among equals is "likable," however, especially when validated by the use of one's real name, and especially when the names one is called are the same names that the speaker applies to herself ("I'm a good old cow," says Laurie, another chorus girl. "[. . .] Aren't I, what's-your-name—Anna?" [p. 17]). The essential, interchangeable anonymity of the men entering the women's sphere illicitly and of the women in theirs (but with that difference) emphasizes one aspect of Rhys's view of the world; these "worlds" are separate.

The world of men and the world of women are separate, and separable: in both worlds "names" are interchangeable, but among women there is an assumed equality of naming, even if it is expressed superficially. Among men, hierarchical differences are implicit. Women may cross the line if they are moneyed, or if they are fully, *legally*, protected by a moneyed man; but things work differently in these separate and unequal contexts. What's-your-name becomes, immediately, Anna. Mr. What's-your-name/'Orace/Jones/ Daniel-in-the-lions'-den remains unnameable (or multi-named) because he *needs* no name. His place is assured before the game begins.

"What I'd like to know is this: why they think they've got the right to insult you for nothing at all?" Maudie asks. Anna already knows the answer to the more experienced Maudie's question: "This business of picking up people and then they always imagine they can be rude to you." We cannot even call such a statement an incomplete sentence, for such a description at least assumes a proposition. Rhys, and her heroine-narrator, supply what could be called a proto-proposition, which can be considered at most to posit only a first or prior element of what we call context. This is all that is within the means, verbal or otherwise, of the women in the circumscribed area of action open to them. Here the truncated statement of context is that in which "people" are rude to you. Laurie is not "rude." Laurie names Anna, as Laurie names herself. Laurie *exchanges* names, identifying, naming their equality, naming herself and Anna. In this she is "better" than Mr. What's-your-name/'Orace/Jones/Daniel-in-the-lions'-den, or, as Naipaul emphasizes, Mr. Blank.

The etiquette of naming, the context of naming oneself and others that Laurie is teaching Anna, is more relevant in their lives than the bluff Maudie's frustrated irony and the use of her "experience," just as it is more to the point in Rhys's writing practice and its significance. Rhys's writing practice in *Voyage in the Dark* is an elaboration of this linguistic and "conversational" etiquette; it depicts the grim consequences of being an unable, if not an inept, performer in the linguistic arena where the crucial dialogic rituals of our lives take place.

AFTER ESTABLISHING the division between "us" and "them" in *Voyage in the Dark*, Rhys reemphasizes the division, the separation between herself and men ("them"). Despite their own seeming differences from one another, which are based on class and relative positions in society's hierarchies, all men share a place of power relative to women. Anna and Mr. Jeffries are at dinner in a private dining room of a "restaurant":

> "This wine is corked," Mr Jeffries said.
> "Corked, sir?" the waiter said in a soft, incredulous and horror-stricken voice. He had a hooked nose and a pale, flat face.
> "Yes, corked. Smell that."
> The waiter sniffed. Then Mr Jeffries sniffed. Their noses were exactly alike, their faces very solemn. The Brothers Slick and Slack, the Brothers Pushmeofftheearth. I thought, "Now then, you mustn't laugh. He'll know you're laughing at him. You can't laugh." (pp. 17–18)

Even a waiter, a relatively poor man, in the very act of serving the wealthier Mr. Blank/Mr. Jeffries, is his image, the two of them bonded in their mutual place of power relative to Anna. They are performing the same action—sniffing. Their noses are "exactly alike," their faces equally "solemn," the "Brothers Slick and Slack." Anna may want to laugh (as we do; the scene is comical), but the two men are in a position to "push[her]offtheearth."

After the meal, Anna turns the handle of a door she hadn't noticed before. Anna's voice "went high," " 'Oh,' [she] said, 'it's a bedroom' " (p. 20). Mr. Jeffries laughed. "I laughed too," Anna says, "because I felt that that was what I ought to do. *You can* [laugh] *now and you can see what it's like, and why not?*" (p. 20) she adds to herself, to us, in one of the other dialogues she carries on while she talks to other characters in the novel. She is referring explicitly to what she had "thought" before: " 'Now then, you mustn't laugh. He'll know you're laughing at him. You can't laugh.' " She laughs now, now that it is permissible, because in the context of the meeting, the conversation, and the cues given her by Mr. Jeffries, she "felt that that was what I ought to do. *You can* [laugh] *now and you can see what it's like, and why not?*" But it doesn't mean much to her now; nor does it mean to Jeffries what it might have before. Its significance is changed, actually inverted by the context. Speech, even laughter, which "means" in conversation as much as speech, is not spontaneous but is something that is allowed her. In this context, the laughter "loses" its meaning as the laugher loses "herself." Her response is the fatigue of helpless cynicism. The significance of her original impulse to laugh is taken from her. But we know, having overheard, its original context, as we know its meaning and its significance in this one.

Anna's own gloss on her original thought—"You mustn't laugh"— shows us how the very words she had used, and is now using, have changed. *"You can [laugh] now and you can see what it's like, and why not?"* "It" carries the burden of the change implicit in the sequential rendering of the progress of Anna's laughter. What is "it" here? Is it still "laughing"—being able to "laugh" out loud, when before she had to suppress that laughter? It is that if we can construe all laughter to be the same, but we know it is not. "It" is no longer laughing *at* him, at him and the waiter, both men. "It" is no longer even laughter; it is "life"—the situation in which Anna finds herself. The joke is on her, on her inexperience upon discovering the bedroom, at which her voice "went high." She laughs because Mr. Jeffries laughs, and he is laughing at her inexperience and her discomfort. To laugh now is to join in laughter at herself, not at him. *"[A]nd why not,"* she ends the thought, and here a note of cynicism is introduced even before the young Anna has entered the bedroom. The "you" has shifted, been displaced, just as Anna's own context and the significance of her laughter have been displaced. The "you" has become the representative of Anna's capitulation to the demands of the "world," to "it," *his* world.

"[A]nd why not?" The whole book can be seen as an answer to that question, because, in the context in which Anna remains, seemingly the answer can't be otherwise. These words are italicized, a typographical aid that Rhys uses sparingly. A reader pays careful attention, then, to Rhys's italicized passages, and here Rhys signals the degradation of her own language in her own mouth—even if it is unspoken. Rather, she points us to the degradation and defeat attendant upon the heroine-narrator's giving voice to her laughter only when it has become falsified. Voicing the laughter earlier, within the context in which she found herself, would have been to disrupt that context, that frame not her own. Her only possible response was to keep silent. Now that the framework itself allows, even encourages, laughter, it is a signal of further suppression, and of submission, which she adopts with hopeful, as well as hopeless, cynicism. Once inside the bedroom, with "red carnations on the table and the fire leaping up," she thinks, "If it could go back and be just as it was

before it happened and then happen differently" (p. 20). "It" again is her situation—the context she wants, instead of the one she is in.

But "it" did not "happen differently," of course. Anna leaves the encounter still a virgin, but that state is soon altered, although in a seemingly more congenial setting, Jeffries's bedroom. This time Anna is practiced in what to expect and performs her lines accordingly.

Afterward:

He came into the room again and I watched him in the glass. My handbag was on the table. He took it up and put some money into it. Before he did it he looked towards me but he thought I couldn't see him. I got up. I meant to say, "What are you doing?" But when I went up to him instead of saying, "Don't do that," I said, "All right, if you like—anything you like, any way you like." And I kissed his hand.

"Don't," he said. "It's I who ought to kiss your hand, not you mine."

I felt miserable suddenly and utterly lost. "Why did I do that?" I thought. (pp. 33–34)

In this scene, the pieces of "unspoken dialogue" are themselves a skeletal outline of Anna's seduction: "He put his hand on my knee and I thought, 'Yes . . . yes . . . yes. . . .' Sometimes it's like that—everything drops away except the one moment" (p. 31). But soon Anna felt "cold, as if someone had thrown cold water over me. [. . .] 'I must go,' I thought. 'Where's the door? I can't see the door. What's happened?'" (p. 32). Then Anna does what she does rarely: she voices, out loud, what she has been thinking: "He wiped my eyes very gently with his handkerchief, but I kept saying, 'I must go, I must go.' [. . .] I wanted to say, 'No, I've changed my mind.' But he laughed [. . .] and I didn't say anything." Later, "I thought, 'When I shut my eyes I'll be able to see this room all my life.'" "I lay quite still, thinking, 'Say it again. Say "darling" again like that. Say it again'" (p. 33). Concerning the actual act, "it," Anna/Rhys doesn't frame her thoughts as dialogue: "I thought that it had been just like the girls said, except that I hadn't known it would hurt so much." Aloud she says, "Can I have a drink? [. . .] I'm awfully thirsty." "I thought, 'Why doesn't he telephone for a taxi?' but I didn't say anything."

There are three italicized passages in this chapter as well. Anna, on her way to meet Jeffries, says/thinks: "*It's soppy always to look sad. Funny stories—remember some, for God's sake*" (p. 30). (Soon Anna will find herself saying to Jeffries, " 'I'm not sad. Why have you got this soppy idea that I'm always sad?' " [p. 33]). At Jeffries's house after Anna has thought, "I must go," and has said repeatedly, "I must go, I must go," she finds herself walking up a flight of stairs to his bedroom; with no other preparation, we read " '*Crawling up the stairs at three o'clock in the morning,' she said. Well, I'm crawling up the stairs*" (p. 32). This is what Anna's landlady "bawled" at Anna after her *first* evening with Jeffries, when she was still a virgin. The landlady's implied accusation was wrong then: soon it won't be: "I don't hold with the way you go on, if you want to know, and my 'usband don't neither. Crawling up the stairs at three o'clock in the morning. And then today dressed up to the nines. I've got eyes in my head" (p. 26). Anna knows, as she walks up that flight of stairs, that her seduction, and violation, is a *fait accompli*: thus she quotes her landlady and verifies the accusation, even if it is retroactive. In a sense, she is fulfilling the implicit accusation of the landlady's remarks, responding to *all* her cues.

As before, the italicized passages represent a displacement and an ironization of previously voiced material (voiced by the landlady originally here, repeated by Anna). Or, in the case of the laughter in the earlier scene, the desire to laugh that had been internally voiced by Anna is itself "voiced" only after the circumstances have altered, after the context has forced a change in the *use* of the words. Anna had hotly denied returning at any such late hour because of its implication. Now she accepts the explicit significance of her "crawling up the stairs" to Jeffries's bedroom; she is on the way to making it reality:

> I stopped. I wanted to say, "No, I've changed my mind." But he laughed [. . .] and I didn't say anything. [. . .]
>
> When I got into bed there was warmth coming from him and I got close to him. *Of course you've always known, always remembered, and then you forget so utterly, except that you've always known it. Always—how long is always?* (p. 32)

The italicized passage here, one of fewer than a dozen in the entire novel, sounds a note to be found in *Wide Sargasso Sea* almost forty years later. Rochester, in bed with Antoinette, "Bertha," thinks to himself parenthetically, "But at night how different, even her voice was changed. Always this talk of death. (Is she trying to tell me that is the secret of this place? That there is no other way? She knows. She knows)."[5]

In *Voyage in the Dark*, the italicized passages tell a story of their own, as the three from this chapter do, culminating in lengthy italicized passages in the last chapter of the novel, in which Anna returns to her childhood. The story begins innocently enough. Before Anna became his mistress, Jeffries has sent her some money to "buy [her] some stockings." Her new life has begun, and her mundane, childish, and womanly thoughts indeed run to clothes: *"A dress and a hat and shoes and underclothes"* (p. 24). Later in the novel Rhys makes explicit what clothes "mean": "The clothes of most of the women who passed were like caricatures of the clothes in the shop-windows, but when they stopped to look you saw that their eyes were fixed on the future. 'If I could buy this, then of course I'd be quite different.' Keep hope alive and you can do anything, and that's the way the world goes round, that's the way they keep the world rolling. So much hope for each person. And damned cleverly done too" (p. 111). But in the immediate context an innocent and hopeful appraisal of her situation reveals itself: *"This is a beginning. Out of this warm room that smells of fur* [a shop run by the two Miss Cohens] *I'll go to all the lovely places I've ever dreamt of. This is the beginning"* (p. 25). Broadening the literal context, in the next italicized passage Anna "thinks": *"This is England, and I'm in a nice, clean English room with all the dirt swept under the bed"* (p. 27). In her capitulation she has apparently even accepted an evaluation of her personal and specific origins and context that is not her own, as she makes plain in many other passages in the novel. The West Indian island where she was born is, by implication, "dirty"; England, "their" context, appears "nice" and "clean" *because* "the dirt" is "swept under the bed." Then occur the three italicized passages discussed previously, which move from innocence to cynicism and hopelessness.

Only two other such passages appear before the lengthy italicization of the final chapter of the novel. One repeats childhood memories of names and identifying details of Negro slaves from an old "slave-list" that she saw once (pp. 46–47). In bed with Jeffries, Anna thinks: "*Maillotte Boyd, aged 18. . . . But I like it like this. I don't want it any other way but this*" (p. 48). She continues thinking: "*Lying so still afterwards. That's what they call the Little Death*" (p. 48).

Anna is beginning consciously to connect these contexts, her own small and immediate one and the larger contexts—of England, of her own background, of owners and slaves, and the unequal interaction between them. She rationalizes ("I don't want it any other way"), even if she has "always known" that there is no "other way."

Anna's inability to "speak," her loss of virginity and innocence and their reflection in the rest of her life are equated through Rhys's deployment of speech on the page. The inability to speak and to be heard when she speaks, her own sexual response, and the whole of her life are displayed in her situation as a speaking subject, the "I" of her unvoiced but "spoken" remarks. The "other half" of the dialogue in which Anna/Rhys is engaged with the "world" is the same dialogue that mirrors and *places* her in that world, by her own implied estimation of herself in relation to it.

How shall we categorize these levels of verbalization, of dialogue? There are the straightforward, usually conversationalized, even formulaic exchanges that are spoken aloud. There are the unspoken remarks and comments and questions preceded by "I thought," or "I imagined myself saying"; "I meant to say"; "I wanted to say." And there are the italicized passages, which are yet another running conversation with herself and the reader. The actual conversation, the dialogue spoken out loud by the characters, is bracketed from the "other" conversation in which the narrator "speaks" to the man (or sometimes a woman) but silently, carrying on a kind of "*sub-conversation*"[6]—although the phrase suggests that the "silent" speech occupies less actual space in the text, or is de-emphasized by Rhys, which is simply not the case. The more infrequent italicized passages are probably more explicitly addressed to the narrator's "self"; she is, in these cases, talking to "herself," often "remembering." Yet for the reader these comments are highlighted, just as the bracketing of the "unspoken" dialogue emphasizes what we gradually perceive to be the "real," the *dominant* conversation taking place *in the text* as we read.

The stories told by the three levels or kinds of conversation are the same, only told from different perspectives. All tell a story of a "drama, of dependence and defeat," but the *narrative* structures are separable. In one case the development is chronological; in the other (still chronological) the other half of the same story emerges; and in the third—the italicized passages—an associative narrative unfolds that is not bound by chronological time. The conventional plot line and the dialogue attendant upon it tell the story conventionally. The "other" dialogue tells the "unspoken" half of the story, placing each in relation to the other. Italicized material suggests another framework, outside the immediate clash of the two idioms presented in the chronological narrative. It places the heroine-narrator (and her speech) in another, larger context, a context that attempts to resolve the clash by capitulation or by memory.

The reader is given all three versions at once, contrapuntally. One way to look at this method of presentation is to consider the conventional story in its narrative presentation as the "real" story, and its dialogue the "real" dialogue. We might then consider the "other" dialogue—that which is "unspoken" within the fictional framework—to be mere commentary. But the deliberate counterpoint, separating one level from the other by obvious marking devices, highlights the sub-conversation that comes finally to dominate the whole by its insistence.

The italicized material marks off the context of these two narratives by being outside the conventional time frame of the novel, by being static, often ostentatiously descriptive, or by offering a view of those thoughts of the heroine-narrator that are not invoked in direct conversation but that mark for us a larger context. These italicized passages serve as tag descriptions or banal explanations of the affective context in or against which the dialogue—spoken and unspoken —is taking place. Their model, too, is speech, and their overall theme is pointedly lack of communication, a lack against which, nevertheless, the heroine-narrator makes incessant, if fatigued, attempts. This expanded notion of context is what Rhys exploits in *Wide Sargasso Sea*; its interaction with our conversations, with our language contexts, becomes the basis for that novel, carrying its message finally, supporting as well as outlining it for us.

The fundamental conversation then is to be found in this counterpoint, in the revelation of the *second* dialogue, which is going on at the same time we are engaged in the first. For a woman, the second dialogue, the "other" dialogue, becomes the dominant mode of expression in the novel. *Voyage in the Dark* establishes this counterpoint as the aesthetic structuring pattern for Rhys's narrative presentation.

This structuring device is highly prominent in Chapter Nine of Part I, in which Jeffries discards Anna in person after the matter had been settled by a friend acting as his agent by means of a *letter*. In this chapter Rhys (as well as her heroine-narrator) insists on an attempt to retrieve the origin "of the letter," to confront the speaker rather than his agent. Their encounter further demonstrates the seeming futility of the gesture. At the same time Rhys locates for us the origin of the power of the process, and of the woman's place relative to it, her power or lack of it in the face of the dominant idiom. But, in this writing of the encounter, she takes a first step toward claiming that sinister power as her own. By revealing the mechanisms at work in the dominant culture's use of its idiom (especially in the written word) to control and manipulate a woman's position relative to it, Rhys begins to inscribe the woman's idiom all the more clearly in the interstices of the uneven dialogue between the two, even as her heroine-narrator seems to succumb to the repressive strategies.

CHAPTER NINE of Part I of *Voyage in the Dark* is the culmination of the heroine-narrator's entry into the full context of the world in which she lives. Her status is revealed to her in her loss of virginity, and her assumption (if one may use that word with its irony, at least, intact) of her place of powerlessness in that context. Her realization of this position of weakness is revealed to her, and to us, through her inability to use speech effectively, her inability to communicate with the powerful of that society. Anna is unable to counter linguistic moves against her (language used as mechanism of control, as obfuscation, or "stick") with a language or speech use of her own. Rhys reveals the course of her heroine-narrator's career through a disposition of these languages—the clash of the two idioms—on the page and within the framework of her novel.

Just as Rhys has previously shown Anna in relation to the conversation of two men in unequal positions of power relative to one another but bonded in their power over her (the waiter and Walter Jeffries), so she uses another man to represent all men's power, "man's power," to control her and other women by means of language. This man does not have direct influence over Anna, as Jeffries does, through an intimate (sexual and economic) relationship; rather, he represents the more abstract quality of that control as it operates through authority bestowed by the kinship system. Notably, this abstract—but therefore all the more efficacious—exercise of power is presented primarily through Rhys's deployment of her ideas about *reading and writing*.

The man, Vincent, is the first of a series of letter writers in Rhys's books; Walter Jeffries's cousin Vincent serves as his intermediary in Jeffries's attempt to drop Anna. As I have already noted, the attempt to settle the matter was initiated by a letter written by Vincent to Anna. Appropriately, we initially only hear about Vincent: he is discussed in a conversation between Walter and Anna after Anna's first meeting with Vincent. Anna doesn't like Vincent. Vincent's place in this "drama, of dependence and defeat" is thus marked by her suspicion of him, and the suspicious place he holds is interwoven through the meetings between Anna and Jeffries as their affair progresses and ends. Notably, it is Vincent, not Walter, who reappears in the latter part of the book, again as Walter's emissary. Walter gives way to his representative, whose entry on the scene is always prefaced by conversation about him, or by letters, and who is "read" correctly by the heroine-narrator from the beginning:

> "Well," [Walter] said, "what did you think of Vincent? He's a good-looking boy, isn't he?"
>
> "Yes," I said, "very."
>
> "He likes you. He thinks you're a darling."
>
> "Oh, does he? I thought he didn't, somehow."
>
> "Good Lord, why?"
>
> "I don't know," I said. "I just thought so."
>
> "Of course he likes you. He says he wants to hear you sing some time."
>
> "What for?" I said. [. . .]
>
> "Because he could probably do something about getting you a job. [. . .]"
>
> "Well, I could go back on tour if it comes to that," I said. [. . .]
>
> "We're going to get you something much better than that. Vincent says he doesn't see why you shouldn't get on, and I

don't see why you shouldn't either. I believe it would be a good idea for you to have singing-lessons. I want to help you; I want you to get on. You want to get on, don't you?"

"I don't know," I said. (pp. 43–44)

Vincent's influence is already emphasized, and we, the readers, have not even "seen" him.

The next letter writers to whom we are introduced are Anna's own relations. Anna has an interview with her stepmother and legal guardian. Hester has written to Anna's Uncle Bo, who lives in the West Indies, concerning his responsibility for Anna. Hester is identified for us by her voice; it would appear that she habitually places herself—and others—through the use of that voice as well: "She had [. . .] an English lady's voice with a sharp, cutting edge to it. Now that I've spoken you can hear that I'm a lady. I have spoken and I suppose you now realize that I'm an English gentlewoman. I have my doubts about you. Speak up and I will place you at once. Speak up, for I fear the worst. That sort of voice" (p. 50). Obviously, this is not the sort of voice that Anna has. She is one of those about whom Hester "fears the worst." But, as a woman, Hester too is speaking defensively; in this instance she is defending herself from a letter from a man, although not a "gentleman." Hester intends to defend herself in writing by telling the man just that: "I shall mean every word of the answer I send," she says. "Your uncle is not a gentleman and I shall tell him so" (p. 55).

Hester reads the letter from Uncle Bo aloud to Anna. We are given the whole of it as she reads. "That's an outrageous letter," Hester says. "That letter [. . .] was written with one solitary aim and object— it was written to hurt and grieve me" (p. 53).

Anna defends her uncle, who used to say about Hester's talking, "Like a rushing river, that woman." She tells Hester that she doesn't suppose he "meant anything." "He's one of those people who always says much more than he means instead of the other way about," implying that most of us, herself especially, say much less than we mean (p. 55). And Hester, by emphasizing that she will "mean" every word of the letter she writes to Uncle Bo, suggests that *she* doesn't always mean what she says.

Concerning the island she comes from and its people, Anna feels she is defending herself. "I'm not going to argue with you," Hester says, "I tried to teach you to talk like a lady and behave like a lady and not like a nigger and of course I couldn't do it. Impossible to get you away from the servants. That awful sing-song voice you had! Exactly like a nigger you talked—and still do. Exactly like that dreadful girl Francine. When you were jabbering away together in the pantry I never could tell which of you was speaking" (p. 56). Anna recalls that Hester "always hated Francine":

> "What do you talk about?" [Hester] used to say.
> "We don't talk about anything," I'd say. "We just talk."
> But she didn't believe me. (p. 58)

The relative positions of people and classes, their racial, sexual, and economic differences, are here, as in "real life," presented according to their speech. Communication (or lack of it) in the usual sense is less relevant than the form of that speech and the context in which it is uttered. As Anna told her stepmother, "We don't talk about anything [. . .]. We just talk." Linguistic attack and relief from it are not a matter of content. Rather, who says it and in what way, to whom one attempts to talk and why, and how one does talk to them are what matters. Anna recalls another interchange from her childhood: "'I don't know what'll become of you if you go on like that,' Hester said. 'Let me tell you that you'll have a very unhappy life if you go on like that. People won't like you. People in England will dislike you very much if you say things like that'" (p. 61).

The lack of communication and the final break between Anna and Hester are presented at the end of the only chapter that shows them together, in conversation. Their break is framed in the context of writing, however, not talking: "I wrote once to Hester but she only sent me a postcard in reply, and after that I didn't write again. And she didn't either" (p. 63). Their break, although a foregone conclusion given the history of their relationship, is precipitated by the letter from Anna's Uncle Bo and marked irrevocably by their final lack of *writing* to one another. (Uncle Bo's letter mentions Anna's lack of communication with him and her aunt: "We hardly ever hear from Anna. She's a strange child. She sent us a postcard from Blackpool or some such town and all she said on it was, 'This is a very windy place,' which doesn't tell us much about how she is getting on" [p. 53].)

Lack of communication, through speech, and the *marking* of it by the material abstraction of *writing*, are Rhys's themes here. The relative positions of power are likewise marked by *speech*—what form that speech assumes, what is "likable," and what is acceptable (or not) to the person in the position of greater power. Although Hester's voice and speech identify her as an "English gentlewoman," a position she counts on and uses to place other people, she herself is vulnerable to a letter that "was written to hurt and grieve [her]." It accomplishes that aim.

In the process, Anna is effectively and finally "orphaned." Her "orphaning" is accomplished through the collusion of three systems of exchange—speech, money, and the relations between the sexes—speech especially as it acquires the abstract expression of both of the others, the legitimizing, as well as punitive, power of writing. Among its other powers, writing offers a moral as well as an aesthetic last chance to make one's chances concrete, to make oneself, one's life and situation, "real."

Writing imaginary letters to Walter takes the place of reading for Anna. This new frame is prefaced by a chorus of what "everybody says":

> [. . .] everybody says the man's bound to get tired. (You make up letters that you never send or even write. "My darling Walter . . .")
>
> Everybody says, "Get on." [. . .]
>
> Everybody says the man's bound to get tired and you read it in all books. But I never read now, so they can't get at me like that, anyway. ("My darling Walter . . .") (p. 64)

As in the first chapter, a sentence fragment giving us a lengthy and detailed subject with no predication outlines what is to follow. We are given what the heroine-narrator prefers to think of as the framework for her life at this point: "Dressing to go and meet him and coming out of the restaurant and the lights in the street and getting into a taxi and when he kissed you in the taxi going there" (p. 64).

Anna is fooling herself, we say. The context she imagines may be what she thinks she wants, but all the while she is "mak[ing] up letters that [she will] never send or even write." "[I] knew," she says, "it was the best way to live in the world, because anything might happen" (p. 64). "Anything," of course, means just that—good *or* bad—and Anna is desperately looking for cues as to how to proceed.

When Anna gets into the car with Walter for a trip to the country, he is "watching" her:

> I was so nervous about how I looked that three-quarters of me was in a prison, wandering round and round in a circle. If he had said that I looked all right or that I was pretty, it would have set me free. But he just looked me up and down and smiled.
>
> "Vincent's coming down by train tomorrow and bringing a girl. I thought it might be fun." (p. 66)

Vincent has intruded again, and still the reader has not "seen" him. While Walter and Anna are together in the country, Walter asks her if they have flowers on her island like the ones in the English countryside: "These little bright things are rather sweet, don't you think?" (p. 67). "Not quite like these," she answers. Rhys then frames the discordance between what Anna might wish and the reality, as we like to call it, of her circumstances: "But when I began to talk about the flowers out there I got that feeling of a dream, of two things that I couldn't fit together, and it was as if I were making up the names. Stephanotis, hibiscus, yellow-bell, jasmine, frangipanni, corolita" (p. 67). Anna concludes with what is almost a non sequitur; certainly it is very nearly inappropriate: "I said, 'Flamboyant trees are lovely when they're flowering'" (p. 67). There is nothing "said" on the page, i.e., in quotation marks, between Anna's insufficient reply, "Not quite like these," and her final, oddly flat and itself "flamboyant" remark: "Flamboyant trees are lovely when they're flowering."

Immediately following, Rhys writes: "There was a lark rising jerkily, as if it went by clockwork, as if someone were winding it up and stopping every now and again" (p. 67). And "Walter said, as if he were talking to himself [and by implication not listening to Anna], 'No imagination? [. . .] I've wanted to bring you to Savernake and see you underneath these trees ever since I've known you.'" "I like it here," Anna replies, "I didn't know England could be so beautiful." "But," she continues to herself, "something had happened to it. It was as if the wildness had gone out of it."

We are given in juxtaposition two literal contexts or environments, her island and his England, the latter which Anna claims to "like" (although "something had happened to it"). Actually, Anna's final spoken reply to Walter's question and its suppositions (flowers, for example, are "little bright things [. . .] rather sweet") puts her context and his into extreme opposition by means of her expansion on those suppositions. The flowers that Anna thinks of are lush, fragrant, and exotic—finally not even flowers at all, but a *tree* rooted and flowering. The species, indigenous to the West Indies, is a tree known to colonials by name as "flamboyant" (royal poinciana). This designation might at first seem merely hyperbolic to the unknowing reader. Walter signals no response at all. His next remarks are of himself and of his imagination, his England, "as if he were talking to himself."

Anna's response to his initial question may be seen as Rhys's gloss on the "text" Anna is forced to "write." Anna's "reading" of the context, of what is missing, of what she is unable to say, forces the written (that is to say, the stated) remarks. Rhys puts in Anna's mouth the signal that she is saying very little, "almost nothing." Rhys signals this absence to us by the oddity of Anna's remarks—the insufficiency of the one; the almost florid redundancy of the other. The dreamlike state of being unable to fit two things together—Anna's present context and the one out there, "her" island, and "his" England (even the England of his "imagination") comes to be felt as a world of automata. Not only is the "lark rising jerkily, as if it went by clockwork," but she too is unable to perform verbally, except "jerkily."

It is as if Anna were moved by fallible "clockwork, as if someone were winding [her] up and stopping every now and again." She cannot bring herself to "name" the flowers of her homeland as if they were real in her present situation, not even to herself, and especially not out loud, so she resorts to a signal of this inability. The inauthenticity of suddenly, spontaneously, being allowed the privilege of naming is not a cue to which Anna can respond. It is too nearly a revelation of her real position vis-à-vis Walter Jeffries.

Soon after this incident Vincent is introduced. As before, it is through conversation between Walter and Anna:

> "That reminds me," [Walter said]. "Vincent must be [at the hotel] by now. I expect he's waiting for us."
> I had forgotten about Vincent.
> "Come on," Walter said.
> We got up. I felt cold, like when you've been asleep and have just woken up. (p. 68)

Walter continues:

> "You'll like the girl he's bringing with him," he said. "[. . .] I'm
> sure you'll like her. She's an awfully good sort."
> "Is she?" Then I couldn't help saying, "Vincent isn't."
> "You don't mean to say you don't like Vincent?" he said.
> "You're the only girl I've heard of who doesn't."
> "Of course I like him. He's certainly very good-looking," I
> said. (p. 68)

As if to ward off "evil" Anna says to herself, "It's unlucky to know
you're happy: it's unlucky to say you're happy. Touch wood. Cross my
fingers. Spit" (pp. 68–69). Immediately when we are introduced to
Vincent in person, we discover that he is a figure against whom no
such warding off can work:

> Vincent said, "Well, how's the child? How's my infantile
> Anna?"
> He was very good-looking. He had blue eyes with curled-up
> eyelashes like a girl's, and black hair and a brown face and
> broad shoulders and slim hips—the whole bag of tricks, in fact.
> (p. 69)

We soon observe Vincent in conversation:

> Vincent began to talk about books. He said, "I read a good
> book the other day—a damned fine book. When I read it I
> thought, 'The man who wrote this should be knighted.' *The Ro-
> sary*, it was called."
> "A woman wrote that book, you fool," Walter said.
> "Oh?" Vincent said. "Good Lord! Well, even if a woman wrote
> it she should be knighted, and that's all I can say. That's what I
> call a fine book."

Vincent's "girl" emphasizes Vincent's place in Rhys's scheme. She remarks, "He ought to be put in a glass case, oughtn't he?" and, cogently, she "finishes" him off: "The perfect specimen" (p. 73).

On their return to London, Anna and Jeffries let Vincent and his
"girl" off at her flat. Anna says, "Good night, Germaine. Good night,
Vincent; thank you very much." She immediately thinks to herself:

What did I say that for? [. . .] I'm always being stupid with this
man. I bet he'll make me feel I've said something stupid.
And sure enough he raised his eyebrows, "Thank me very
much? My dear child, why thank me very much?" (p. 75)

This is the beginning of the end, as one might say melodramati-
cally. Typically, Rhys suggests as much, but she puts the statement in
the mouth of Anna's landlady: " '[T]his is no way for a young girl to
live,' Mrs Dawes said" (p. 78), and Mrs. Dawes's view is a partial one.
Anna herself says she "didn't know what to answer" to Mrs. Dawes—
"placid and speaking softly, but a bit as if she were watching me
sideways" (p. 78).

After a few weeks Anna receives a letter from Walter "saying that
he might be in England again sooner than he had expected." One
day "Mrs Dawes said, 'There's a letter for you. I took it up to your
room. I thought you was in.'" When Anna got upstairs, "It was lying
on the table, and right across the room I thought, 'Who on earth's
that from?' because of the handwriting" (p. 78).

The handwriting, of course—as the writing on the wall has already
told us, as Rhys has already "written" it for us—is Vincent's.

In the long, condescending, and familiarly toned letter, Vincent
tells Anna that "Love is not everything—especially that sort of love—
and the more people, especially girls, put it right out of their heads
and do without it the better. That's my opinion."

Life is chock-full of other things, my dear girl, friends and just
good times and being jolly together and so on and games and
books. Do you remember when we talked about books? I was
sorry when you told me you never read because, believe me, a
good book like that book I was talking about can make a lot of
difference to your point of view. It makes you see what is real
and what is just imaginary. (p. 80)

He concludes, "I believe that if you will work hard there is no reason
why you should not get on. I've always said that and I stick to it" (pp.
80–81). In a postscript Vincent gets to his real point: "P.S. Have you
kept any of the letters Walter wrote to you? If so you ought to send
them back" (p. 81).

Vincent reiterates what "everybody says" ("Everybody says the
man's bound to get tired. [. . .] Everybody says, 'Get on.' [. . .] Every-

body says the man's bound to get tired and you read it in all books"). In his condescension, he deliberately confuses the "real" and the "imaginary," reminding Anna that "books" can help one see, that they can make "a lot of difference to your point of view."

His own letter, however, is preeminently a part of the real world. It marks the effective "truth" of what "everybody says" by *writing* it down. By means of this letter Vincent exerts the paralegal power of society, of the men of that society, to control a woman's life through their conventional language practices. The inevitability of this control is what Anna is encouraged to see as real. Vincent's explicit messages are two: Walter wants to disassociate himself from Anna, and he wants any letters he wrote to her returned, so that she does not have that "capital" to use against him (to use V. S. Pritchett's word for Rhys's diaries—another kind of written "capital").

"I believe that [. . .] there is no reason why you should not get on. I've always said that and I stick to it," Vincent writes, reemphasizing his role as agent of that society, an agent with the seeming power to say a thing and cause it to be. Naturally, in a world that legitimizes its control by the writing down of what "everybody" says as the ultimate mark of that control, Vincent urges Anna to "send [. . .] back" any letters Walter wrote to her. She "ought to," he says, in a postscript, as if idly, asking her to return the one thing which, in that world, might give her some control (illegitimate, of course—blackmail) over Walter, which would in effect represent some semblance of control over all of "them" who control her—"Mr. What's-your-name/'Orace/Daniel-in-the-lions'-den/Mr. Blank."

Anna's overworn reflex is to try again to communicate with Walter. She does not finally write those letters she imagined writing, "My darling Walter . . ."; instead she sends a straightforward telegram that yet retains an air of supplication: "I would like to see you tonight if possible please Anna" (p. 81). She thinks, "He won't answer," but at half past seven Mrs. Dawes "brought up a telegram from him: 'Meet me tonight Central Hotel Marylebone Road 9.30 Walter'" (p. 82). The conversation between the two is not yet at an end. Anna thinks, if they can continue to *talk*, the letter of the law won't be invoked. "He won't be able to, he won't be able to," she thinks as she dresses for their meeting. If she can bypass the letter, bypass the message delivered by his agent and talk to Walter himself, perhaps her idea of reality can be maintained. Perhaps she will remain in the circuit of exchange represented by Walter's permission of a continuance of their "talk."

CHAPTER NINE represents the culmination of the drama acted out in Part I of *Voyage in the Dark*. The pieces of the framework Rhys has established are here thrown into relief and the prominent aesthetic patterning of the novel becomes even clearer. The first words typographically indicated as "spoken" are not literally spoken to anyone. ("I thought," Anna says, " 'He won't be able to, he won't be able to' " [p. 82]). The first words actually spoken are those of Mrs. Dawes: " 'You'll get wet,' she said. 'I'll send Willie as far as the Tube station to get a taxi for you.' " But Mrs. Dawes immediately withdraws the effect of her solicitous suggestion. She "began to click her tongue and mutter, 'The poor boy—out in the pouring rain. Some people give a lot of trouble.' "

Anna makes no reply. Instead, she "thought," " 'When you have fever your feet burn like fire but your hands are clammy,' " indicating her solicitude for the boy Willie through herself, how one (she) *feels* when one (she) is ill, the presumed consequence of being out in "the pouring rain."

When Anna is in the taxi, she thinks, " 'I ought to have given Willie a bob. I know Mrs Dawes was annoyed because I didn't give him a bob. It was just that I didn't think of it. Tomorrow some time I must get hold of him and give him a bob' " (pp. 82–83). When she meets Walter, she says, "Hullo," and then "I'll have coffee." But *she imagines herself saying*, "very calmly," " 'The thing is that you don't understand. You think I want more than I do. I only want to see you sometimes, but if I never see you again I'll die. I'm dying now really, and I'm too young to die' " (p. 83). And then she says out loud: "That letter I had from Vincent—." Walter's first words are "I knew he was writing." "You asked him to write?" she says. He replies, "Yes, I asked him to write."

"All right," Anna says. "Listen, will you do something for me?" She appeals to him directly and he answers:

> "Of course," he said. "Anything. Anything you ask."
> I said, "Well, will you get a taxi, please, and let's go back to your place, because I want to talk to you and I can't here."
> (p. 84)

But "I thought," the heroine-narrator says: "'I'll hang on to your knees and make you understand and then you won't be able to, you won't be able to.'" (Here Anna is echoing the first "unspoken" words of the chapter: "'He won't be able to, he won't be able to.'" Anna is trying, in the sub-conversation she is carrying on with Walter, to make viable, to make material, what she wants and what she knows is contrary to what Walter most certainly *will* "be able to do."

Walter answers the "unspoken" half of Anna's part of the "conversation": "He said, 'Why do you ask me the one thing you know perfectly well I won't do?'" (p. 84). He had offered her a lie: "Of course [I will do] anything you ask." When she does ask, Walter knows what Anna's unspoken intention is; his reply is to that, to her intention to try to "make [him] understand."

Anna, of course, has no reply to this verification of the lie that was the answer to her original appeal. The "lie" itself is in fact Jeffries's own "verification" of the rationale for his position and his actions, which were and are his way of telling what is at least for him *his* "truth." She says nothing aloud. She "didn't answer." Instead, she "was thinking": "'You don't know anything about me. I don't care any more [*sic*]'" (p. 84). But of course Walter knows almost everything about her that he needs to know *for his own purposes*. This is a typical scenario acted out between a man of his kind and a woman of hers, as he defines them and their relative positions—even including what she has "said" in this specific instance, but not spoken aloud to him.

"And I didn't care any more," the narrator continues: "It was like letting go and falling back into water and seeing yourself grinning up through the water, your face like a mask, and seeing the bubbles coming up as if you were trying to speak from under the water. And how do you know what it's like to try to speak from under water when you're drowned?" (p. 84). Anna also knows that the fundamental conversation in which they are engaged is the unspoken one. It is the "other" conversation in which anything she might say is superseded by the circumstances of Jeffries's control as it is demonstrated *here*, in the extreme stereotypicality of the situation. They both know beforehand what to expect, even though Anna hopes to circumvent the conventional format and its outcome. She capitulates again: "I didn't care any more."

Of course a woman "drowned" in such circumstances cannot speak and be heard; she has no effect on circumstances controlled by powerful others for their own purposes. Those who cannot "know what it's like" are those whose own language constitutes the medium in which she is "drowned," those, like Jeffries, whose language practices become the element in which she tries to live and by which she is suffocated, "drowned," muted, even silenced.

Meanwhile, Walter is heard to be speaking. He "was saying, 'I'm horribly worried about you. I want you to let Vincent come and see you and arrange things. I've talked it over with him and we've arranged things'" (p. 84). Vincent, his agent, "society's agent," is to "arrange things." Naturally, Anna resists:

> I said, "I don't want to see Vincent."
> "But why?" he said.
> "I've talked it over with him," he said. "He knows how I feel about you." (p. 84)

Walter feels that Vincent, in his emphatic role as agent, can "speak" for him even better, certainly more *effectively*, in that role, than he himself could. When Anna says, "I hate Vincent," Walter replies, disingenuously and cruelly,

> "But, my dear, you don't imagine, do you, that Vincent's had anything to do with this?"
> "He had," [Anna] said, "he had. D'you think I don't know he's been trying to put you against me ever since he saw me? D'you think I don't know?" (p. 84)

Anna's accusation is accurate, even if she is forced to "talk about it" in the context of a personal relationship that Walter is at pains to depersonalize through the agency of Vincent.

He continues the linguistic charade:

> He said, "It's a damned poor compliment to me if you think I'd let Vincent or anybody else interfere with me."
> "As a matter of fact," he said, "Vincent's hardly ever spoken about you. Except that he said once he thought you were very young and didn't quite know your way about and that it was a bit of a shame." (pp. 84–85)

In other words, since Vincent hasn't "spoken" about Anna, she cannot expect him to acknowledge her seriously; she can make little or no claim to any effective identity in Vincent's eyes, or—it goes without saying—in Walter's.

Anna's attempts to prove that, on the contrary, the *sort* of things Vincent *says* shows that he "knows" about her, and about himself and Walter, who both know their way about (in their world) as Anna evidently does not. Vincent also knows their positions relative to one another. Rather than Vincent's lack of "speaking" about her proving his indifference, the *kind* of language he regularly uses demonstrates just how specifically he knows what he can and cannot do, what Walter can and cannot do, to her. Anna recognizes in this situation a direct relationship, whether Walter, or Vincent, acknowledges it or not: "I said, 'I know the sort of things he says: I can hear him saying them. D'you think I don't know?'" (p. 85). She *can hear him saying them*. The *manner* of saying—how and why, to whom and by whom things are said—is the crux, the proof of knowledge, and the verification—the "truth" for her this time—of *what* they are really saying. She can "hear" them, and thus she "knows."

But knowledge, particularly of this kind, is not power. On the contrary, power resides in control of the silences, which themselves border and frame the "real" conversation of the society in which one lives. Anna speaks freely (a "freedom" qualified by some of the same constraints that are imposed on the outside) only within those silences, those holes and gaps in masculinely controlled discourse, a discourse shaped by their desire and their relative position of power. Men can, when forced, respond to the more habitual "unspoken" dialogue presented to them. But their recognized language, the idiom of power and the powerful, resides in *what is spoken*; hers resides in what is not. Anna's language or idiom "suffers silently . . . in the unsaid, or in the non-sense," as Gauthier describes it.[7] Anna here attempts, and Rhys in her novels succeeds, in making "*audible* that which agitates within us," and she does so precisely in the "*intervals* . . . in the *gaps*, in all that which is not a continuation of their discourse," as Wittig prescribes.[8] Significantly, however, even Anna's own discourse adheres to the grammar and other conventions of "their" language. Only much later in the continuing development of Rhys's heroine-narrator in *Wide Sargasso Sea*, are the grammatical conventions of a woman's language revealed to her and to us.

Walter now ends a conversation he feels is getting out of hand: "He said, 'I can't stand any more of this.'" As Anna is getting into a taxi,

Walter says, "O God, look what I've done," and Anna "wanted to laugh." Instead, she replies, "I don't know what you mean[. . .]. You haven't done anything."

What Walter still seems concerned about—given what he proceeds to say and given that most of their ostensible conversation has been about Vincent—is emphasized again in his penultimate attempt to "say" something to Anna: "You've got hold of absolutely the wrong end of the stick about Vincent. He's awfully fond of you and he wants to help you" (p. 85). This is patent doublespeak, even triplespeak, if we consider that Walter is trying not only to convince Anna of his good will through an assertion of Vincent's, but also to convince Anna that her reading of him, and of Vincent, is wrong. He is also— perhaps especially—trying to convince her that her reading of their *conversation* is wrong.

Knowing, at least, what the right "end of the stick" is, knowing that Vincent embodies the abstract power of the "stick" and that this abstraction has real and hurtful consequences, Anna, on the point of leaving, says, "Hell to your beloved Vincent. Tell him to keep his bloody help. I don't want it" (p. 85). To emphasize her point, Rhys returns us at this moment to Walter and his twin, the waiter, and their music hall turn: "[Walter] looked shocked, like that waiter, when he said, 'Corked, sir?'" And what a world of power and the response to power is invoked in that word—"Corked?"—given the context in which it was originally spoken.

Walter's final words, "I shouldn't wonder if I got ill with all this worry," are silly in the extreme. The superficiality of his attempt overall, despite its devastating effect on the young heroine, is revealed in Rhys's parodic rendering of the man's limp response, which was, in the first place, a deliberately strategic use of parody by the man himself. The parody is common, often observable in men when they find themselves discomfited in social situations. It is an attempt to mimic in all seeming seriousness "the Woman," whose frailer nerves might cause physical upset over an emotional situation. In this instance it is the woman who "curses," and the man who figuratively waves a wan hand in the air.

THE NEXT DAY Anna writes Walter and tells him not to "write here because I'm leaving. I'll let you know my new address" (p. 86). This is Anna's next-to-last direct communication with Walter. She is still attempting to maintain the idea that *writing* is somehow possible, and that she can at least do that, no matter how unlikely a prospect it is. She "writes" and pretends that he may, even will, "write." But out in the street, when "a man passed," she thought that "he looked at me funnily and I wanted to run, but I stopped myself" (p. 86). Mr. Slick and Mr. Slack have become "a man" she passes in the street—the collective Mr. Blank, who can, as she puts it earlier, "pushmeofftheearth." "I walked straight ahead. I thought, 'Anywhere will do, so long as it's somewhere that nobody knows'" (p. 86). She might as well have said, "Anywhere will do so long as it's somewhere that I can escape from what *everybody says*." Anna's "knowing" and her attempts to "say" what she knows, as she reiterates to Walter—"D'you think I don't know [. . .]? D'you think I don't know? [. . .] D'you think I don't know?" (pp. 84–85)—are no safeguard against *their* "knowing," and especially against their *saying*.

AFTER SOME MONTHS of life as a semi-prostitute, Anna discovers that she's pregnant. Laurie, Anna's friend from the touring company, the one who taught her the etiquette of the linguistic rituals that Anna would encounter, is discussing Anna's having an abortion:

> "What about that man you talked about who used to give you money? Won't he help you? Or were you kidding about him?"
> [. . .]
> "I don't know what to say," I said.
> "Don't be a fool. Say Dear Flukingirons or whatever his bloody name is. I'm not very well. I'd like very much to see you. You always promised to help me. Etcetera and so on."
> From a long way off I watched the pen writing: "My dear Walter . . ." (p. 144)

(We may note that Mr. Jones/Jeffries/What's-your-name/'Orace/Daniel-in-the-lions'-den/Walter/Vincent—Mr. Blank, has a new name: "Flukingirons or whatever his bloody name is.") It is as if Anna is not really doing the writing: the "pen" is, and she is "watching" it: "My dear Walter. . . ."

As one might expect, Walter doesn't respond to Anna in person. Vincent does. Walter, however, did write and tell Anna that Vincent was coming. When Vincent asks Anna, "What's the matter?" and she tells him, "he sat forward in his chair and stared at me, looking very fresh and clean and kind, his eyes clear and bright, like blue glass, and his long eyelashes never still for a second. He stared at me—and he might just as well have said it" (p. 146). Anna *answers* what Vincent "might just as well have said" but didn't: "Oh, I don't mean it's Walter's. I don't know whose it is." "What do you want to do?" Vincent asks Anna. "I want not to have it," she answers. "'I see,' he said. And he went on talking, but I didn't hear a word he was saying. And then his voice stopped." Anna responds, although she hasn't "heard a word he was saying." She responds to "his voice" stopping:

> I said, "Yes, I know. Laurie's told me of somebody. She wants forty pounds. She says she must have it in gold. She won't take anything else." [. . .]
> "Poor little Anna," making his voice very kind. "I'm so damned sorry you've been having a bad time." Making his voice very kind, but the look in his eyes was like a high, smooth, unclimbable wall. No communication possible. You have to be three-quarters mad to even attempt it.
> "You'll be all right. And then you must pull yourself together and try to forget about the whole business and start fresh." [. . .]
> "D'you think so?" I said.
> "Of course," he said. "You'll forget it and it'll be just as though it had never happened." (pp. 146–47)

With this, Anna asks if he'll have some tea.

No communication possible: that Anna already realizes this is signaled by the fact that she is not trying to "talk" to Vincent. She listens instead to "his voice"—its starting and stopping. The "sound" of it is "very kind," but the "look in his eyes" signals the barrier: "high, smooth, unclimbable." She is reckless enough to answer *his* unspoken questions, to disregard the etiquette of keeping her silence while he speaks.

The conversation continues desultorily. Vincent's discomfort in a verbal situation that is not completely under his control is emphasized by his frequent coughing, that psychological stammering often associated with the clinical symptoms of hysterical young females' speech repressions (Dora's, for example).

The exchange of money and that other form of capital—writing and letters; and Vincent's place as agent for both—is touched upon, necessarily. Vincent attempts to be as offhand as possible, just as he was in his postscript to his first letter to Anna: " 'Quite,' he coughed again. 'Well, you must let me know. When you write, write to me—not to Walter. He's going to be abroad for some time.' " Anna does not reassure him. Instead, she offers him a formulaic reply: " 'Thank you very much,' I said. 'You're awfully kind.' " After more perfunctory exchanges, Vincent zeroes in again on the real matter at hand:

> "By the way," he said, "there's just one thing. If you have any letters of Walter's I must ask you to give them to me."
> "I'm sorry, I must insist on that," he said. (p. 148)

Again, Vincent asks for the letters as if they were an afterthought rather than goods that were being paid for, which at this point Anna understands they are. That Vincent knows she understands this is emphasized by his "insistence."

"Are these all?" Vincent asks when Anna brings him the letters. "They're all I kept," Anna answers. "I don't keep letters as a rule. There's the one he wrote from Paris, too, saying you were coming— you'd better have it as well" (pp. 148–49). "You're a nice girl, you really are." Vincent begins. He continues making reassuring noises for the space of a few sentences, and then he breaks off again, unable to help himself: ". . . Are you sure these are all the letters?" Anna answers with equanimity: "I've told you so." Vincent answers: " 'Yes, I know.' He pretended to laugh. 'Well, there you are. I'm trusting you' " (p. 149). "Yes, I see that," she answers. The cat is out of the bag, and Vincent knows it. His role is clear, his pretense obvious. The "real" conversation is on a new footing, and Anna's responses are "glassily" clear, ringing with a straightforwardness that Vincent is not used to in "my infantile Anna."

As if casually, in the remainder of their conversation Anna brings up the letter that *Vincent* wrote to her. Anna asks about Vincent because, she says, she likes to "be able to imagine things" (p. 149). He's going into the country, he tells her.

> "It must be lovely in the country."
> He said, "It smells good."
> "You told me about it," I said, "in your letter."

"What letter? Oh, yes, yes, I remember."

"It's no use asking me for that one," I said. "It wasn't one I kept." (p. 149)

This ironic reminder of Vincent's own letter is an ultimately pathetic display of one-ups-"man"-ship insofar as the details of the heroine's story are concerned. What the last dialogue between Vincent and Anna does accomplish, however, is the pinpointing of some of the usual gaps and holes in the framework of the masculine discourse, ignored here by Anna, which she would previously have rushed to fill with her own half of the unspoken dialogue.

Vincent is forced, at least once, in feminine fashion, to "speak" silently a question essential to the meeting. At the same time, he exercises the masculine prerogative of making his demands overt, rather than indirect, in order to ensure return of the letters. Notably, he forgets his own letter, of which Anna reminds him, in his now overt role as agent. What is really at issue here becomes clear: money and control through the capital of written evidence, documents of the possibility of an ultimate dominance. This clarity is achieved through the new, uncomfortable rearrangement of their habits of discourse, which is brought about by the (no matter how momentary) possibility of Anna's exerting new control. Theoretically, Anna could refuse the return of the letters. Already, out of sheer weariness, she ignores some of the old rules of the dialogue with the dominant idiom. The situation itself, however, precipitates this momentarily new dialogic rearrangement and finally demands her capitulation. She returns the letter, and Vincent, in fact, has the last word: " 'Look here, cheer up,' he said. 'It's going to be all right for you. I don't see why it shouldn't be all right for you'" (p. 149).

IN THE final chapter the abortion is botched. Anna is lying delirious in her room, a doctor on the way. Over half the short chapter is italicized, consisting primarily of memories from Anna's childhood. In the first of these Anna is half-listening to her father, her stepmother, her Uncle Bo, and her aunt while she watches the Carnival Masquerade, a parade of blacks on the island:

Hester said Gerald the child's listening—oh no she isn't Father said she's looking out of the window and quite right too [. . .].

I was watching them [. . .]—the masks the men wore were a crude pink with the eyes squinting near together squinting [. . .] the masks the women wore were made of close-meshed wire covering the whole face and tied at the back of the head—the handkerchief that went over the back of the head hid the strings and over the slits for the eyes mild blue eyes were painted then there was a small straight nose and a little red heart-shaped mouth. [. . .]

I was watching them [. . .] Uncle Bo said [. . .] Hester said [. . .] Uncle Bo said [. . .]—their voices were going up and down—I was looking out of the window and I knew why the masks were laughing and I heard the concertina-music going. (pp. 156–57)

"A pretty useful mask that white one watch it and the slobbering tongue of an idiot will stick out—a mask [. . .] with an idiot behind it I believe the whole damned business is like that," her father had said (p. 156). An image of carnival as aftermath of a forced abortion is not inappropriate, yet here, too, Rhys's use is singular: the heroine-narrator's vision of society as carnival marks a moment of brutal injustice rather than, as in the male reading, a conservative moment of saving play.

"Masks" with "idiots behind them": the masks the men wore "with the eyes squinting" and "near together squinting" (the men cannot see very well?), and the women wore masks that covered their *whole* faces, with "mild blue eyes painted" on (the women are not intended to see at all?). Both masks hide the color, the status of their wearer except for the marking "man," the marking "woman." The child hears voices going up and down, and she is looking as well as listening. What she sees, in the context of what she hears, allows her to "know" why "the masks were laughing." Anna learned her language or idiom as a girl-child from the context of masks; its meaning is only superficially hidden behind them. The function of the carnival masks is the marking of difference between the empowered and the relatively powerless—blacks "hidden" under "white" masks; but even within this caricature of the assumption of power, the masks themselves continue to retain the more basic masquerade, the marking of sex and gender. The "color" is "changed"; blacks wear "white" (or pink) masks: this difference is exploited and parodied. But gender marking is explicit and integral to the mask, as it is to the reality of empowerment and dominance. Gender marking is not left behind in the masquerade; it is emphasized. The masks of the men are characterized solely by the eyes; the women's masks, in contrast, cover "the whole face" and are tied at the back of the head where the handker-chief "hid the strings" (which manipulate the "doll" whose face is painted on?) and emphasize other features ("a small straight nose and a little heart-shaped mouth"). The parody, caricatured here, points us to characteristics of *seeing* and *being seen*. Indeed, Anna seems to corroborate her father's description of her primary activity: *"the child's listening,"* her stepmother says; *"oh no she isn't Father said she's looking out of the window and quite right too."* Her father notes the centrality of "watching" in Anna's responses, but he neglects to give corresponding weight to her stepmother Hester's also accurate ob-servation and to realize the interrelatedness of the two for a woman. The full description of the child's observation of the scene empha-sizes the bonding of sight and hearing. Anna learns the lesson of the mask while she listens; she listens while seeming to concentrate on watching. The "voices go up and down," weaving the context for the "watching." They are the backdrop for, as well as the fundamental and binding element of, the context of seeing and knowing.

> "I fell," [the grown-up Anna] said. "I fell for a hell of a long time then."
>
> "That's right," Laurie said. "When [the doctor] comes tell him that." [. . .]
>
> "Tell him you had a fall," she said. "That's all you've got to say. . . ."
>
> "Oh, so you had a fall, did you?" the doctor said. [. . .]
>
> He moved about the room briskly, like a machine that was working smoothly.
>
> He said, "You girls are too naïve to live, aren't you?"
>
> Laurie laughed. I listened to them both laughing and their voices going up and down.
>
> "She'll be all right," he said. "Ready to start all over again in no time, I've no doubt." (pp. 158–59)

These are the novel's last lines of dialogue. The last words we hear spoken are those of the doctor, condescending, complacent. They echo, although in a more sinister register, Vincent's last words to Anna. The doctor's words, and Vincent's, are spoken in the context of "voices going up and down," *their* voices going up and down. The doctor is like a machine; the dreamlike world of automata is invoked again. This world becomes simply "voices going up and down," the context *of* the masks, of the language that issues forth only from a "mask." Take the mask off and "you" are no longer part of the conversation defined by masculine discourse. Keep it on and "you" do not speak, or you are not heard when you do. Take it off, ask them to remove theirs, and the conversation comes to an end. You have introduced the fundamental conversation that is no longer under their seeming control. If you persist, they will simply exclude you from further conversation.

When their voices stopped. These are the first words of the last paragraph of the novel: "When their voices stopped the ray of light came in again under the door like the last thrust of remembering before everything is blotted out" (p. 159). Rhys had intended the original version of this sentence to be the end of the novel. She had written, "And a ray of light came in from under the door like the last flash of remembering before everything is blotted out and darkness comes."[9] Her editor, Michael Sadlier, wanted her to change the ending. The following is their conversation as Rhys recalls it in her autobiography:

"Why do you end it like that?"
"Because that's the way it must end."
"You mean the girl dies?"
"Of course; there is no other end."
"Oh, I don't know; so gloomy; people won't like it. Why can't she recover and meet a rich man?"
"But how horrible," I said. "How *all wrong.*"
"Well, then, a poor, good-natured man," he said impatiently.
"No, I won't change the end. I won't change one single word," I said, and rushed out of the office, for I was afraid of bursting into tears.
The next morning he rang me and asked me to go back to his office. I did. I said, "But can't you see that a girl like that would be utterly bewildered from start to finish? She's dying and there's no more time for her as we think of time. That's how she feels, I'm certain."
"Oh, give the girl a chance."

> So I spent several gloomy weeks trying to think of two or
> three paragraphs that wouldn't spoil the book, trying to give the
> girl a chance.[10]

What Rhys does in the "changed" version of the last paragraph is emphasize the speech-language-communication context of the novel by inserting the phrase "When their voices stopped" at the beginning of her original sentence, dropping the phrase "and darkness comes" at its end. In other words, as her editor wanted, the "girl" does not "die." What Rhys's editor wanted her to do was to "give the girl a chance," to avoid saying or doing what "people won't like." Rhys argued that "a girl like that would be utterly bewildered from start to finish[.] She's dying and there's no more time for her as we think of time." We can recall here Anna's "unspoken" words to Walter: "'if I never see you again I'll die. I'm dying now really, and I'm too young to die.'" If the "conversation" between them ends, she will "die"; she's "dying" then "really," as the literal conversation is falling apart around her. The context of the relationship on which she depended can no longer be attenuated.

As I have observed, writing was a kind of figurative last chance for Rhys, a reworking of her life in and through language. In that sense, the "girl's" last "chance" can be found in the text, not in her fictional life. Rhys's heroine-narrator here has "no more time as we think of time." She may not have "died," but she *has* died to the possibility of change in her situation. We may also consider the image of phallic penetration and of the "Little Death," given in the second version, to reflect and reinforce the cultural and contextual violation implicit in the sexual encounter as she has described it. In substituting an image which is at the least invasive, its quality and direction moving only toward darkness ("*the* ray of light [. . .] like the last *thrust* of remembering" [my emphasis]) for an internal, self-contained, not necessarily sexual image of enlightenment ("*a* ray of light [. . .] like the last *flash* of remembering" [my emphasis]), Rhys underscores her original point while seeming to comply with yet another masculine demand. She uses "their" imagery just as she uses "their" words. Significant here as well is the use of the definite article in the second instance to emphasize the specificity and determinateness of the first half of the simile—that "ray of light." In the "new" version that "ray of light" seems to serve as stimulus for or causative agent of the second half.

In the original version, the first half of the simile is not catapulted beyond its grammatical boundaries or immediate metaphorical function: the heroine-narrator, and the functional elements of the simile, remain intact.

Rhys actually avoided "saying" in her novel what the editor wanted her to say. Instead of Anna's dying conventionally, Rhys has simply shown that, through language, Anna has "died" anyway, died to the attempt to make herself heard. She has given up attempting the context of the "voices going up and down." The voices stopped. The active language context is stilled, and what Anna repeats, what Rhys writes in the "new" last paragraph of the novel, is a near repetition of what Vincent said, what the doctor said—*their* last spoken words: Vincent said, "Look here, cheer up [. . .]. It's going to be all right for you. I don't see why it shouldn't be all right for you," and earlier, "[. . .] try to forget about the whole business and start fresh" (pp. 149, 147). The doctor said, "She'll be all right. [. . .] Ready to start all over again in no time, I've no doubt."

Rhys writes, her heroine-narrator records—but not within quotation marks; Anna is not *saying* the words—the last words of the novel, which echo the men: "I [. . .] thought about starting all over again. And about being new and fresh [. . .] when anything might happen. And about starting all over again, all over again. . ." (p. 159).

There is some hope here, however, at least insofar as the text itself leads us to believe: "When their voices stopped the ray of light came in *again* like the last thrust of *remembering*" (p. 159; my emphasis). In the first version of this sentence, Rhys doesn't use the word "again." ("And a ray of light came in from under the door like the last flash of remembering before everything is blotted out and darkness comes.") "Again" suggests repetition, and "the ray of light [. . .] again" is "like remembering." It is precisely through "remembering"—that is to say, through repeated "reviewing"—that we constitute for ourselves a knowing.

But actually Rhys has not changed the ending of her novel. I agree that the first version was better. She managed, apparently, to cause her editor to assume that she had "changed" the meaning of the ending, when in fact her heroine-narrator merely repeats the last words of the representative men in the novel, emphasizing what Rhys has already "said."

For us as readers, to recognize, to reknow, is to remember ourselves. In remembering, we effect the wholeness of self that we achieve when we see ourselves "framed" in the presentation of other women's lives. We don't believe that the heroine will be able to "start all over again" "new and fresh," "utterly bewildered as she is from start to finish." And neither does she, we believe. "Time," as "we think of it," is over for Anna Morgan. The context is closed for her, closed *to* her; there is "no more time," the arbiter of any context, "for her." Rhys chose the kind of irony that a male reader, a native speaker of the dominant idiom (her editor specifically, no doubt), can assume answers his objections. She could count on the persuasiveness of the language practice of saying what one doesn't *mean*, assured that the habituated user of the language of power and dominance— the sophisticated reader of either sex—will be persuaded to the contrary. The assumption is that, in the terms of the dominant idiom, saying what one doesn't mean is a sure way of "getting it 'said.' "

Voyage in the Dark presents Rhys's heroine-narrator as she first encounters the world. This world—England, "their" world, "his" world —presents itself to her antagonistically and counters her own successfully by trivializing her. The sentence that signals this conflict— "Flamboyant trees are lovely when they're flowering"—is reinvoked and expanded forty years later in *Wide Sargasso Sea* (p. 151). In that novel the sense of time, and the context of which it is a part, is raised to a higher point of artistry. It is from a particularly feminine vantage point that Rhys presents the expanded context of *Wide Sargasso Sea*. There, especially, Rhys's heroine-narrator is given another chance, as she gives Charlotte Brontë's anti-heroine another chance.

It is appropriate to close on the autobiographical note that points up that aspect of her ruse in this last paragraph of *Voyage in the Dark*. Rhys sidestepped her editor's reading of her text in a double move. He asked her to give her heroine-narrator, the "girl," a "chance." The only chance Rhys has left her is in the text itself. In looking for "two or three paragraphs that wouldn't spoil the book, trying to give the girl a chance," Rhys produced one paragraph and made her point even more explicit. "*When their voices stopped*," there was at least the *possibility* of "*remembering*" (my emphasis). Anna echoes the men's "words" with the kind of irony a male reader can assume "tells the tale." The female reader (a native speaker of the "other" language) knows this use of irony bespeaks another. She recognizes the possibility of her own voice speaking *through* the echo, in the echo, within the agitating space it leaves in the text. We read just such an "absence" in the last paragraph of *Voyage in the Dark*. The "agitation" is made audible to us; its resonance remains even when the narrator has abdicated the seeming place of the attempt. Anna remains "elsewhere. . . ."

CHAPTER SIX.

THE INTRATEXT

She would ask me to read the different versions [of work on the autobiography], she would choose what she thought the best, and then tell me to tear up the others. . . . She seemed to get satisfaction from this, as if getting rid of something was a great clarification.
—David Plante on Jean Rhys

MANY STRAIGHTFORWARD statements concerning the composition of *Voyage in the Dark* can be found in Rhys's autobiographical writing and in interviews she gave late in her life. The notebooks in which she wrote a diary when she was not quite twenty years old, and from which *Voyage* was later to be composed, were bought on impulse to cheer up her grim room and its ugly table:

> It was after supper that night [. . .] that it happened. [. . .] I pulled a chair up to the table, opened an exercise book, and wrote *This is my Diary*. But it wasn't a diary. I remembered everything that happened to me in the last year and a half. I remembered what he'd said, what I'd felt. I wrote on until late into the night, till I was so tired that I couldn't go on, and I fell into bed and slept.
>
> Next morning I remembered at once, and my only thought was to go on with the writing. [. . .]
>
> I filled three exercise books and half another ["They were not at all like exercise books are now. They were twice the thickness, the stiff black covers were shiny, the spine and the edges were red, and the pages were ruled" (Plante, p. 248)], then I wrote: "Oh God, I'm only twenty and I'll have to go on living, and living and living." I knew then that it was finished and that there was no more to say. I put the exercise books at the bottom of my suitcase and piled my underclothes on them. After that

whenever I moved I took the exercise books but I never looked at them again for seven years.[1]

In this scene Rhys shows us a girl or young woman, like the autobiographical heroine of *Voyage in the Dark*, at a time equivalent to that immediately after the period described in *Voyage*. The passivity of the heroine-narrator of the novel is pushed aside in the cause of the writer's assertions of her experience in the diaries that were to form the basis for the novel. The peculiar "naming" of the diary—"*This is my Diary*"—can be seen as an accession to self by language-distancing; Rhys herself immediately disavows its commonplace function in the sentence that follows its naming.

The activity of writing furnished the heroine-writer Anna/Rhys with a sufficient sense of her own need to say what she wanted and to do as she needed: to write the diaries that became *Voyage in the Dark*, Rhys's favorite among her novels:

> I wrote it because it relieved me. I never wrote for money at the start. I wrote the makings of *Voyage in the Dark* long, long ago. I wrote it in several exercise books and then I put it away for years. . . . Then, twenty years later, fate had it that I tackle it again. I hadn't really written a book; it was more or less a jumble of facts. From the notes I'd done ages before I managed to put together *Voyage in the Dark*.
>
> And is it still your favorite? [the interviewer asked]
>
> I suppose so. Because it came easiest.[2]

In the same interview, Rhys remarked that "there's very little invention in my books": "What came first with most of them was the wish to get rid of this awful sadness that weighed me down. I found when I was a child that if I could put the hurt into words, it would go. It leaves a sort of melancholy behind and then it goes. . . . I would write to forget, to get rid of sad moments. Once they were written down, they were gone."[3]

Rhys's published novels and short stories, however, her *public* work, were not merely personal musings, even if they afforded her "relief." Full relief obviously came from her presentation *to* the world of her considered version *of* the world.

Concerning her "singular instinct for form," as Ford Madox Ford called it,[4] Rhys said: "The things you remember have no form. When you write about them, you have to give them a beginning, a middle, and an end. To give life shape—that is what a writer does. That is what is so difficult."[5] David Plante relates, concerning similar remarks, "Jean often talked of the 'shape' of her books: she imagined a shape, and everything that fit into the shape she put in, everything that didn't she left out."[6] Concerning both of these impulses—the "relief" Rhys got from "ridding herself" of "sad" feelings, and the "shaping" that she was looking for—Plante tells us that, in working on her autobiographical writing,

> She would ask me to read the different versions, she would choose what she thought the best, and then tell me to tear up the others. I tore up wastepaper baskets full. . . . (And, in fact, she told me that to her writing was a way of getting rid of something, something unpleasant especially. She asked me once to write down for her a short poem that was going round and round her head. "Two hells have I/Dark Devon and Grey London—/one Purgatory: the past"—And after I wrote it down she said, "Thank God, now I can forget that.")[7]

In her "real life" she can "forget"; *writing* does the remembering for her. She doesn't actually abdicate, as she seems to here. As she says elsewhere, in a "confession," "I have plenty to say [and] I am bound to say it. [. . .] I must write."[8]

Voyage in the Dark was a re-presentation of a part of Rhys's life in words, a re-vision of the dialogue that constituted the affair and is its central drama. What she is "shaping" is "life"—her own life—the better to present what seemed to her fundamental to its expression. In writing that life in her diary she "remembered" what he *said* and what she *felt*; however, in re-viewing it as a reader of her own life in order to shape the novel, what Rhys accomplishes is the *re*-constitution of the self that was and the constitution of the self that now writes the life. This constitution of self interweaves the two into a "shared text," and it is the text that expresses their continuous present. Both are present in the process and the result of that self-constitution. In writing the novel Rhys "remembers" not only what "he said," but also what she said and didn't say, in a remembering that, indeed, itself expresses what she felt. She *says* it—for both "selves"—in her writing. She had not yet, however, effected the presentation of the interweaving of selves so that we see the likeness, as we do in *Wide Sargasso Sea*.

In an interview Elizabeth Vreeland said to Rhys, "You wrote that you have such a great memory . . . that you can shut your eyes and remember conversations." Rhys answered, "That's what I've tried to do, but it's a very long time ago now."[9] The conversations that make up the greater part of *Voyage in the Dark* were written down, or at least noted, one assumes, almost immediately after they happened, when Rhys was not quite twenty. The affair in which "Anna Morgan" was engaged was one involving Rhys and her own "Walter Jeffries."

In fairness, since Rhys herself was concerned to get the record straight, we can infer only so much. But we can suppose or infer some things. We can suppose that Rhys is telling us some things we can believe, as well as interpret: (1) She remembered conversations with great accuracy; (2) the conversations recorded in *Voyage in the Dark* convey what he "said," what she "felt,"—the implicit framework for the "fundamental conversation" between them; and (3) the conversations related in *Voyage* are in all likelihood accurate representations of actual conversations. These conversations are the basis for the novel's shape, which, in Rhys's words, gives "form" to "life."

Sections of the unfinished autobiography *Smile Please* can be read as a gloss on, or a continuation of, *Voyage in the Dark*. The section called "Interval" picks up the heroine-narrator after the end of the affair recounted in *Voyage*:

> When my first love affair came to an end I wrote this poem:
> > I didn't know
> > I didn't know
> > I didn't know. (p. 92)

This "poem" echoes negatively the heroine-narrator Anna Morgan's defensive-aggressive question repeated three times in the climactic Chapter Nine of Part I of the novel: "D'you think I don't know [. . .] D'you think I don't know [. . .] D'you think I don't know?" (*Voyage*, pp. 84–85).

"Then I settled down to be miserable," she continues.

But it still annoys me when my first object of worship is sup-
posed to be a villain. Or perhaps the real idea at the back of this
is that his class was oppressing mine. He had money. I had
none.

On the contrary, I realise now what a very kind man he must
have been. I was an ignorant girl, a shy girl. And when I read
novels describing present-day love-making I realise I was also a
passive, dull girl. Though I couldn't control my hammering
heart when he touched me, I was too shy to say, "I love you." It
would be too much, too important. I couldn't claim so much.

When I first met this man I rather disliked him, and why I
came to worship him I don't quite know. I loved his voice, the
way he walked. He was like all the men in all the books I had
ever read about London. (p. 92)

Concerning the question "Do books 'lie' or not?" Rhys seems, in some
ways, to think not, especially in relation to a man's placing of himself
in relation to the world and to the women in it. Just as the man with
whom she had her first affair was "like all the men in all the books I
had ever read about London," so the heroine-narrator in *Voyage* discovers that what "everybody says" and what "you read . . . in all
books" is true to her experience of the man with whom she has her
affair. "Everybody says the man's bound to get tired and you read it
in all books" (*Voyage*, p. 65). The "men in all the books," the men in
her own books, and the men in her own early life would seem to be
cut from the same pattern, as revealed by their mutually reinforcing
presentation of themselves in "their" world and in "their" books.
Rhys, however, allows men to continue to define themselves in *her*
books, a prerogative generally disallowed women in the masculine
text of self-constitution in or out of books.

Descriptions of Rhys's reading in childhood and adolescence provide an explanation of her seeming generosity toward male characters. When her nurse tried to frighten her, the young Rhys was reading a "bowdlerized version of *The Arabian Nights*" (p. 21), an illicit
book whose heroine saves her life by her telling of tales. Rhys recalled: "No one ever advised me what to read or forbade me to read
something. I even looked at the rare and curious shelf [in the library,
"a new Carnegie Library"] but I don't remember any of it making
much impression. I liked books about prostitutes, there were a good

many then, and vividly recollect a novel called *The Sands of Pleasure* written by a man named Filson Young" (pp. 50–51).

However, Rhys tells us, "The older I grew the more things there were to worry about":

> Religion was then as important as politics are now. [. . .] There was the business of black, white [. . .] coloured. [. . .]
>
> There was also the business about ladies and gentlemen and that was terribly complicated and very important. [. . .] "Nature's gentlemen" existed, but apparently no "Nature's ladies." That was probably right.
>
> So as soon as I could I lost myself in the immense world of books, and tried to blot out the real world which was so puzzling to me. Even then I had a vague, persistent feeling that I'd always be lost in it, defeated.

We can recall that for Rhys even earlier, "Before I could read, almost a baby, I imagined that God, this strange thing or person I heard about, was a book. Sometimes it was a large book standing upright and half open and I could see the print inside but it made no sense to me" (p. 20). The "real world" and "God," one of whose halves was the father-book whose print she could see but which, like the world, "made no sense" to her, "were all about the same thing." She could accept "it," the "real" world and the puzzlement—"in books." From books, "fatally," she tells us, "I got most of my ideas." To rearrange the world, Rhys would write her own books, rewrite her life, try to write away that part of it that was inimical to her. But she could not, of course, write in "their" language, the language of the father-text.

To write her own books Rhys looked to the mother-book, the other half of the book that was "God," for a model. She could not write in "their" language, just as she does not "speak" it. Another section of *Smile Please* seems to carry forward the story of Anna Morgan after the close of the novel *Voyage in the Dark*. Rhys writes that her ex-lover sent her a Christmas gift, a tree with gifts attached; it was delivered to her room, where she was going to spend Christmas alone. She did not want the tree and the gifts. She writes, "The star at the top. I don't want that either. I don't know what I want. And if I did I couldn't say it, for I don't speak their language and I never will" (p. 100).

Other incidents described by Rhys in later life concern her time in

England before the affair, while she was still at the Academy of Dramatic Art, and immediately following, when she was an actress with the touring company. Still others foreshadow her adult view of language and of "them." Concerning her aspirations as an "actress," Rhys told Elizabeth Vreeland, "It seems as if I was fated to write . . . which is horrible. But I can only do one thing. I'm rather useless, but perhaps not as useless as everyone thinks. I tried to be an actress—a chorus girl—and the whole thing ended when I was handed a line to say: 'Oh Lottie, don't be so epigrammatic.' But, when the cue came, the words just disappeared. That was that."[10] Elsewhere Rhys mentions that, in response to something she wanted to deny, she "didn't know whether to answer 'It isn't true!' or 'We didn't do that!' " So, as usual, she "said nothing" (p. 46). Saying what she did not say out loud in the "real world" was what her writing was; and in *Voyage in the Dark* there is a representation of that very cross-hatching of saying and not-saying.

In Dominica, when she was still a child, Rhys's mother told her, "You are a very peculiar child [. . .]. There are times when I am very anxious about you. I can't imagine what will happen if you don't learn to behave more like other people" (p. 75). Hester, the "stepmother" in *Voyage*, puts it more aggressively, specifically in terms of language and of race and/or class: "I tried to teach you to talk like a lady and behave like a lady and not like a nigger and of course I couldn't do it" (*Voyage*, p. 56). As the adult Rhys puts it: "I don't speak their language and I never will" (p. 100).

In Rhys's next book, *Good Morning, Midnight*, this opposition is presented in the first paragraph. We hear the "speaking" voice of the room that is like so many others in which Rhys and the heroine-narrator have lived:

> "Quite like old times," the room says. "Yes? No?"
> There are two beds, a big one for madame and a smaller one on the opposite side for monsieur. The wash-basin is shut off by a curtain. It is a large room, the smell of cheap hotels faint, almost imperceptible. The street outside is narrow, cobble-stoned, going sharply uphill and ending in a flight of steps. What they call an impasse. (*Midnight*, p. 9)

Outside belongs to them, to "monsieur," whose bed is the smaller: he doesn't need the larger (or even the smaller) bed for the short duration of his stay in the room; her bed is his. He speaks to her in the voice of the structure that constrains her, the "large room." Were she to leave the room, break the constraints, and travel "sharply uphill" to take that "flight of steps," she would encounter "what they call an impasse." This is the result when the two idioms clash: an impasse, for the woman at least.

IN 1980 V. S. Pritchett, reviewing *Smile Please: An Unfinished Autobiography*, observed (accurately, I think) that, for Rhys, "Autobiography was a special torture. Not because she thought her private life was her own business but because she had already written it out in her very autobiographical novels and stories. She was being asked to winnow away her remarkable art and reveal, if she could remember them, the 'real' facts in a continuous narrative."[11] "Her private life" had already been "written . . . out" in her work. Yet to put the record straight was a cliché next to impossible for an artist who had been, as Pritchett calls Rhys, "instinctive." Pritchett's statement seems to suggest that Rhys was writing of her self and from her self, with little artistic distance and shaping. If we consider the self on display in Rhys's novels, some comment on a psychological approach to the writing would give a further understanding of the women's self that Rhys displays in her novels when they are viewed as art.

Psychological, specifically schizophrenic, analogues are found by many readers of much important women's fiction. Doris Lessing's work, for example, is often analyzed this way. The schizoid response to one's surroundings—a duality of perception, an objectifying of oneself—readily offers the kind of presentation that leads male commentators especially to characterize the style of a successfully achieved woman's work as "detached" or "indifferent." On the other hand, as Elizabeth Abel points out in "Women and Schizophrenia: The Fiction of Jean Rhys," such a doubleness of perception and thus of presentation is an appropriate response to situations in which women often find themselves. Abel stresses "Laing's insistence that schizophrenia is a legitimate and not uncommon response to certain interpersonal interactions"; this insistence or observation provides "a clue to understanding Rhys's heroines and thus the nucleus of Rhys's fiction" (as it can also help us with Doris Lessing's).[12]

Laing's paradigm of the divided self [which consists of "a real internal self and a false external one that complies mechanically with the desires of others"] is particularly useful in analyzing the behavior of Rhys's heroines in her middle novels, in which Rhys moves from the third-person narration of her first two novels to first-person narration by the heroines themselves, with a consequent new emphasis on the heroines' subjective lives. In *Voyage in the Dark* (1934) Rhys suggests that her heroine suffers from a sense of internal division between a responsive but covert inner self and a mechanical external one. This split is not identical to that which Laing describes: Anna Morgan's real self is the product of a happy childhood and not an escape from parental demands. Once this self is formed, however, Anna can find no way of confirming it in the England to which she moves, and it retreats within the mechanical being she becomes in response to her daily life. It is the relationship of these two selves within the person of Anna Morgan that constitutes the psychological interest of this novel, whose tale of unrequited love seems almost intentionally banal.[13]

This duality of response indeed marks a "responsive but covert inner self and a mechanical external one." But the "selves" (the self) we are talking about remain, preeminently the *speaking subject* (that "first-person" narrator). It is not the "relationship of . . . two selves" which, for me, "constitutes the . . . interest"—not even the psychological interest—of the novel. The interest and the drama are achieved in the presentation of the idiom, the language, of this "responsive but covert inner self." What is crucial is the "real . . . self," in contrast to and in conflict with the language of the so-called external world, that is, a world that is not part of us or under our control. In my view, there is no such entity as the "external self." There is one self ("oneself") and what is external to it. This is not to say there is no relationship or interaction between this self and the external world, that oneself is not versionalized according to context and circumstance.

What is "mechanical" or "false" is a person's attempt to speak exclusively in a language or idiom that is not her or his own; worse, to be forced by circumstances to speak in that language rather than in her own. For a person to reject her own language is tantamount to rejecting herself. As Elizabeth Abel points out, the problem Rhys explores is that "Once this self is formed [Anna's "real" self] . . . Anna can find no way of confirming it in the England to which she moves."[14] Unquestionably, Anna's problem of self-constitution is originally based in literal context, but that is only a beginning.

In *Voyage in the Dark* Rhys's presentation of the problem highlights the conflict in terms of *language context*. The conflict, the opposition, is real enough, and it is not internal, as the novel reveals it to us. Pressure is brought to bear from the outside. Dialogue, both spoken and unspoken, reveals the "real self" in conversation with this "external" world, which is not the world itself, but others in it—men and their agents, specifically. The narrator does not desert her task or her self; she carries on the dialogue even if it is unspoken. And Rhys gives this "unspoken" dialogue a place of its own *in her writing*.

In the opening paragraph of *Good Morning, Midnight* the act of writing is established immediately as a revelation of the speech context that is a metaphor and an instrument of oppression and power. One notes the constraining quality of the "speaking" room, which is like all the others in which the heroine-narrator has found herself— the rooms "going on endlessly" just as the words on the (masculine) page do. It is a context Rhys intends to disrupt if she can by writing it "out." She outlines its structures for us on the page, interjecting her own voice into the seemingly uninterruptible flow and structure of "their" context, which speaks here in the "voice" of the room.

Is this paradigmatic schizophrenia? It is difficult to think so. The schizoid personality may fit the woman's situation, and understandably so; the girl-child is brought up to respond, at least externally, to other people's desires. Working out of this "Olympia complex" is part of the business of a thoughtful woman's growing up, but a residue remains in the form of automatic language responses that a woman sheds incompletely and only with deliberate, considered action. However, the woman's idiom that remains *was* schooled in this "dual mode of response,"[15] and her language, her native idiom, is forever marked by its initial displacement. What she chooses to make of it, literally and figuratively, is preeminently a woman's choice, subject not only to the residual effects of the complex through which her language comes to be identified as *her own*, but also to the laws and conventions of its making, which she discovers are held in common with other women.

As Elizabeth Abel has observed, some of the heroine-narrator Sasha's "tenderest feelings" in *Good Morning, Midnight* are for women. Sasha "suggests in her relationship to her midwife a fundamental contact that endures between women and communicates more fully than the novel's slippery verbal labels: 'She speaks to me in a language that is no language. But I understand it. . . . Speaking her old,

old language of words that are not words.'"[16] Whereas some might reject the evident sentimentality in the stereotype of a woman giving birth and the midwife's possession of almost magical qualities, we recognize that the impulse is accurate. It is accurate because even though Rhys describes this language *as* language, its "words"—the stuff of which it is made—are "not words," not, apparently, like that "endless procession of words." Something else is happening in the language women speak. However, she goes no further here in suggesting what that "something else" might be; the exploration is confined to the dialogue between the dominant and the oppressed idioms. Only in *Wide Sargasso Sea* is the dialogue expanded to show us what a woman's language is made of, what its structure is like, and how it works—how it can be used to speak to men as well as to other women.

In the early novels, especially in *Voyage in the Dark*, Rhys demonstrates the problematical dialogue with men rather than the other-directed dialogue that engages women writing today. What is valuable for us in Rhys's early presentation is the identification of the locus of our speech. Rhys's placing of speech helps us enunciate what we now have to say and helps us understand the dynamics of our past and present responses to the "dominant" idiom.

I WANT to make only a few observations concerning *After Leaving Mr Mackenzie*, the novel written and published after *Quartet*, the first. I point to two representative incidents that end on the same note, incidents in which the heroine, Julia Martin, is dismissed from the minds and lives of two other characters—Mr. Horsfield, an Englishman with whom she has been having an affair; and her sister's friend and household companion, Wyatt, a suggestively masculine, perhaps lesbian, partner to her sister Norah.

After their mother's death, Norah shows some concern for the sister to whom she is not close. Wyatt assures her that everything is as it should be:

> Norah was sitting up on the sofa. She said, "Where's Julia?"
> "She's gone home," answered Miss Wyatt. "Much better for her."
> "Oh, no," said Norah in a hysterical voice. "We can't send her away like that. I don't believe she's got any money."

"My dear," said Miss Wyatt, "just you lie down and keep yourself still. Your sister's going to write."

"Oh," said Norah.

"Of course," said Miss Wyatt with contempt. "She'll write."[17]

This is Mr. Horsfield after he's gotten rid of Julia:

On his way home Mr Horsfield tried to put Julia entirely out
of his mind.

As he was opening the door of his house he thought: "Well,
that's all over, anyway." And then he wondered how he should
send money to her if she did not write. "But, of course, she will
write," he told himself.

He shut the door and sighed. It was as if he had altogether
shut out the thought of Julia. (*Mackenzie*, p. 127)

Writing is the end of all communication—the logical result of the
attempt to communicate that erases all the talk and certainly any
communication that went before. Just as Rhys has told us: "I found
when I was a child that if I could put the hurt into words it would
go. . . . I would write to forget, to get rid of sad moments. Once they
were written down, they were gone."

That is what writing was for Rhys, a halting of the "endless procession of words [that] gave me a curious feeling—sad, excited and
frightened. It wasn't what I was reading, it was the look of the dark,
blurred words going on endlessly that gave me that feeling" (*Voyage*,
p. 9). Anna/Rhys is here reading a man's book. In following her own
"book," her own reading of herself and others, fixing her language
on the page in contrast to his, structuring the frame, displaying the
"real" and the unspoken dialogue, Rhys wrote her own. And, indeed,
in doing so she clarifies the "blur" that is the masculine language
context.

The "sad moments" for Rhys are fixed most particularly in the
words people say and don't say to others, as well as in their looks
and evaluative stares. From her own "watching" and "listening" she
chooses words finally—if they are written—as the instrument, the
signal, and the marking of the oppression perpetrated on a person if
she is a member of an underclass, or if she is, rather, seemingly
classless. The most pervasive of such markings are those that have
historically classed women as a group without a right to speak, effec-

tively muting—even silencing—them in the society in which they move and attempt to speak. The writing down of the words, both spoken and unspoken, in the repressive pattern within which Rhys has experienced them, accomplishes two things. First, it gives her access to the power words have, especially the written word; it allows her the stage upon which to speak. At the same time, it allows her dangerous access to the means of killing that structure on the page— through writing. She exploits this structural system, a structure and a system which itself has exploited and used her in "real life," on the page.

Writing, for Rhys, is not a stoic thing, not that aesthetic achievement that reveals her "indifference" or "detachment." It is a presentation of a body of language, the corpse of masculine discourse as she experiences it. Into the body of the masculine idiom she inserts her own, that "unspoken" half of the dialogue, the fundamental conversation as it is constantly, consistently, and perniciously carried on in "our" language. She brings her own idiom to bear upon the oppressor's in preparation for the making of the woman's text in her last novel, *Wide Sargasso Sea*. Rhys performs a verbal operation on the body of language that constitutes the male idiom, and her incisive craft results in the excision of the cover of the male idiom to expose its almost inflexible frame. This frame will later serve as the warp of the feminine text in *Wide Sargasso Sea*. The "other half" of the discourse, the weft of the "woman's language"—all that is "not a continuation of their discourse" and that had heretofore "suffered silently" in the holes of that discourse—begins to move in the movement of the shuttle and becomes the dominant pattern in the weave of the text of *Wide Sargasso Sea*.

I N *Smile Please* Rhys recapitulates a series of interrogations and answers that she wrote in 1957, most of which is headed "The Trial of Jean Rhys." She begins, "Someone told me that after long torture the patient, subject, prisoner, whatever the word is, answers every question with 'I do not know'" (p. 129). Later, the interrogator reminds her, as if harking back to her original remark: *"The phrase is not 'I do not know' but 'I have nothing to say'"* (p. 132). She replies that she has plenty to say—"Not only that, but I am bound to say it." "I must," she says. "I must write." The voice reminds her that it is dangerous to do so, "under the circumstances." She insists, and the voice "says": *"All right, but be damned careful not to leave this book about"* (p. 133).

Rhys of course did precisely that: she left her books "about." She wrote and published the things she did not say, thus saying them irrevocably and ridding herself of them at the same time. She wrote her own books, "needle-sharp." She wrote the "other book," which was small and inside of which were "sharp, flashing things." In this writing Rhys spoke to her idea of God by including and countering the father-book, while modeling her own on that of the mother. "Sad, excited and frightened" she may have been in her life, but she understood the dangerous enterprise of writing her own books to say the "unsaid things."

Rhys did not rewrite men's books. In her own books she rewrote conversations with men by interpolating her own unspoken words, writing those words *as speech*. She used the conventions of our public writing (quotation marks, speaker and addressee indicated) to record that speech in the fixative provided by masculine conventions of publishable discourse.

Likewise, by hewing closely to the subjective, even the heightened sense of oneself vis-à-vis other people that is labeled paranoid or schizoid, Rhys demonstrates the borders of her language and those of the dominant language structure. Rhys found this voice in *Voyage in the Dark* after she had used the third-person, so-called omniscient point of view in *Quartet* and *After Leaving Mr Mackenzie*. In *Voyage* she discovered that the otherness of a woman's voice is best displayed by adhering to that otherness. In making this technical shift, Rhys gives us not only a portrait of the "victim," as her heroines are often described, but also, and more importantly, a portrait of the victimized *speaker*. She is a speaker whose native language practices are in profound contrast to, and collusion with, those very language practices that are the instrument of her victimization.

In *After Leaving Mr Mackenzie* Mr. Horsfield, a man who picks up the heroine after she has been cast aside by MacKenzie, attempts to draw her out by asking her to talk about herself. She does so finally by talking about her attempt to "explain" herself to a woman some years before. Neither Horsfield nor the woman before understands what she is trying to say. But it is significant that she (Anna/Rhys) uses a description of an attempt to explain to a woman in order to explain her situation to a man, and presumably to her general audience as well.

The attempt is highlighted by a picture of a woman that Ruth, the woman to whom Julia was talking, "had on the wall":

> "And all the time I talked I was looking at a rum picture she had on the wall—a reproduction of a picture by a man called Modigliani. Have you ever heard of him? This picture is of a woman lying on a couch, a woman with a lovely, lovely body. Oh, utterly lovely. Anyhow, I thought so. A sort of proud body, like an utterly lovely proud animal. And a face like a mask, a long, dark face, and very big eyes. The eyes were blank, like a mask, but when you looked at it a bit it was as if you were looking at a real woman, a live woman. At least, that's how it was with me.
>
> "Well, all the time I was talking I had the feeling I was explaining things not only to Ruth—that was her name—but I was explaining them to myself too, and to the woman in the picture." (*Mackenzie*, p. 40)

All this explanation is not what Horsfield wanted or expected: "It seemed to him that for a festive evening it had not been very festive" (*Mackenzie*, p. 43). For Rhys and for us, however, the scene represents something we do want and even expect: we see in the description the possibility of the beginnings of a conversation, not just between but *among* women, "real" women, "live" women, who have themselves taken off their masks.

As if realizing that trying to "explain" directly didn't work well even for Rhys herself, in the next novel—*Voyage in the Dark*—she finds the technical means to say and to show what she wants us to see and to hear. The first-person narration, in which all that we hear is from a seemingly central, subjective point of view, expands that subjectivity: "All the time I was talking," Rhys's narrator says, "I was explaining things not only to Ruth [. . .] but to myself too, and to the woman in the picture," the woman still caught in the frame of the masculine conception. Because of this strong narrative-structuring principle, we are disturbed when the heroine-narrator seems, as she does on occasion, to slip into another character's mind. This is because she has focused our attention on the dialogue—spoken and unspoken—that we are following, not on the individual character's response or reactions (which is what Rhys attempted to present in her first two novels). It is Rhys's chorus of voices, under her single direction, to which we attend.

For the fundamental conversation to continue, we depend on all the voices being controlled by the single speaker, the writer as heroine-narrator. Paradoxically, if she deserts this role of conductor, the other voice seems wrong, discordant. Another voice jars, except in direct exchange (and except for the heroine-narrator's "other" voice —that italicized "voice"). In *Voyage*, for example, when Walter Jeffries and Anna are talking, the narrator lapses into speculation concerning what Jeffries is thinking or feeling: "When he talked his eyes went away from mine and then he forced himself to look straight at me and he began to explain and I knew that he felt very strange with me and that he hated me, and it was funny sitting there and talking like that, knowing he hated me" (*Voyage*, p. 83).

Without the mediation/presentation of the writer's record of what a character says, of what "they" say, such description loses life. In this sense, the "I" of the heroine-narrator is deleted. The spoken language, recorded for us in the writing, evokes our response. The structure we are following is created by the positing—through the heroine-narrator's subjectivity—of multiple intersections at work in the constitution of self and language that begins here. The only voice we trust in the novel is rendered in the context of written *dialogue*. We believe what the writer has reported or recorded, not what the heroine thinks other people say or feel. We are responding to a visual medium that depends on words overheard or repeated by the reader/writer. The dialogue is, in this sense, concrete, especially as it is perceived, heard, and repeated to us through the consciousness of the heroine-narrator. When she departs from this structure, we feel that the writer has slipped. Rhys's technique wavers when the narrator speculates outside the framework of reported dialogue and attempts to break into any consciousness other than her own, except as we discern the mechanics of it in reported speech. Rhys's major structuring and narrative device—reported dialogue, both spoken and unspoken—commands our fullest attention.

Rhys responds to her interrogator in "The Trial" concerning her autobiographical writing: "I have plenty to say. Not only that, but I am bound to say it. [. . .] I must." She repeats this injunction to herself: "I must write. If I stop writing my life will have been an abject failure. It is already that to other people. But it could be an abject failure to myself. I will not have earned death." Her interrogator continues, "*You are aware of course that what you are writing is childish, has been said before. Also it is dangerous under the circumstances.*" "Yes," she answers, "most of it is childish. But I have not written for so long that all I can force myself to do is to write, to write. I must trust that out of that will come the pattern, the clue that can be followed."

"*All right,*" her interrogator concludes, "*but be damned careful not to leave this book about*" (p. 133). Rhys is Theseus here, as well as Ariadne. She follows the clue (the "clew," the thread) to make her way through the labyrinth that constitutes the woman and achieves or finds her text. Rhys deliberately "left her books about," as I have already emphasized. She was "bound to say" what she had to say, and the only way she could do so was to write. And in speaking she offers us the "pattern, the clue that can be followed," in her own words. She places for us both her language and her life in that "dangerous" context in which a woman speaking can place our own language for us—in *writing*, that map showing the territories and borders of the particular place of our living that we call "language."

CHAPTER SEVEN.

THE WOMAN WRITER

AS READER: THE

DREAM-TEXT OF

WIDE SARGASSO SEA

Who blames me? Many no doubt; and I shall be called dis-
contented. I could not help it: the restlessness was in my na-
ture; it agitated me to pain sometimes. Then my sole relief
was to walk along the corridor of the third story, backwards
and forwards, safe in the silence and solitude of the spot and
allow my mind's eye to dwell on whatever bright visions rose
before it . . . and, best of all, to open my inward ear to a
tale that was never ended—a tale my imagination created,
and narrated continuously: quickened with all of incident,
life, fire, feeling, that I desired and had not in my actual
existence.
——Jane Eyre in Charlotte Brontë's *Jane Eyre*

EAN RHYS'S *Wide Sargasso Sea* (1966) was published
long after *Good Morning, Midnight* (1939), the last of her
early novels. Concerning her attitude following the
publication of this earlier novel, Rhys told Elizabeth Vreeland, ". . . I
was very hopeful. But then war was declared, almost immediately,
and they didn't want books . . . I was forgotten and gave up writing. . . . And then I wrote some short stories. And then there was this
thing about doing *Good Morning, Midnight* on the BBC radio. And
then I started *The Wide Sargasso Sea*."[1] When Vreeland asked, "Where
did the idea come from of reconstructing Bertha's life—the Jane
Eyre heiress who sets fire to the house and jumps from the parapet?"
Rhys answered,

When I read *Jane Eyre* as a child, I thought, why should she think Creole women are lunatics and all that? What a shame to make Rochester's first wife, Bertha, the awful madwoman, and I immediately thought I'd write the story as it might really have been. She seemed such a poor ghost. I thought I'd try to write her a life. Charlotte Brontë must have had strong feelings about the West Indies because she brings the West Indies into a lot of her books, like *Villette*. Of course, once upon a time, the West Indies were very rich, and very much more talked about than they are now.[2]

Rhys did not say that she wanted to give a life to Brontë's Bertha or even that she wanted to explain Bertha or her life. What she wanted to do was to "write her a life." Rhys's response tells us much about what the act of reading can mean for a woman, since a woman has not had a satisfactory share of "reality," and it reveals Rhys as a writer. Rhys tells us how a woman joins the two acts, reading and writing, into one.

As a reader, a woman, psychosexually conditioned as she is, invariably takes into account the eccentric relational contexts as well as the explicitly centered text of what she reads. Rhys used one such contextual reading as the structuring principle of *Wide Sargasso Sea*—the dialogic response to our own dreams which our reading of Freud has helped us to understand. This response necessitates reading our own text as if it were the text of another. Such an ex-centric model, as we realize in reading Rhys's novel, is a way of maintaining our difference(s) while at the same time affirming the strength to be found in a collective, collaborative response to the texts and contexts in which we find ourselves.

Rhys placed her response as a reader not only in relation to Brontë's text, but also within the context to which she felt Brontë was responding, one that Rhys claimed as her own. Rhys's background was West Indian, Creole, and colonial, a culture already in decline in the mid-nineteenth century while still being a source of profit for the British. In responding to her reading of Brontë's text, Rhys sought not only to correct an omission, but also to correct what she considered a misreading of "Creole women," part of whose identity was shaped by the British exploitative context. In short, Rhys writes as a reader of both text *and* context. And since her own text, instructive as it is, is inevitably drawn from and produced within her own historical and cultural context, the text that she produces invites a similarly writerly response from her own readers. The pattern that Rhys presents depends on the reader's response to a text that she recognizes, in which she sees herself, and that, as a writer, she—the reader—continues with the addition and inscription of her own difference.

In *Voyage in the Dark* Rhys shows us the heroine-narrator's language practice, her muted idiom in contrast to the dominant idiom. In *Wide Sargasso Sea* her presentation expands to include a full delineation of contexts in opposition. *Wide Sargasso Sea* focuses on the woman's idiom by showing it in relation to other women, who are also "native speakers" of the muted idiom. The completed movement represented by *Wide Sargasso Sea*, the full delineation of our textual space, is mirrored in the "completed sentence" we find there, in contrast to the "incomplete sentence" that Anna Morgan/Jean Rhys—co-narrators of co-texts—were unable to complete in the earlier novel. The movement toward completion displaces the text of the dominant idiom, using it both as fixed place of metaphor for the definition of her own text and as a fixed frame for its weave. Rhys inverts the place of metaphor that has allowed the masculine sentence to stand, inadequately, as the sole model for a completed discourse in the cultural tradition that is itself modeled after "their" sentence.

Just as woman-as-metaphor has served as the place to fix a man's desire in the aesthetic and institutionalized structures of our culture, so here Rhys makes use of a man's text, the place of that text, to fix the desires of her own. The displacement of the male text and the structural metaphor it represents ultimately display a woman's text. While Rhys's presentation of the masculine text is rigorous in the seemingly accurate psychological narration of itself, of "himself" as Rochester is read, especially by male critics, Rhys nevertheless uses the male text as a fixing place in much the way that the discourse of "Man" in our culture has used "Woman," but with a difference. The placement of the masculine text does not silence his text—he still tells his own story—as the woman's text has been silenced. In his displacement, he becomes the defining litany of his own speech, and a recital of the reasons for it.

In examining her own life, in writing her own text, and in allowing the primacy of her heroine-narrator's text to dictate its relation to the dominant text, Rhys created a novel that demonstrates one kind of appropriate feminine aesthetic. The whole of *Wide Sargasso Sea* can be seen to complete the "woman's sentence" that, more than fifty years ago, Virginia Woolf despaired of finding.[3]

The completed sentence is a metaphor emphasizing the relation of the woman's muted text to that of the dominant text of our culture. Rhys's text offers another, more serviceable metaphor that emphasizes the relationship among women. I suggest that in *Wide Sargasso Sea* the "clue," the "pattern," in Rhys's words, is the movement of the shuttle of the dream as it moves among the women in the novel (and the women of Brontë's novel, including Brontë herself; and the women of Rhys's other books; and Rhys herself; and us, her readers). The dream, the "sub-conversation" of *Voyage in the Dark*, has here become explicit in the narratives that form the novel. The fixed initial framework or warp of the text can be construed as the masculine text (represented by Rochester's narration and motivation) through which the moving shuttle of the woman's text weaves the pattern we come to see, the weft or woof of the text.

Rochester is not among the dreamers in the dream. He offers only the initially flexible, finally resistant warp against and through which the women weave the text of the dream. The shuttle is passed from dreamer to dreamer, woman to woman. Rochester is not left out of this web of text, but he can only resist, as the already taut thread of the warp set up on the loom is prepared to do. The resistant framework, the warp of the dream, is "his" world. As Rochester tells Antoinette, "But my dear, you do not know the world." That is his "reality," as he tells us. Antoinette, a woman, knows another reality, expressed in the dream she has seen with her own eyes. This reality can be seen in the way that Antoinette reads her own context, and that of others, and it is expressed in the way Rhys reads and rewrites Brontë's text and its context, as well as her own.

Rhys presents the masculine text in the place it has claimed, defining and redefining itself while the woman's text works around and through it. In so placing her text, in writing outside the confines of the masculine text, using the spaces of silence that the self-imposed borders of the dominant text clearly mark, Rhys isolates the dominant text as a fixed point in the weave of her own.

If we view the presentation of a woman's text as a kind of dream ("a tale," as Brontë's *Jane Eyre* says, "that was never ended—a tale my imagination created, and narrated continuously"[4]) to which another woman, the reader, responds in terms of the language practice we share, we see that our response to that text is analogous to the relationship we have to our own dreams. Just as Rhys, in writing *Wide Sargasso Sea*, is responding as a reader to Brontë's text, to her own life, and to her own earlier texts, so are we both writer and reader of our own dreams. Brontë's text uses Jane Eyre's dream-texts at crucial points, adding a dimension to the text that also emphasizes its difference from that of Rochester, the conscious teller-of-tales. In picking up the strand of the dream-text of Brontë's novels as the structural principle of her own, Rhys shows us how we can read another woman's text: as our own dream, and at the same time as an "other's" dream.

Brontë could point to her "double" but she could not overcome the internalized censor who prevented her from actually *writing* her. Over a century later Rhys could do so, but she was able to overcome the censor only by shaping an apparently accurate *transcription* of what in itself could be construed as a "dream," a "fictitious narration" resembling those from which Freud drew his ideas about the dream-work.

Dreams, as Freud has shown us, constitute themselves as both place and language. The narrator of a dream can be identified only in our recognition that she is *in* the dream, that she has a place in the network of relationships producing the narrative of the dream. She is not, specifically, its *narrator*; she is part of the narration, of what is being narrated. As a reader of her own or of another's dream, the dreamer writes her response in her reading of the dream, a reading that is a continuation of the dream to which she is responding. She narrates her continuation of it and thus interlaces the continuation, her reading, into the first narration. The "narrator" remains herself and an "other" at the same time. She remains the same and yet different from herself.

The narrative, the dream, is thus collectively authored—even if its several "authors" are the same person, first as indeterminate writer, then as responding reader—but without the finality the word "authored" suggests. The narrative of the dream is passed on; it invites its continuation. Each reader in her turn, even if she is the "same" reader, and each reading in its turn participates in the narrative and continues it.

The relationship between parts of a dream furnishes its meaning for us; we do not find a meaning imposed by a subject who places herself at the center of the construct as its "author." Rhys's choice of this structuring principle, which emphasizes relationships and the process of how things and people interrelate, creates the woman's text and allows the metaphor of the dream to represent it.

Rhys was herself under the constraint(s) of what we might call the "check and stimulus" of Brontë's dream-text.[5] "Check and stimulus" refers to those points of recognition—of likeness, as well as of difference—that produce our own reading of a text. Rhys's culture resembled Brontë's in many respects. Yet Rhys was born more than seventy years later and into a colonial culture, that first difference Rhys noted even as a child. This notation was a first point in the building of the "spectral architecture" of her own novel. This spectral architecture is what we see as individual readers; it is the text we begin to build in response to the text we read. Her position as a reader in her own context allows Rhys to provide us with a sense of similar constraints in our reading of her novel. The dream—Antoinette's dreams, Rhys's response to Jane Eyre's dreams, Brontë's text, and her own—provides the narrative framework of the novel; at the same time, as a dream, it narrates itself, constituting within itself both context and language. The checks and stimuli of this dream-principle expand our fundamental conversation.

Freud's description of our dream-work explains some of the reasons why we recognize the artistry of *Wide Sargasso Sea*. Freud's analysis of a case of hysteria in the young woman he called Dora in some ways represents the masculine text that offers the framework, or warp, for the weave of the feminine text. His reading of the "uncanny"—which, according to Julia Kristeva, can be related to the "unsaid"[6]—helps to reveal the mechanisms within both the muted feminine and the dominant masculine texts in Rhys's book. This double exposure is a narrative of the irreducible difference between a woman's reading and a man's.

Such an expanded view is what *Wide Sargasso Sea* affords us. Rhys makes the collective enterprise clear, the reading of ourselves and others that compels our own writing. The model offered by her text invites response and continuation, not only of another woman's text, but of other texts of difference as well.

THE BLUEPRINT FOR *Wide Sargasso Sea* derived from the "spectral architecture" of Rhys's reading of *Jane Eyre* is the basis of the realized structure of Rhys's novel.[7] This text, both response-representation and outline, provides the overtly identifiable, direct links with Brontë's novel.

The second dream-text entails the transformative processes of Rhys's own novelistic dream-work, contrasted with Brontë's novel. Rhys's dream-text is constituted by a set of relationships dependent on the prior relationship of mother and daughter-narrator; in contrast, the relationship to the father determines the masculine text, Rochester's narrative.

The foremost element in the first dream-text emphasizes what Rhys's own contextual reading defines as the conspicuously silent, unvoiced moment in Brontë's novel. This is the moment of the Creole madwoman, whose laughter and night visits are her only manifestations in the life she and Jane Eyre share in Thornfield Hall. Rhys's novel seeks to emphasize that the two women do indeed share a text.

Another structural link with Brontë's novel, and a major constraint on Rhys's, is the fated quality of Antoinette's life. This element unwinds in Antoinette's literal dreams as they are described serially, beginning in the narrative of her childhood and culminating in the narrative of her life and final actions at Thornfield Hall. Descriptions of the dream(s) foreshadow and shadow—that is to say, follow or double—the unfolding formal text of the novel. Serial description, the evolution of Antoinette's dream, parallels the progress of the life, the story told to us in and by the narratives that form the novel. Rhys's inclusion of these literal dreams can be seen as one technical response to Brontë's own use of Jane Eyre's dreams; as such, it emphasizes a sharing-of-the-text: Antoinette/Jane's; Brontë/Rhys's. Rhys's writerly response includes an answer in technique as well as a readerly response to content.

The third link uniting Brontë's text and Rhys's is the point at which Rhys's novel explicitly intersects Brontë's. For a time the two texts cohabit the same space, when Grace Poole, another of the silent women of *Jane Eyre*, begins to speak in Rhys's novel. Grace Poole's speaking voice, which is silent or monosyllabic in Brontë's novel, offers the overt signal of the origin of Rhys's *Wide Sargasso Sea*. With Grace Poole's *voice*, Rhys links her text to Brontë's and bridges Brontë's with her own, entering Brontë's text at the same time, interrupting its narrative arrangement to complete her own. Antoinette's narrative also places her text in the "present tense" of Brontë's. After Grace Poole's introduction, Antoinette's narrative begins in the simple, present tense of description, a static locating of self in a place:

> In this room I wake early[. . . .] Grace Poole, the woman who looks after me, lights a fire[. . . .] The woman Grace sleeps in my room. [. . .] There is one window high up[. . . .] There is no looking-glass here[. . . .] The door [. . .] is kept locked. It leads [. . .] into a passage. [. . .] When night comes [. . .] it is easy to take the keys. [. . .] I [. . .] walk into their world. [. . .] They tell me I am in England but I don't believe them. [. . .] This cardboard house where I walk at night is not England. (pp. 146–48)

The narrative then resumes in a more conventional past tense and continues so to the end of the novel. We are "with" Antoinette in Thornfield Hall, where Brontë's novel places her and where, from the beginning of Antoinette's dream, she was predestined to find herself and to "end" her dream, as that "dream" of Brontë's directed her to do. Antoinette, and Rhys, faithfully execute the scenario of Brontë's dream, telling us that she has done so: "That was the third time I had my dream, and it ended" (p. 153). *That* dream may be ended; her own is not, however, and Antoinette/Rhys's narrative continues to its own conclusion.

Grace Poole's introduction to the culminating narrative also raises a voice for the collective case. Grace Poole's point of view is specifically that of a servant, a position that she is allowed to explicate. The entire introductory passage (pp. 145–46) is italicized, further emphasizing her voice and point of view. Drawing the other women of Brontë's into a relation to one another, she also places Antoinette in relation to herself and to the others:

> *"I know better than to say a word. After all the house is big and safe, a shelter from the world outside which, say what you like, can be a black and cruel world to a woman. Maybe that's why I stayed on."*
>
> *The thick walls, she thought. [. . .] above all the thick walls, keeping away all the things that you have fought till you can fight no more. Yes, maybe that's why we all stay—Mrs Eff and Leah and me. All of us except that girl who lives in her own darkness.* (p. 146)

In the same passage that returns us to Brontë's text, we are also given verbal and conceptual cues that return us to the thoughts of the child Antoinette after she has awakened from the first and inchoate version of her dream, a "bad dream." Afterwards the little girl "lay thinking": "I am safe. There is the corner of the bedroom door and the friendly furniture. There is the tree of life in the garden and the wall green with moss. The barrier of the cliffs and the high mountains. And the barrier of the sea. I am safe. I am safe from strangers" (p. 23). Grace Poole's adult concerns echo the child's sentiments; " '. . . *a shelter from the world outside.*' . . . *The thick walls . . . keeping away all the things that you have fought till you can fight no more.*" We could also put it the other way around: the child's sentiments echo Grace Poole's adult concerns. Interweaving of texts and narrative creates circularity, as well as vertical intersecting and horizontal continuing effects. These are informed by the repetition-with-difference inscribed by the speaker's or the narrator's context and narrative starting point. With Antoinette's childhood dream we are given the forecast of the novel's development and of Antoinette's "fate" as predetermined broadly by Brontë's text.

Rhys's narrator, even as the child Antoinette, both underscores her predestination and suggests the strategic open-endedness of Rhys's narrative method: "I woke next morning knowing that nothing would be the same. It would change and go on changing" (p. 23). This passage, along with the adult Antoinette's brief description of the shipboard crossing, locates the significance of the novel's title. Neither the "barrier of the cliffs and the high mountains," the fastness of the island of Dominica, which shelters Antoinette in her own context, or finally and especially the "barrier of the sea"—the wide Sargasso Sea—that lies just northeast of her island, between her island and the passage to England, proves a barrier.

When Antoinette woke on board ship, "it was a different sea. Colder. It was that night, I think, that we changed course and lost our way to England" (p. 148). Even the original destination—the England she had early imagined with curiosity and interest—is "lost" in the crossing of that sea that is finally no "barrier." "This cardboard house," she tells us, "where I walk at night is not England" (p. 148). It is the illusory, but by no means benign, legally sanctioned construct of her husband—the "stranger," the "someone who hated me," as he is called in the first dream (p. 23); "the man who hated me," as he is more specifically identified in the last dream (p. 155). He is a stranger who crosses geographical "barriers" but who cannot or will not attempt to traverse the cultural and psychological boundaries that separate him from the woman who becomes his wife. In this sense only is the wide Sargasso Sea a "barrier." It marks an impassable psychological boundary. It could have served as a crossing point, a conduit; it remains a gulf, impassable except superficially and by force. The "wide Sargasso Sea" marks the place of Rochester's trespass, and of his failing. It is at the same time a barrier that Antoinette—wrenched out of her own context, wherein she had already tried to cross "barriers," of color, culture, and class—discovers to be a means of her own passage to self-discovery.

In the false England to which she was forcibly brought and in which she is forcibly incarcerated, Antoinette finds the means to identify herself. She writes the end of her dream: "Now at last," she tells us in the last few lines of her narration, "I know why I was brought here and what I have to do" (pp. 155–56). The joining of Brontë's text and Rhys's "brought" Antoinette to Rochester's (and Brontë's) "England." It is Rhys's text alone that discovers her. The two dream-texts come together in Part Three of the novel to form a single dream-text. In the final paragraph we are returned to the single individuating text of Rhys's narrative.

Rhys's last novel is the logical culmination of the whole of her written text, the end of the "voyage in the dark" that she and her heroine-narrator began in the early novel. Anna Morgan, the heroine-narrator of *Voyage in the Dark*, could see the "ray of light," external to her and not in her control, not "in her hands," which "came in again under the door like the last thrust of remembering" (*Voyage*, p. 159). Antoinette, the *"girl who lives in her own darkness,"* completes the voyage, shielding the flame of the candle with her hand so that it can light her "along the dark passage," so that the "remembering" may be continued in a writing of the dream-text which can be seen as a common text of our lives. "I will remember quite soon now," she assures us shortly before the endings of both dreams—Brontë's and her own, the one that isn't "her own," and the one that is.

Wide Sargasso Sea represents Rhys's achievement of the aesthetic destination toward which the early novel *Voyage in the Dark* sets itself. The closing passages of *Wide Sargasso Sea* show the heroine-narrator's arrival at a psychological destination, one consistent with the overall achievement, both cultural and conceptual, that has been actively at work in women's lives and intellectual pursuits for more than a hundred years. Grace Poole's words, quoted above, expressly set the stage for the enactment of what Gilbert and Gubar identify as a characteristically nineteenth-century drama of "enclosure and escape."[8] Rhys carries the drama the crucial step forward. As Grace Poole's introduction concludes: "*Yes, maybe that's why we all stay—Mrs Eff and Leah and me. All of us except that girl who lives in her own darkness. [. . .] she hasn't lost her spirit. She's still fierce. I don't turn my back on her when her eyes have that look. I know it*" (p. 146). It is Antoinette's *look* that Grace knows, the "look" in Antoinette's eye (the metaphoric as well as physiologically moving organ of dreaming) where her "spirit," which she has not lost, remains.

The rhetorical surfacing of this inner activity is the public presentation of a woman's constitution of herself in the practice of her writing. As dream-subject and narrator, she is the author of the text of difference represented by a dream-text. The dream-text is addressed directly to members of her audience who themselves want to address and engage "others," readers for whom, indeed, the figurative "look in the eye" is something they "know." These readers respond by recognizing the possibility of a figurative writing of their own texts of difference in relation to people with whom they feel a mutuality of experience, but from whom they nevertheless and inevitably differ. In the response of these readers, as well, is a recognition of their asymmetrically constrained dialogue with the already established, dominant text.

The narrative model derives from a woman's relation to her mother. By extension, such a model can be applied to a person of either sex. Rhys's textual model can ultimately be considered a gender-free paradigm. At this moment in our culture's history, however, it is women who "naturally" partake of this process—of its advantages and disadvantages. The woof or weft of the text remains the "feminine," and the warp, the "masculine"; the feminine text is the dream-text that forms the weft of the novel *Wide Sargasso Sea*.

As I noted earlier, the dream as it is used in *Wide Sargasso Sea* is the "explicitation" of the "sub-conversation" of *Voyage in the Dark*. The "muted idiom" has been expanded to delineate and display the woman's context that had formerly been all but invisible, specularly and textually muted. The sub-conversation formerly had not been *spoken*;

the woman's context had not been *displayed*. Rhys reveals this context in the interplay of text(s) and subtext(s) that forms the aesthetic base of her novelistic presentation and technique.

The relationship between text and subtext, and the distinction between them, is central to a description of a dream-text as it is offered in *Wide Sargasso Sea*. To show this I will use definitions provided by two disparate sources: Stanislavski, the teacher, and Freud, the psychoanalyst. These descriptions, both provided by men near the turn of the century, are not as disparate as they might seem at first glance if we consider them in terms of the theater metaphor that I discussed previously.

The word "subtext," wrote John Russell Brown, comes "from Stanislavski's writings about the actor and is still particularly associated with the 'method' of acting that was first developed while Chekhov was writing for the Moscow Art Theatre."[9] The subtext was defined as

> the manifest, the inwardly felt expression of a human being in a part, which flows uninterruptedly beneath the words of the text, giving them life and a basis for existing . . . a web of innumerable, varied inner patterns inside a play and a part, . . . all sorts of figments of the imagination, inner movements, objects of attention, smaller and greater truths and a belief in them, adaptations, adjustments and other similar elements. It is the subtext that makes us say the words we do in a play.[10]

We might put beside Stanislavski's definition of "subtext" Freud's almost contemporaneous description of how we can view the "dream-work" that produces the dream we experience:

> The dream-thoughts and the dream-content are presented to us like two versions of the same subject-matter in two different languages. Or, more properly, the dream-content seems like a transcript of the dream-thoughts into another mode of expression, whose characters and syntactic laws it is our business to discover by comparing the original and the translation. The dream-thoughts are immediately comprehensible, as soon as we have learnt them. The dream-content, on the other hand, is expressed as it were in a pictographic script, the characters of which have to be transposed individually into the language of

the dream-thoughts. If we attempted to read these characters according to their pictorial value instead of according to their symbolic relation, we should clearly be led into error.[11]

Freud described the method of reading these "symbolic relations" by likening them to a picture puzzle, a rebus in which we "try to replace each separate element by a syllable or a word that can be represented by that element in some way." Words lose their usual meanings and stand in for something else, even for some *thing*, and vice versa. Words themselves can become "things" in dreams: "The words which are put together in this way are no longer nonsensical but may form a poetical phrase of the greatest beauty and significance. A dream is a picture-puzzle of this sort."[12]

These two passages share similar impulses toward an analysis of preconscious "expression"—of seemingly different kinds. Stanislavski's "adaptations, adjustments, and similar elements" are readily comparable to the explicit mechanisms of the dream-work ("condensation," "displacement," the capacity for "representability," and "secondary revision") as Freud defines them in *The Interpretation of Dreams*.[13] Similarly, just as the process by which the manifest content of a dream becomes a picture-puzzle as a result of the transformations accomplished by the dream-work, so the process of the actor's interpretation of his or her role through a response to the subtext is similar to the production of the manifest content of the dream. The latent content, the "dream-thoughts" especially, as they are transformed in the dream-work, can be likened to that "inwardly felt expression" of Stanislavski's, which "flows uninterruptedly beneath the words of the text, giving them life and a basis for existing."[14] Indeed, the text that the actor presents and the subtext have a relationship with the dream-content and the dream-thoughts respectively, although Freud's view that they are like two versions of the same subject matter in two different languages is potentially more textualist and more radical. Just as the two cooperate in the process of the dream-work, just as the dream-thoughts are transcribed by the dream-work to produce the manifest content (the dream we perceive and recollect after the work), so, similarly, does the subtext flow "beneath" the words of the text that is represented by the actor's performance. As Brown points out concerning Shakespeare's dialogue, it is the "subtext" that has "for centuries, been sought out and expressed through gesture, bearing and elocution, in order to give a 'personal and exact life' to [the] dialogue."[15] This attempt can be viewed as the professional actor's mimicking of the more literal *transcription* of the dream process.

In basing the text of *Wide Sargasso Sea* on the subtext of Brontë's novel in relation to the subtext of her own/her heroine-narrator's life, patterning the presentation of the novel on the relationship between the two, Rhys gave "a personal and exact life"—her own in part, specifically Antoinette's—to her text. This endeavor began in her attempt to "try to write [Brontë's Bertha] a life"; not to "describe" her life, but to *write* it. In doing so, she has written *a* life for many women, at least as we discern our life in our language practices.

Implicit in any text are numerous subtexts, one of which, in all likelihood, will dominate a given reader's response. Rhys makes this relationship clear in her response to Brontë and in the methods of presentation she chooses for the display of her own text. Any subtext is likely to erupt into a full-blown text, the latent content of the one becoming the manifest content of the other. The unwritten dream-thoughts of the first "dream," the first text, become the manifest, written text of its successor. The "lie" in the text is the mark of a subtext, what is latent in the newly manifest material; in other words, the lie, the silence in the text, is the marker of the subtext of the newly found, the most recently written, text.

As a writer, Rhys may be said to be conscious of what is only implicit in our recognition or analysis of our dreams, and of the "dream-work" that produces a dream rather than a novel. The system of the dream-work is closed and self-referring to the extent that it is accessible to the interpreter. Its processes transcribe material that is confined and bounded by internal relationships. Neither the dream nor the system that produces it can go outside itself; the dream and its "meaning" exist only within the relationships that make up the "work." Rhys's overt thematic and technical attempt concerns the problem of communication with another system. Thus Rhys's novelistic attempts at communication are outside the private grammar of our dreams. It is Rhys's achievement that she has captured some of the sense of a "simultaneity in time," characteristic of dreams, in a *narrative* structure: "dreams take into account in a general way the connection which undeniably exists between all the portions of the dream-thoughts by combining the whole material into a single situation or event. They reproduce *logical connection* by *simultaneity in time*. Here they are acting like the painter who, in a picture of the School of Athens or of Parnassus, represents in one group all the philosophers or all the poets. It is true that they were never in fact assembled in a single hall or on a single mountain-top; but they certainly form a group in the conceptual sense."[16]

Rhys's use of the "dream-thoughts" of the subtexts is a technique by which she transcribes Antoinette's life onto the page while at the same time remaining within the constrained framework of Brontë's text. She gives one voice to more than one text, moving from the dream-thoughts to the manifest content of her novel, in which text and subtext are, indeed, "like two versions of the same subject-matter in two different languages." She interweaves the texts and the subtexts with which she is working into a single text, *Wide Sargasso Sea*, achieving the intersection and synchronicity that mark a dream-text. The "performance" that Stanislavski emphasized becomes integral to a representation of the dream-structure, to the presentation of a dream-text—a narrative—written and read "in time," that nevertheless achieves the "simultaneity in time" that characterizes a dream.

Efforts to communicate with another system or context and the barriers to such a communication are both given in the metaphor of the dream. Dreams operate both thematically and stylistically in Rhys's more overt expressions of theme, especially in relation to Rochester, and, more significantly, in the technique that allows the dream-text to emerge as an expression of the context shared by the women in the novel.

Two elemental idioms are opposed in Rhys's novels. There is the muted idiom of women—here white, black, and colored women (the black and colored men, with the exception of Daniel Cosway and the "Young Bull," occupying a position auxiliary to the women). And there is the dominant idiom of white men. The two are represented in *Wide Sargasso Sea* by the mutually exclusive contexts we are given for Antoinette and for Rochester. Their contexts are seemingly "fixed"; and they meet but do not blend. The original lack of the one's understanding of the other and of the other's background is, early in the novel, tagged a "dream," something blurred and "unreal." These "dreams," Dominica and England, are blatantly opposed in a verbal interchange early in Rochester's narration:

> "Is it true," she [Antoinette] said, "that England is like a dream? Because one of my friends who married an Englishman wrote and told me so. She said this place London is like a cold dark dream sometimes. I want to wake up."
>
> "Well," I [Rochester] answered annoyed, "that is precisely how your beautiful island seems to me, quite unreal and like a dream."
>
> "But how can rivers and mountains and the sea be unreal?"
>
> "And how can millions of people, their houses and their streets be unreal?"
>
> "More easily," she said, "much more easily. Yes a big city must be like a dream."
>
> "No, this is unreal and like a dream," I thought. (p. 67)

The explicit struggle between the two idioms or contexts represented by Antoinette and Rochester are specifically their "ideas" of themselves and the world: this is the thematic starting point for the novel. The technical expression of Rhys's thematic concerns, however, opens up this dialogue to more crucial concerns: the circuit of the dream that represents the relationship and the "conversation" between, and among, the women's texts. The "self" Antoinette asserts in her last narrated action(s) in the novel is constituted in its relationship to many others, all women. The act of self-assertion and self-constitution that the act of writing itself signals for Rhys is drawn for us as a circuit exclusive to women. All of the women share the dream in contextual—as well as "textual"—opposition to the men.[17] The dream is finally the overriding metaphor for "context" as well as of "text," both of self and of idiom.

Note that Rochester's last remark in the interchange is not spoken aloud. He *thought*, "No, this is unreal and like a dream." Significantly, Antoinette here speaks of writing between women for what is perhaps the only time in the novel: "one of my friends who married an Englishman wrote and told me [. . .] this place London is like a cold dark dream." This is another kind of marking in the text, the marking of a male/female difference, as well as an indicator of where to look and where not to look for the operation of this feminine circuit. A written exchange between women is the starting point for an attempted conversation and hoped-for exchange with Rochester. Antoinette's response to her friend's letter is very unlike Rochester's present response, or his later response to Daniel Cosway's letter. (Cosway's letter serves Rochester only as proof that his own biased misgivings about his wife are "true," rather than affording an opportunity for possible understanding.) The "dreams" of the two, Rochester and Antoinette, remain to be acted out in a conflict in which the "dream" sanctioned by "law" is forcibly dominant. But the dream set , in motion among the women empowers their own placing of themselves in the textual dialogue.

The subtext, then, is by no means "hidden"; rather, it is strongly marked. The interplay between text and subtext becomes the vehicle for the display of the mechanisms for the achievement of Rhys's text, Antoinette's individuation, and their novelistic representations. Subtext thus becomes all important to the woman's text. Unlike the masculine model of discourse, it is a consciousness of myriad subtexts that engenders the production of our texts and our reading and understanding of them. Brontë's subtext becomes "versionalized" in Rhys's manifest text; the subtext that Stanislavski suggests is imperative for the manifest performance of the actor indeed becomes the technique for the performance of the novel's text. Finally, consciousness of subtexts becomes the model for the presentation of ourselves to ourselves.

What is muted in Brontë's text becomes the occasion for Rhys's more audible orchestration. As she transcribes her version, she marks new subtexts that are themselves silent in her own text. On another level, we, the readers, are brought back to that most elemental concern, the formulation of our own subjectivity, a making of ourselves as subject. Rhys has taken us the extra step. She has turned the nineteenth-century plot inside out. The subtext, the "hidden plot," becomes the basis for the technique that itself opens the plot, revealing the narrative technique itself to be the key that opens the door, as well as our eyes, to the full display of the plot. We see not only *what* it is, but *how* it works.

The power of the dream places the women in the textual dialogue. The fundamental conversation with which Rhys began her work is expanded into an exploration of a woman's context, through its dialogue with a man's and, more crucially, through the conversation between and among women. "Subtext" becomes the crucial element in the presentation of any text of difference. Subtext can become the text of the woman's novel through differentiation from a man's or from another woman's, by building upon its predecessor's marked subtext. Differentiation from the masculine text versus differentiation from another female text reveals that the masculine narrative serves only as a fixed frame for the weave of the feminine dream-text. The feminine text has a unique relation to another woman's text; its crucial elements are derived from the other's text, the one a direct response to the other. The source of origin here is "The Other." But this Other is another woman.

Wide Sargasso Sea, as Angela Williams has observed, is "the only novel which Jean Rhys says she *chose* to write." The first four novels seem to have been written from a "psychological necessity, from 'a wish to get rid of this awful sadness which weighs me down so much.'"[18] These problems, however, are not a particular type of woman's alone, and the model of representation that Rhys uses has more than personal application. "[P]ossibly because it was not primarily written for therapeutic reasons," Williams suggests, "[it] may be seen as an analysis of these problems rather than a delineation."[19] Rhys's novel thus offers a critical analysis, underscoring the modes of our perceptions and the arena of their action. Rhys's analysis resides in the pattern of the novel's narrative strategies and in the central mode of re-presentation, that is to say, in the working out of the dream-text.

Two characteristics are essential to the model for a woman's novel that I call a "dream-text," to the aesthetic pattern it assumes, and to its rhetorical appeal—its ability to evoke persuasively an active response from its readers. First, the narrative processes of the text suggest a collaborative authorship, a plurality of narrators or near-narrators; second, the text overtly suggests the presence of its own subtexts. The subtexts are those texts of difference that are (almost) censored in the narrative but that are negatively present as "gray" areas in the text.[20] They can be rendered positively through the process of a reader's response, that response lifting the subtext into plain view. The "spectral architecture" produced in the response offers the text that becomes the manifest text in a continuation of the prior text.

In *Wide Sargasso Sea*, for example, Rhys is completing what is for her the salient subtext of her own early novel, *Voyage in the Dark*, as well as the salient subtext of Brontë's *Jane Eyre*. There is, however, another subtext in *Voyage* that remains a subtext in *Wide Sargasso Sea*. That subtext is the text(s) of the colored and the black women in the novel; much less marked, although present, is the text of the black and the colored men. This women's text remains unwritten by Rhys, although some of its component parts are incorporated into the subtext that has surfaced in *Wide Sargasso Sea*, and, as we see in examining the manifest text of that novel, this unwritten text, the marking of it, is crucial to what Rhys apparently considers her own text.

Both of these essential characteristics—the plurality of voices and the marking of the salient subtext—are signaled in the beginnings and endings of Antoinette's two *enclosing* narratives. The first words of the novel's first section echo the ominous and emblematic talisman—"they say"—that we recognize from *Voyage in the Dark*: "They say when trouble comes close ranks, and so the white people did. But we were not in their ranks. The Jamaican ladies never approved of my mother, 'because she pretty like pretty self' Christophine said" (p. 15). In these few lines we are given three verbal links with the subtext of *Voyage in the Dark*: (1) the contextual placement of the heroine-narrator ("outside" and ambivalently placed in relation to her "whiteness," this itself a movement toward the subtext); (2) her identification with her mother, which will form the basis for the intertextuality among all the women; and (3) the initial and most overt markings of the salient subtext of this novel, that of the black woman who also serves as "spokeswoman" for the heroine-narrator. "Also," I say, when the very fact of her "use" in Rhys's narrative presentation marks this salience. The ease with which I speak of her "serving," especially in a technical capacity helping a discussion of "aesthetics," "literature," "culture," is itself a mark of the context that Rhys and I share. The ending of this first narrative section closes not with Antoinette's voice, but with that of Sister Marie Augustine, one of the many female caretakers in the novel: "She said, as if she was talking to herself, 'Now go quietly back to bed. Think of calm, peaceful things and try to sleep. Soon I will give the signal. Soon it will be tomorrow morning'" (p. 51).

The two enclosing narratives move from one woman's voice to another, voices significantly *not* the primary narrator's. Part One ends with one woman's voice—Sister Marie Augustine's; Part Three, the final section of the novel, begins with the voice of another woman, Grace Poole. These narratives move also from saying to knowing, the movement with which we are familiar from our reading of *Voyage in the Dark*. Grace Poole's words "They knew . . ." are an appropriate bridge from Rochester's text to Antoinette's. They also perform the more crucial function of interweaving the women's voices into the text of the heroine-narrator. Grace Poole's introduction begins with a discussion of Rochester gleaned from what "they" say, offered, according to Grace, as what "they knew": "*'They knew that he was in Jamaica when his father and his brother died,' Grace Poole said. 'He inherited everything, but he was a wealthy man before that. Some people are fortunate, they said, and there were hints about the woman he brought back to England with him'*" (p. 145). This transition from Rochester's text to Antoinette's—Grace Poole's voice reported within quotation marks—moves effortlessly in the weave of the woman's text. Her introduction concludes with a description of Antoinette: "*I'll say one thing for her, she hasn't lost her spirit. She's still fierce. I don't turn my back on her when her eyes have that look. I know it*" (p. 146).

Antoinette's voice takes up the narration at this point, linking her text, in her turn, with what has come before, in her relation to Sister Marie Augustine and in the interrelation between the voices of her caretakers:

> In this room I wake early and lie shivering for it is very cold. At last Grace Poole, the woman who looks after me, lights a fire with paper and sticks and lumps of coal. [. . .]
> The woman Grace sleeps in my room. [. . .] She drinks from a bottle on the table then she goes to bed[. . . .] But I lie watching the fire die out. When she is snoring I get up and I have tasted the drink without colour in the bottle. [. . .] When I got back into the bed I could remember more and think again. I was not so cold. (pp. 146–47)

Sister Marie Augustine's functions are comparably described, and the two descriptions are "like two different versions of the same subject-matter," similar actions *performed* by different women in different situations. The "situations" are the "same," one that Antoinette as dreamer and Rhys as writer are rewriting as they approach the culmination of the manifest dream-text, the formal achievement of the novel. Specifically, the Sister's response is to the young Antoinette's awaking from a dream, the *dream* that is at the core of the narrative dream-text and that culminates in the narrative that Grace Poole introduces:

> Now Sister Marie Augustine is leading me out of the dormitory, asking if I am ill, telling me that I must not disturb the others and though I am still shivering I wonder if she will take me behind the mysterious curtains to the place where she sleeps. But no. She seats me in a chair, vanishes, and after a while comes back with a cup of hot chocolate.
> I said, "I dreamed I was in Hell." (pp. 50–51)

Shortly afterward the narrative closes with the words of Sister Marie Augustine, to be picked up and threaded into the narrative in the novel's final section by the final female caretaker of Antoinette's dream, Grace Poole.

Although the most important caretaker figure is Christophine, her strong and clarifying voice is omitted from this section, as is any image of her person. Her notable absence in this section is the strongest marking of a "missing" text, a crucial subtext. Antoinette does call to her, but this call is not "voiced" in the text; it is not given within quotation marks, and when she calls, "a wall of fire" answers her. As a *spokes*woman for Antoinette, however, Christophine is central to the drama acted out in the events reported in Rochester's section, both in dialogue with him, and with Antoinette in the nine-page portion of "Rochester's" narrative that Rhys pointedly gives Antoinette for narration (pp. 89–98). Here Rhys gives us the unravelling point of her manifest text.

In an uncharacteristically clumsy passage, Rhys connects Antoinette's dreaming (not her dream-text) with Brontë's novel. Christophine has suggested that Antoinette leave Rochester, but the passage following seems to reveal that she cannot because, as she puts it, she must "dream the end of my dream." Antoinette's dream is the fate that the plot of Brontë's novel has already provided for her. We may read that "end" as inescapable; if it is within the framework of a "dream-text" that Rhys writes her own way out of that end, then it is within the confines of Antoinette's dream(s), the dream-text as Brontë has already defined it, that Rhys's fictionalized *character*, Antoinette, must remain, even if her text does not. She must seek out the end of the dream that Brontë has foreordained for her:

I have been too unhappy, I thought, it cannot last, being so
unhappy, it would kill you. I will be a different person when I
live in England and different things will happen to me. . . .
[. . . .] I must know more than I know already. For I know that
house where I will be cold and not belonging, the bed I shall lie
in has red curtains and I have slept there many times before,
long ago. How long ago? In that bed I will dream the end of my
dream. But my dream had nothing to do with England and I
must not think like this, I must remember about chandeliers
and dancing, about roses and snow. And snow. (p. 92)

In this passage Rhys appears to want it both ways: Antoinette "knows
the house" and "the bed" where she "will dream the end of [her]
dream." In other words, she may be read to know, as we do, that she
is "in" Brontë's novel. On the other hand, "my dream had nothing to
do with England and I must not think like this," she admonishes
herself. Antoinette's *own* text, Rhys's own text, finally has "nothing to
do with England," i.e., Brontë's context, Brontë's version of their
shared text. Her narrative-constituting of herself—Antoinette's self,
the text of self that is Rhys's novel—is *different* from the preordained,
constrained text originating in someone else's needs or desires.

Rhys's text continues, with Christophine questioning the reality of
such a place and of such a placing for Antoinette:

"England," said Christophine, who was watching me. "You
think there is such a place?"
"How can you ask that? You know there is."
"I never see the damn place, how I know?"
"You do not believe that there is a country called England?"
She blinked and answered quickly, "I don't say I don't *believe*.
I say I don't *know*, I know what I see with my eyes and I never
see it. [. . .] If there is this place at all, I never see it, that is one
thing sure." (pp. 92–93; emphasis in original)

Christophine here speaks for the dreamers, who trust their eyes,
their seeing. Antoinette manifests, for the moment, the influence
that Rochester's "dream" ("I knew that my dreams were dreams," he
says [p. 137]), his idea of reality, has had on her, despite his suspi-
cions of his failure to influence her. She even uses his word—"obstinate" (p. 78)—for Christophine. "I stared at her," Antoinette narrates

her response, "thinking, 'but how can she know the best thing for me to do, this ignorant, obstinate old negro woman, who is not certain if there is such a place as England?' She knocked out her pipe and stared back at me, her eyes had no expression at all" (p. 93). And in this moment their gazes are fixed, the one in the other. "I sleep so badly now," Antoinette says to her. "And I dream." "I don't meddle with that for you," Christophine answers, referring specifically to aiding her with "obeah," knowing that Antoinette must continue to "see" with her own eyes, must continue her dream.

"When she bent her head she looked old and I thought, 'Oh, Christophine, do not grow old. You are the only friend I have, do not go away from me into being old'" (p. 94). Antoinette knows that Christophine is her "friend" precisely in response to Christophine's firm convictions of what she "knows," what she *sees*. And later Christophine helps Antoinette sleep. She will not "meddle with" her dreaming, but she does induce and watch over its prerequisite, her sleep. Our active dreaming, our seeing with our own eyes, helps us awake from Antoinette's dream.

The dream as constraint and as necessity is created thematically as well as structurally. It moves through all the narratives of the novel and oversees them as well. The dream frames that narration that is (almost) Rochester's alone, and it shapes the dimensions of the woman's context in the book as it is revealed to us through Antoinette's narration. The feminine weavers, the other "dreamers," are revealed in their more integral place in the text, in their relations to Antoinette's specific dreams, and in their relations to her and to one another; in short, in their part in the plot or action of the story told by the narrative and by Rhys's interweaving of them into the strategy of *her* narrative.

AFTER SHE HAS WOKEN from her dream, the seventeen-year-old Antoinette remembers trying to pray after her mother's death. She recalls that "the words fell to the ground meaning nothing" (p. 51). She then notes in an emphatic one-line paragraph: "Now the thought of her is mixed up with my dream." Indeed, the caretaker role played by Antoinette's mother—no matter how inadequately in the actual events of their life together—is central to the casting of the form of the dream-text as Rhys develops it. *The words,* which "made no sense" to Rhys or to her character Anna Morgan in

Voyage in the Dark, are a part of that "large book" identified with the father. They are not the metaphor of choice for the making of her world, even if they offer the means for her expression of it. The symbolic cast of Rhys's world, and of Antoinette's, is dependent on the mother and her text.

The story of this dream is in part a rewriting of the fairy tale of the princess who wakes from a long sleep. But here no prince serves as the agent of her awakening. Rather, the heroine-narrator wakes to a world of the women in her life, and finally she wakes to herself. Antoinette wakes after her first dream, the first and inchoate version of the dream given to her by Brontë, to her mother; then she awakes to her Aunt Cora, who assures her, "you are safe with me now," after her mother has been taken away; then to Sister Marie Augustine; and to Christophine (Christophine, who, finally, would not wake her to "misery"); and finally to Grace Poole in the attic of Thornfield Hall.

There is, too, the shadow form of a woman present during the shipboard incident in which Antoinette is given something to make her sleep, but, in fact, Antoinette has been abandoned by the caretakers who have helped her dream. The unidentified woman is present, but it is not she who asks Antoinette to drink, and she is not there when Antoinette awakes. Antoinette awakes alone and to "a different sea." "A woman came and then an older man[. . . .] The third man said drink this and you will sleep. I drank it and I said, 'It isn't like it seems to be.'—'I know. It never is,' he said. And then I slept. When I woke it was a different sea" (p. 148). The other important female figures in Antoinette's dream-text are Amélie and Tia, both images of self or "mirror-images" for her. Amélie is an ambivalent figure; Tia is the defining mirror-image whose recognition awakens Antoinette to herself, and revives her from the dream-as-sleep of Brontë's dream.

As one of the markers of the subtext, Tia's *name* resolves the heroine-narrator's text momentarily for its formal closure. Tia remains the "looking-glass" for the heroine-narrator's resolution of self and narrative. Amélie, Antoinette's ambiguous double, is not present in the final narrative; nor is Christophine, her caretaker and spokeswoman, except for the "unvoiced" call to her for "help." Only Tia, her mirror-self, is present in image and gesture: we *see* her. Other caretakers are there: her mother, especially in her question, as well as her presence "in" Antoinette herself; her Aunt Cora, in her "work"; even the caretaker Sister Marie Augustine is present, a reverberating voice as Antoinette's narrative is passed from her care to Grace Poole's.

Christophine's voice is notably absent, as her person is absent, except for the dubious apotheosis represented by her embodiment in the "wall of fire" that Antoinette sees "protecting" her, the fire that Christophine's earlier consistent support and example "allow" Antoinette to set herself. Amélie has long since withdrawn. The space these two figures might have occupied looms large. Their silence "speaks"; it is "telling." This silence, their absence, reveals the subtext which is not *written*. This is the text that Rhys has omitted in the culmination of her writing, from the construction of her final manifest dream-text. The outline of some of her dream-thoughts, however, can be seen in the marking of the censored subtext. And it is relevant with regard to the written male text (which includes, as Christophine calls it, "Letter of the Law") that Christophine and Amélie figure as *spokes*woman and ambivalent mirror-image, respectively, for Antoinette, the white Creole colonial, in *her* narration and in the completion of her narrative. Similarly, Antoinette, the white woman in relation to the white man, the Creole in relation to the Englishman, is the figure for the completion of his desires, the writing of his text. Well might Christophine remark that she has nothing to do with reading and writing. When Rochester asks her if she wants to say good-bye to Antoinette, she replies:

> "I give her something to sleep—nothing to hurt her. I don't wake her up to no misery. I leave that for you."
> "You can write to her," I said stiffly.
> "Read and write I don't know. Other things I know."

And "she walked away without looking back" (p. 133). Significantly, this is the last time we see her, although Rochester recapitulates some of her conversation, her dialogue with him, later in his narrative.

Some reference points in Brontë's text are helpful here, bringing together as they do some of the half-formed images of Brontë's own dream-text. Figures who remain "unspeaking" or silent in Brontë's text, except as they appear in a dream or in specular images, are revealed to Jane Eyre only in the "looking-glass" of the symbolism of the dream, or in the literal looking-glass of her bedroom at Thornfield Hall. They are images that bear the label "censored" in the very form of their manifestation in the talkative Jane Eyre's narration. In a "trance-like dream" that occurs after Jane has refused to live with Rochester, she is "transported to the scenes of childhood":

> I dreamt I lay in the red-room at Gateshead; that the night was dark, and my mind impressed with strange fears. The light that long ago had struck me into syncope, recalled in this vision, seemed glidingly to mount the wall, and tremblingly to pause in the centre of the obscure ceiling. I lifted up my head to look: the roof resolved to clouds, high and dim; the gleam was such as the moon imparts to vapours she is about to sever. I watched her come—watched with the strangest anticipation; as though some word of doom were to be written on the disk. She broke forth as never moon yet burst from cloud: a hand first penetrated the sable folds and waved them away; then, not a moon, but a white human form shone in the azure, inclining a glorious brow earthward. It gazed and gazed and gazed on me. It spoke to my spirit: immeasurably distant was the tone, yet so near, it whispered in my heart—"My daughter, flee temptation!"

"Mother, I will," Jane answers (*Jane Eyre*, p. 281).

We may recall several interconnections as we read the text of this dream. We also see the contrast between Rhys's text and Brontë's, especially as revealed in those dreams of Jane Eyre's that are integral to Brontë's presentation of the manifest text of the eponymous novel *Jane Eyre*. Jane Eyre's dream can be compared with two other of Brontë's visions—that of the actress Vashti in *Villette*, and that of the figure Jane sees in her bedroom and whose appearance and actions she describes to Rochester and therefore to us. This figure, as emphasized traditionally, is a monstrous "double" for Jane. This double, we discover, is similar to two other female figures who inspire Jane/Brontë with awe: her mother, the Moon, and Vashti, the inflammatory actress. Both of these figures, like the monstrous Bertha in her night visitation to Jane, wake Brontë's heroine from a kind of sleep, literal or figurative. This is Jane's description of Bertha's night visit:

> "On waking, a gleam dazzled my eyes: I thought—oh, it is daylight! But I was mistaken: it was only candlelight. . . . a form emerged from the closet: it took the light, held it aloft, and sur-

veyed the garments pendent from the portmanteau. . . . The shape standing before me had never crossed my eyes within the precincts of Thornfield Hall before; the height, the contour, were new to me. . . . It seemed, sir, a woman, tall and large, with thick and dark hair hanging long down her back. I know not what dress she had on: it was white and straight; but whether gown, sheet, or shroud, I cannot tell. . . . presently she took my veil from its place; she held it up, gazed at it long, and then she threw it over her own head, and turned to the mirror. At that moment I saw the reflection of the visage and features quite distinctly in the dark oblong glass. . . . Just at my bedside the figure stopped: the fiery eye glared upon me—she thrust up her candle close to my face, and extinguished it under my eyes. I was aware her lurid visage flamed over mine, and I lost consciousness: for the second time in my life—only the second time—I became insensible from terror." (*Jane Eyre*, pp. 249–50)

The "scenes of childhood" to which Jane Eyre refers, in which her mother, the Moon, appears to her, are, of course, that scene at Gateshead when the child Jane was unjustly and cruelly confined to the "red-room." The result of this experience, as she describes it to Rochester, was that for the first time in her life she "became insensible from terror," here described as being "struck into syncope." She provides us with this direct link to her childhood in her ongoing dream-text, just as Antoinette's dream-text begins in childhood and is directly linked to childhood experiences of the dream and of "reality."

Jane's discussion with Rochester concerning the visit from the "form," the "shape" that Jane had never seen before in Thornfield Hall, expressly locates all of these events in the context of the ongoing dream-text that Jane is writing in conjunction with the events of the novel, a dream-text that Rhys incorporates into her own. When Rochester suggests that the visit from Bertha—a figure he knows and recognizes—is "the creature of an over-stimulated brain," she replies, "Sir, depend on it, my nerves are not at fault; the thing was real: the transaction took place" (*Jane Eyre*, p. 250). "And your previous dreams: were they real too?" he questions, just as the Rochester of Rhys's novel more destructively questions Antoinette's "dream" and her "reality." These earlier dreams form "the preface," as Jane says (*Jane Eyre*, p. 249), to the visitation from Bertha, the form or figure she cannot, and will not, recognize.

Jane's earlier dreams offer details that Rhys incorporates into Rochester's own "dream" of the Dominica he encounters and of the Thornfield Hall "in ruins" that he will come to know. Jane's dreams seem to link past and future within Brontë's text, as Rhys's dream-text does on a larger scale, incorporating Brontë's own text. More cogently, however, these earlier dreams of Jane's closely parallel the dreams of the "stranger" that the child Antoinette experiences and the "reality" she encounters in her life with him. For both women, the dreams originate in childhood; they focus on the role of "the mother" in the child's life, and, in her absence or inadequacy, on the role of other female caretakers.

The dream that immediately prefaces the appearance of Bertha, the woman to whom Jane awakes from her dreaming, contains elements of the dreams of Antoinette as child and as adolescent, the first and second versions of Antoinette's dream. In the case of each woman's dreams, the woman (or girl) who is the narrator-protagonist is fleeing. Jane flees the "temptation" of sexuality. It could be argued that the young Antoinette also flees what is usually called "budding sexuality." More pertinently, Antoinette flees an intimacy with the stranger, who proves himself to be the one who flees *her* sensuality. In Jane's dream she is pursuing Rochester (even if in fact he is the pursuer). In Antoinette's dream there is no pursuit. In the first, she is "not alone," "someone who hated me" is present. In the second, "someone" has become the "man who is with me." In her first dream she has not yet fully entered Brontë's; in the second dream she has, and the situation is given, and the end of the pursuit accomplished. Only struggle and possible escape remain.

The immediate framework for Jane's prefatory dreams is the evening Rochester is away from Thornfield Hall. It was dark, the wind rising. "On sleeping," Jane tells him,

> "I continued in dreams the idea of a dark and gusty night. I continued also the wish to be with you, and experienced a strange, regretful consciousness of some barrier dividing us. During all my first sleep I was following the windings of an unknown road; total obscurity environed me; rain pelted me; I was burdened with the charge of a little child: a very small crea-

ture, too young and feeble to walk, and which shivered in my cold arms and wailed piteously in my ear. I thought, sir, that you were on the road a long way before me; and I strained every nerve to overtake you, and made effort on effort to utter your name and entreat you to stop—but my movements were fettered; and my voice still died away inarticulate; while you, I felt, withdrew farther and farther every moment." (*Jane Eyre*, pp. 247–48)

"I dreamt another dream, sir:" Jane continues,

"that Thornfield Hall was a dreary ruin. . . . I thought that of all the stately front nothing remained but a shell-like wall, very high, and very fragile-looking. . . . I still carried the unknown little child: I might not lay it down anywhere, however tired were my arms—however much its weight impeded my progress, I must retain it. I heard the gallop of a horse at a distance on the road: I was sure it was you; and you were departing for many years, and for a distant country. I climbed the thin wall with frantic, perilous haste, eager to catch one glimpse of you from the top: the stones rolled from under my feet, the ivy branches I grasped gave way, the child clung round my neck in terror, and almost strangled me: at last I gained the summit. I saw you like a speck on a white track, lessening every moment. The blast blew so strong I could not stand. I sat down on the narrow ledge; I hushed the scared infant in my lap; you turned an angle of the road; I bent forward to take a last look; the wall crumbled; I was shaken; the child rolled from my knee, I lost my balance, fell, and woke." (*Jane Eyre*, pp. 248–49)

Following this narrative, Rochester says, "Now, Jane, that is all," with an air of finality and admonishment for letting "these dreams weigh on your spirits." He also says, "I am close to you," noting a state of affairs that is all too central to Antoinette's dreams. "All the preface, sir; the tale is yet to come," Jane replies (*Jane Eyre*, p. 249). The tale yet to come is a description of Jane's visitation from Bertha, Rhys's Antoinette. Rochester denies Bertha's reality, says that "the woman was—must have been—Grace Poole." The rest, he claims, are "fig-ments of imagination; results of nightmare" (*Jane Eyre*, p. 251).

The child of Jane's dream is the child she was at Gateshead, locked in the red-room by her Aunt Reed. Rhys conflates the child Antoinette and the woman she becomes with Brontë's (Jane's) child and woman, dreaming herself into Brontë's arms and rescuing the child Jane into a single individual. Jane might see herself as caretaker of the child who was herself; Rhys extends this condition of the constitution of self to the caretaker figures who people her dream-text, the kinds of figures who, in fact, offer Jane the model for the care of self that she can only "dream" in her relation to Rochester. Preeminent among them is her mother, the Moon, whose dream takes her back to the "scenes of childhood."

The "mother" figure of the Moon, who speaks to Jane and reveals herself to her in "human form," comes from the waking dreams she has while incarcerated in the red-room; an actual caretaker is at her bedside when she awakens from the "first time" in her life that she "lost consciousness." The red-room is identifiable with the attic of Thornfield Hall, both places of incarceration and the "madness" of intensified or exacerbated introversion.

"Daylight," in Jane's narrative of her imprisonment in the red-room, "began to forsake the red-room":

> I wiped my tears and hushed my sobs, fearful lest any sign of violent grief might waken a preternatural voice to comfort me, or elicit from the gloom some haloed face, bending over me with strange pity. . . . Shaking my hair from my eyes, I lifted my head and tried to look boldly round the dark room. At this moment a light gleamed on the wall. . . . while I gazed, it glided up to the ceiling and quivered over my head. I can now conjecture readily that this streak of light was, in all likelihood, a gleam from a lantern, carried by some one across the lawn: but then, prepared as my mind was for horror . . . I thought the swift-darting beam was a herald of some coming vision from another world. My heart beat thick, my head grew hot; a sound filled my ears, which I deemed the rushing of wings: something seemed near me; I was oppressed, suffocated: endurance broke down; I rushed to the door and shook the lock in desperate effort. Steps came running along the outer passage; the key turned, Bessie [the lady's maid] and Abbott [the housekeeper] entered. (*Jane Eyre*, pp. 13–14)

Bessie "pleads" for her, but Mrs. Reed "thrust" her back in the room and locked the door. ". . . and soon after she was gone," Jane concludes, "I suppose I had a species of fit: unconsciousness closed the scene" (*Jane Eyre*, p. 15). At the beginning of the next chapter, she describes her awakening from the "fit":

> The next thing I remember is, waking up with a feeling as if I had a frightful nightmare, and seeing before me a terrible red glare, crossed with thick black bars. I heard voices, too, speaking with a hollow sound, as if muffled by a rush of wind or water: agitation, uncertainty, and an all-predominating sense of terror confused my faculties. Ere long I became aware that some one was handling me; lifting me up and supporting me in a sitting posture, and that more tenderly than I had ever been raised or upheld before. I rested my head against a pillow or an arm, and felt easy.
>
> In five minutes more the cloud of bewilderment dissolved: I knew quite well that I was in my own bed, and that the red glare was the nursery fire. It was night: a candle burnt on the table; Bessie stood at the bed-foot with a basin in her hand, and a gentleman sat in a chair near my pillow, leaning over me. (*Jane Eyre*, p. 15)

A basic similarity to the child Antoinette's feelings of "security" upon awakening from her dream in familiar surroundings is found in the next paragraph, along with a contrast that is at extreme variance with Antoinette's ideas of what constitutes this "security." "I felt an inexpressible relief," Jane tells us, "a soothing conviction of protection and security, when I knew that there was a stranger in the room, an individual not belonging to Gateshead, and not related to Mrs. Reed."

This passage marks a fundamental break between *Wide Sargasso Sea* and Brontë's dream-text, even an opposition to it. Bessie, the female caretaker here, is Jane's staunchest ally in the house, although her status in the house and in society is depicted as vitiating her support. However, the male figure is precisely a "stranger," and Jane remarks that his presence provides "an inexpressible relief, a soothing conviction of protection and security." The stranger himself asks a question similar to that which Antoinette's mother's parrot Coco

would ask of any stranger who approached. "Well," he asks, "who am I?" and Jane realizes that she does know him. He is Mr. Lloyd, "an apothecary, sometimes called in by Mrs. Reed when servants were ailing: for herself and the children she employed a physician." It is Bessie who asks, "Do you feel as if you should sleep, Miss?" "I will try," Jane answers. As befits a servant, Bessie's place is "at the bed-foot"; the man, the "stranger" is seated comfortably at Jane's bedside, leaning over her.

It is appropriate that in Jane's awakening from the real childhood experience that was like a "nightmare," she wakes to two figures, a woman and a man. Her awakening is not exclusively to women, and there is no primary caretaker, like Christophine, who can offer the example of the waking dream, of seeing with her own woman's eyes. When Jane awakens as an adult to the figure at her bedside who looks with her "fiery eye" upon her, "close to my face," she "became insensible from terror." She could not return the look; she could, in fact, only look at her when she saw "the reflection of the visage and the features quite distinctly in the dark oblong glass." She could see "Bertha" *only* in the looking-glass, the actual woman she could not see without terror. The shape at her bedside looking her straight in the eye was a caretaker she could not admit. Her own identification seems to be with the masculine caretaker, and, in fact, in the dreams that preface the visitation from Bertha, it is in attempting to follow Rochester that she "fell, and woke." In contrast, at the end of that dream of Antoinette's, which is Brontë's, the dream that signals the beginning of the "real" ending of Antoinette's narrative, Antoinette "jumped and woke" in response to her recognition of her mirror-image, Tia. She did not "fall"—she jumped. And, as I have already observed, the dream passes on to Grace Poole, who awakens with the remark, "I must have been dreaming" (p. 155).

On the other hand, when Rochester says with finality, "Now Jane, that is all," she answers, "All the preface . . . the tale is yet to come." The tale yet to come is "Bertha's" story, the story of the woman care-taker to whom Brontë cannot directly respond. In completing this tale, Brontë's as well as her own, Rhys signals a drawing together of texts (which includes her own *Voyage in the Dark*) by returning her own text to the image of Brontë's "mother," the Moon, an image that frightened Jane as a child and offers her the "answer" when she is an adult. The "moonlight" that frightened her as a child, but which at the time she thought "some coming vision from another world," becomes in the later dream the "white human form" who resolves her problems for her. This, so she tells us, was the dream in which she "lay in the red-room at Gateshead": it is patently a rewriting of that waking dream. Jane herself identifies it for us as "the light that long ago had struck me into syncope, recalled in this vision." Rhys incorporates this rewriting in her own dream-text in the figure of the "real" mother and "real" female caretakers. These caretakers help her, and Brontë, achieve the end of the text that Brontë set in motion, but that Brontë could not complete in her own manifest text, in her own time and place.

The light, the mundane "lantern" of conjecture, becomes the candle on the table that reveals Bessie and the male caretaker standing by. More significantly, it is the candle that Bertha, with her "fiery eye," held aloft to look finally into Jane's face, into her eyes if Jane could have returned the look. Bertha "thrust the candle close to my face," she tells Rochester, the candle whose "gleam dazzled" her eyes and woke her from her dream of him to the figure of Bertha. This candle, in Rhys's text, becomes the candle that lights Antoinette to the end of her "voyage," to the end of her text and of Brontë's: "the flame flickered and I thought it was out. But I shielded it with my hand and it burned up again to light me along the dark passage" (p. 156).

In Antoinette's early dreams we may note some details placed in seemingly deliberate opposition to those of Jane's dreams. In Antoinette's second dream, the one most comparable to Jane's prefatory dreams (in which the night is not only dark but "gusty"), the narrator specifically tells us "there is no wind." Most importantly, however, there is no light—not candle, or lantern, or moonlight—until the light of the fire in her culminating dream-text. But here, at the last, Antoinette/Rhys has taken Brontë's "light," that of the mother Moon, and of Bertha's light, the candle, as the guiding light for her final dream and text.

Brontë's (Lucy Snowe's) response to the actress represented by Vashti in *Villette* is similar to her response to the Moon. At the same time, however, it contains a key to her rejection of a similar figure in *Jane Eyre*. *Jane Eyre*, published four years after *Villette*, represents an odd and significant retrogression, one that casts doubt on this aspect of Brontë's presentation and piques our interest. In appearance

Vashti is not unlike the "white human form" of the mother, Moon, who "spoke" to Jane's "spirit," "immeasurably distant . . . the tone, yet so near, it whispered in my heart." Both of these figures resemble Bertha as first described, "a woman, tall and large, with thick and dark hair hanging long down her back," her dress "white and straight; but whether gown, sheet, or shroud I could not tell." This is the description of Lucy Snowe/Brontë's encounter with the performance and figure of the actress Vashti as it is recorded in *Villette*:

> She rose at nine that December night; above the horizon I saw her come. She could shine yet with pale grandeur and steady might; but that star verged already on its judgment day. Seen near, it was a chaos . . . an orb perished or perishing—half lava, half glow.
>
> I had heard this woman termed "plain," and I expected bony harshness and grimness—something large, angular, sallow. What I saw was the shadow of a royal Vashti: a queen . . . turned pale now like twilight, and wasted like wax in flame.
>
> For a while . . . I thought it was only a woman, though a unique woman, who moved in might and grace before this multitude. By-and-by I recognised my mistake. Behold! I found upon her something neither of woman nor of man: in each of her eyes sat a devil. These evil forces bore her through the tragedy, kept up her feeble strength—for she was but a frail creature; and as the action rose and the stir deepened, how wildly they shook her with their passions of the pit! They wrote HELL on her straight, haughty brow. They tuned her voice to the note of torment. They writhed her regal face to a demoniac mask. Hate and Murder and Madness incarnate she stood.
>
> It was a marvellous sight: a mighty revelation.
>
> It was a spectacle low, horrible, immoral. (*Villette*, pp. 233–34)

In the movement of this description, and in the one-line descriptions with which it concludes, we see the two conflicting responses at work in *Jane Eyre*. The Vashti in whom Lucy Snowe "found . . . something neither of woman nor of man," "in each" of whose "eyes sat a devil," is at once the mother, Moon, "inclining a glorious brow," who can gaze and gaze and gaze at Jane with benevolence and who can speak to her "spirit," as a "daughter," and the figure of "Hate and Murder and Madness incarnate," the one Jane sees in the figure of the woman looking at herself in a mirror with a wedding veil (Jane's) thrown over her head. Her "visage" Jane describes as "fearful and ghastly to me—oh, sir, I never saw a face like it! It was a discoloured face—it was a savage face. I wish I could forget the roll of the red eyes and the fearful blackened inflation of the lineaments" (*Jane Eyre*, p. 249). "Shall I tell you of what it reminded me?" Jane asks Rochester. The sensational answer is that it reminds her "Of the foul German spectre—the Vampyre" (*Jane Eyre*, p. 250), an answer calculated to warm the heart of any Victorian gentleman.

The two images of Vashti, then, can be split into the two we find in *Jane Eyre*: the benevolent and strengthening mother, the Moon, in "human form"; and the "foul German spectre—the Vampyre," the figure of Bertha, "a spectacle low, horrible, immoral." This last assessment, of course, is Rochester's view of Bertha in Brontë's *Jane Eyre*, and it is also his view of Antoinette in Rhys's *Wide Sargasso Sea*. Brontë chose the "immorality" of the vision in her text of *Jane Eyre*. In this sense, Rhys herself incorporates not only the censored text of *Jane Eyre*, but the other text of the same figure that Brontë included in her initial response to the woman (the French actress Rachel, Elisa Felix), a real woman, and the response a response to an actual performance, recorded in *Villette*.

Note again the lack of *voice* in the presentation of the "spectre" who is Bertha, contrasted with the explicit and central place given to the speaking voice of the mother, Moon, and to Vashti (whose "passions" "tuned her voice to the note of torment"). Brontë's description of Vashti includes the visual, aural, and emotional impression of her performance; finally, however, the total impression and "incarnation" of her being that so passionately moves Lucy/Brontë is summed up in the key words of her final, formulaic descriptions: "sight," "revelation," and "spectacle." The impact of the woman Vashti on the woman Charlotte Brontë/Lucy Snowe is visual, and it is in Vashti's "eyes" that "a devil sat." What this implies is "something neither of woman nor of man." In other words, Vashti crosses a gender barrier, crosses the conventional borders of a woman's presumed context, to make the spectacle of herself that Brontë sees. It is there—in the eyes—that the immorality of the unconventional, passionate, and powerful woman resides. And it is in her own "eyes" that Brontë measures the power and the shock of it. The presence—or absence—of voice here is significant.

The only voice that speaks aloud in Jane's dreams is the mother's, the Moon's. When Jane is "straining to overtake" Rochester, she "made effort on effort to utter [Rochester's] name and entreat [him] to stop—but my movements were fettered," she says, "and my voice still died away inarticulate," in contrast to Antoinette, who voices her cry to Tia, voices the crucial name of recognition. Jane cannot voice Rochester's name; she has no voice in her dreams except to "hush" the "feeble" infant in her arms. In her encounter with Bertha, neither of them speaks, and Jane, as already emphasized, cannot exchange or maintain the fixing or the searching look of the other woman.

Conversely, it is not the voice alone that renders the impression of a woman in active response to another woman, as Brontë's response to Vashti's visual impact makes clear. It is the movement from sight to a voicing of recognition—the melding of the two in that movement— that results in the aesthetic expression of that recognition. Joining hand and eye to create the possibility of a voicing is the crux. This joining is a crucial step in the constitution of self and of a woman's "text," both literally and figuratively.

In that place of "recognition," the eyes, is the subjective designation of the relative state of madness or sanity, woven into *Wide Sargasso Sea* as an element given by Brontë's text. According to Rochester's narration, Antoinette is a lunatic and he is "sane." In a description of the mad Antoinette, whom Rochester distinguishes from himself, the "voice," important as it is, comes after the fixing in place of this crucial and relative distinction. As the description continues, the voice gains importance: "She lifted her eyes. Blank lovely eyes. Mad eyes. A mad girl. [. . .] I scarcely recognized her voice. No warmth, no sweetness. The doll had a doll's voice, a breathless but curiously indifferent voice. [. . .] the doll's smile came back—nailed to her face. [. . .] I was [. . . .] Sane" (pp. 140–41). The voice is finally inseparable from the marking that can be attributed to the "eye," and the "doll's voice" itself is silenced, so that the eyes remain the characterizing vehicle for "sanity" or "madness." The voice is *stopped*, proving the mark of the eyes: "the doll's smile came back—nailed to her face," effectively stopping the voice. The eyes remain the receptacle for the mark of one who has taken the "mistaken" path, the "mistake," as Rochester calls it, the "mis-take," the "wrong path," the "wrong" dream (pp. 78, 85). Antoinette, too, later attempts to explain to Rochester how he is "mistaken" (p. 107).

In the opposition of these two dreams, these two "takes" on reality, the written word—specifically letters—and "Letter of the Law," as Christophine calls it, effects the seeming ascendancy of Rochester's dream over Antoinette's. Rochester knows that the dream is what he attempts to dislodge. He cannot follow Antoinette into that dream, since he knows, as he tells us in his narration, that *his* "dreams were dreams" (p. 137). He knows the difference between the "real" world and "dreams," and the "real world" is his. "Ah," Brontë's Rochester cries in *Jane Eyre* when Jane has just announced that her "uncle in Madeira is dead, and he left me five thousand pounds"—"Ah, this is practical—this is real!" (*Jane Eyre*, p. 382). We hear the same voice in even a seemingly minor comment from the unnamed "Rochester" in *Wide Sargasso Sea*. ("She was undecided, uncertain about facts—any fact" [p. 73].) Rochester's world can only serve as that fixed frame—threads in the pattern, but frame nevertheless—the warp, through which the shuttle of the women's dream passes and repasses as Rhys, the woman writing, weaves the text of their dream, her dream-text.

As Rochester's plaint emphasizes ("Nothing that I told her influenced her at all" [p. 78]), he first attempts to mute or silence Antoinette into conformity with his view of a woman's role by verbal persuasion or coercion. Proof of his successful coercion is Antoinette's silence—marked by the mask, the "doll's smile stopping the voice," the smile "nailed to her face." The doll's face is worn by the black women at Carnival; the men's masks are characterized solely by the "squinting" eyes. The basic marking of difference, however, lies in the eyes; more, in the seeing.

This marking of difference holds true for a woman's writing as well. The seeing, more than the voice, differentiates a woman's text. The presentation of a woman's seeing, a display of what and how she sees, distinguishes her writing (writing, which is made to be seen, which signifies the convention of seeing) from a man's. Imposition of the mask is an analogy for the marking of the literary subtext, a marking ritualized and parodied but, in its parody and ritual, clear in its implications. The ritual is a public acting out of the opposition inherent in living within a culture's subtext, and of the necessity of that subtext for the dominant text's expression.

Rhys is "writing" the "dream," and the preeminent organ meta-phorized as the agent of dreaming is the eye (and the "I" that is pluralized in the dream-work). By means of the voices that pass on the narrative in a kind of relay—Sister Marie Augustine's, Grace Poole's, Brontë/Jane's *lack* of a dream-voice, Bertha's silence being given voice in Rhys's text—and by the explicit passing on of the dream shown us in the conjunction of Antoinette's "I jumped and woke" and Grace Poole's "I must have been dreaming," we see a con-tinuous weave. Early in the novel Sister Marie Augustine would not take Antoinette "behind the mysterious curtains to the place where she sleeps" (p. 50). By the end of the novel the "transfer" of the dream is completed. The "sleeping" and the "dreaming" are in the open, a common place.

Who, we might well ask, is dreaming here? The only sure answer is that it is a woman. Recall Xavière Gauthier's emphatic *"If there is a madman, then it's definitely the Woman,"* or, as Helen Nebeker puts it, "a poor mad woman—who sees so clearly."[21] The dream we are given seems common property, belonging to the women throughout the text of Rhys's novel, both in the intratext (the continuous narrative of all Rhys's heroine-narrator's, especially Anna Morgan of *Voyage in the Dark*, and of her own life), and in the intertext that brings the women of Brontë's text(s) into the circuit of the dream. The circuit of exchange for the writing of this dream-text is closed to the men in the text(s), including Brontë's, of course; the dream is open to all the women involved.

The dream is preeminently Rhys's. She inscribes, in a woman's hand, in a woman's voice, the dream that Charlotte Brontë and her heroine-narrator Jane Eyre—Brontë's "text"—could only describe as a partially seen "vision." This vision is of a ghostlike figure, indeed Jane Eyre's "mad double," a figure that of necessity she kept "hid-den," even from herself, perhaps especially from herself. The ac-count of what is made "real" in Antoinette's dream-text is not given to the reader as "real action" that she, and we, "see" in Brontë's novel. In Brontë's original text the action happened off-stage; this is also an omission that Rhys sought to correct. Brontë's depiction of the actions that Antoinette's final dream foresees is told to Jane Eyre and fleshed out in part by hearsay in the account of the fire given to her by a man who witnessed it. This male witness could give Jane

Eyre only a partial view, one made up in great measure of what "they say" about the events.

Rhys's achievement is that she writes the dream collectively without sacrificing the compelling narrative device of an individual protagonist, that single voice we are accustomed to "trust," with whom we conventionally identify as we read. The only sure dreamer is given us, however, in our realization that in Rhys's dream, as described by Freud's general description of our dream-work, the full expression of the narrator and of the narration can be found only in the process of relationships that constitutes this woman's text. This process includes all the women in Antoinette's world and, by extension and example, all of us.

THE FIRST VERSION of the dream that represents Brontë's subtext is given to the child Antoinette. "I went to bed early," Antoinette tells us, "and slept at once":

> I dreamed that I was walking in the forest. Not alone. Someone who hated me was with me, out of sight. I could hear heavy footsteps coming closer and though I struggled and screamed I could not move. I woke crying. The covering sheet was on the floor and my mother was looking down at me.
> "Did you have a nightmare?"
> "Yes, a bad dream."
> She sighed and covered me up. "You were making such a noise. I must go to Pierre, you've frightened him." (p. 23)

As we see, Antoinette's mother, Annette, is there when she wakes up, and she provides some comfort, although the child's brother is foremost in Annette's mind. The little girl seems not to care. After her mother leaves her, she continues, "I am safe. [. . .] I am safe from strangers." However, the dream has begun; the continuation of Brontë's subtext is set in motion. "I woke next morning," we are told, "knowing that nothing would be the same. It would change and go on changing" (p. 23).

The impetus of the dream is an interchange with Tia, the little black girl with whom Antoinette plays. Christophine seems to have arranged for Tia to come to Coulibri precisely to fill a need in the white girl's life. On the morning of the day that closes with the

dream, Tia dares Antoinette to turn a somersault in the bathing pool, "like you say you can" (p. 20). "I never see you do it," Tia says. "Only talk." Antoinette attempts the somersault, accepts the dare that is recapitulated in the final dream of Part III. Tia announces that she's lost the bet anyway; the somersault wasn't "good." They exchange words. Antoinette calls Tia a "nigger"; Tia responds, "Old time white people nothing but white nigger now, and black nigger better than white nigger" (p. 21). "All that evening," Antoinette says, prefatory to describing her dream, "my mother didn't speak to me or look at me and I thought, 'She is ashamed of me, what Tia said is true.'"

Later in the narration, the scene of the fire at Coulibri offers the mirror-image of Tia for Antoinette—each the negative of the other. It is the last scene of Antoinette's childhood at Coulibri; it is also the last time she is with her mother, who wouldn't "speak" or "look" at her on the evening of the dream, the last time she is with her before her mother disappears from her life:

> Then, not so far off, I saw Tia and her mother and I ran to her, for she was all that was left of my life as it had been. We had eaten the same food, slept side by side, bathed in the same river. As I ran, I thought, I will live with Tia and I will be like her. Not to leave Coulibri. Not to go. Not. When I was close I saw the jagged stone in her hand but I did not see her throw it. I did not feel it either, only something wet, running down my face. I looked at her and I saw her face crumple up as she began to cry. We stared at each other, blood on my face, tears on hers. It was as if I saw myself. Like in a looking-glass. (p. 38)

Unlike Jane Eyre, who can see her double, her "other" self, *only* in a literal looking-glass, for the time being these two children seem able to acknowledge their separation and one another, even if only with "blood" and "tears." On the other hand, the description is Antoinette's; we can read Tia as her alter ego. Tia remains silent, however. We do not know, except through their fixed and mutual stare, and her tears—and the "jagged stone" *in her hand*—what Tia sees. Certainly part of what Antoinette "sees" is the jagged stone, although she "did not see her throw it." But the effects of that stone, or one like it, *its* "double," produce the tears and the blood that are integral to the doubled image in the "looking-glass."

The second time Antoinette describes the dream, she specifically announces its serial nature: "This was the second time I had my dream." The dream and her description of the circumstances that set the stage for it arise after a visit from her stepfather at the convent. He allows her to know what fate has in store for her. She is fearful of what it may mean to be outside the world of the caretaking sisters and the company of the other girls, with "strangers"—not only men, but people outside her own milieu:

> Again I have left the house at Coulibri. It is still night and I am walking towards the forest. I am wearing a long dress and thin slippers, so I walk with difficulty, following the man who is with me and holding up the skirt of my dress. It is white and beautiful and I don't wish to get it soiled. I follow him, sick with fear but I make no effort to save myself; if anyone were to try to save me, I would refuse. This must happen. Now we have reached the forest. We are under the tall dark trees and there is no wind. "Here?" He turns and looks at me, his face black with hatred, and when I see this I begin to cry. He smiles slyly. "Not here, not yet," he says, and I follow him, weeping. Now I do not try to hold up my dress, it trails in the dirt, my beautiful dress. We are no longer in the forest but in an enclosed garden surrounded by a stone wall and the trees are different trees. I do not know them. There are steps leading upwards. It is too dark to see the wall or the steps, but I know they are there and I think, "It will be when I go up these steps. At the top." I stumble over my dress and cannot get up. I touch a tree and my arms hold on to it. "Here, here." But I think I will not go any further. The tree sways and jerks as if it is trying to throw me off. Still I cling and the seconds pass and each one is a thousand years. "Here, in here," a strange voice said, and the tree stopped swaying and jerking. (p. 50)

Ending her account of the dream, Antoinette continues her narration with a description of the actions of Sister Marie Augustine, whose "part," as Helen Nebeker accurately observes, is "brief but not minor."[22]

Antoinette refers to the continuation of her dream and dreaming in "her" portion of Rochester's section (pp. 89–98). This portion of the narration also describes her journey to Christophine's, which is synchronous with Rochester's journey into the forest. For both of them it is a time of crisis and explanation. They both seek a kind of knowledge, the "magic" that controls or might help each of their lives. Both "see" something finally, but what Rochester "sees," or at least its important element, doesn't concretely exist. That element resides in his own unstable psychological construction of the events. In Antoinette's case, it is initially put more simply. "It's you, Antoinette?" Christophine calls out when she sees her approaching, "Why you come up here so early?" "I just wanted to see you," Antoinette answers (p. 89).

In the narration of her conversation with Christophine, Antoinette interjects her own thoughts about England, about her ideas of England, and about her unhappiness. Rhys concludes these thoughts of Antoinette's with an overt reference to the "end" we know is coming for her, the end of the dream as Brontë's text has ordained it for her: "I must know more than I know already. For I know that house where I will be cold and not belonging, the bed I shall lie in has red curtains and I have slept there many times before, long ago. How long ago? In that bed I will dream the end of my dream. But my dream had nothing to do with England and I must not think like this. I must remember about chandeliers and dancing, about swans and roses and snow. And snow" (p. 92). "This must happen," as Antoinette observes in the narration of "the second time" she had her dream. Here Antoinette claims the dream that is not her dream but that is the continuation of another woman's text, the subtext of which she does indeed claim in order to make it a text. Here she also makes manifest the influence that Rochester has had on her, even though he thinks (despairingly, as has already been noted) that he has had no influence over her at all (p. 78).

Christophine then continues the conversation that Antoinette's narrative has momentarily broken off. She pointedly signals the disruption, and the continuation, that is Antoinette's contemplation of her dream. Her instinct concerning the kind of "help" Antoinette's own "dreaming" needs is accurate. Christophine reminds her that she hasn't *seen* England and that it is only with a woman's own seeing that she knows a thing. A woman's dreams must be her own. When Antoinette tells her, "I sleep so badly now. And I dream," Christophine necessarily replies: "I don't meddle with that for you" (p. 94). The value of the dream-text consists in the seeing, the writing of one's own text. To be, to remain, another's subtext—to remain in, or live out, another's dream—is the lie.

The dream that is used as general metaphor for context in Antoinette's early exchange with Rochester and as the structural recapitulation of Brontë's censored dream-text takes on its full power as the book comes to its conclusion and Antoinette's "dream" in the last section becomes "reality." Rhys's text, Antoinette's narrative, moves in its weave from the voice of one caretaker figure to another. Finally we hear Antoinette's own voice, the voice that begins the narration of this text and that will ultimately claim the dream, and the dream-text, as its own: "In this room I wake early and lie shivering for it is very cold. At last Grace Poole, the woman who looks after me, lights a fire with paper and sticks and lumps of coal. [. . .] In the end flames shoot up and they are beautiful. I get out of bed and go close to watch them and to wonder why I have been brought here. For what reason? There must be a reason. What is it that I must do?" (p. 146).

Later Antoinette looks at her red dress on the floor—the dress that, to her, represents her island—and recalls herself on her island in her own context. In her movement toward remembering, Antoinette knows the red dress is significant; we can contrast its color with that of the dress she was wearing in her second dream—a white dress, the color of a wedding dress, the color given her by Brontë's text. Most of all, the red dress represents the mark of herself for Antoinette, her name. In the convent, stitching her signature into a canvas of "silk roses on a pale background," she tells us, "Underneath, I will write my name in fire red, Antoinette Mason, née Cosway, Mount Calvary Convent, Spanish Town, Jamaica, 1839" (p. 44). Herself, her name, her place, her time—in "fire red," the color she chooses for the signing, the *writing* of her name. Antoinette thinks the dress should be able to effect recognition of her; as she tells Grace Poole, for example, her stepbrother, Richard Mason, would have "known" her if she had worn the red dress. Grace Poole looks at her and says, "I don't believe you know how long you've been here, you poor creature." Antoinette answers strongly: " 'On the contrary,' I said, 'only I know how long I have been here. Nights and days and days and nights, hundreds of them slipping through my fingers. But that does not matter. Time has no meaning. But something you can touch and hold like my red dress, that has meaning' " (p. 151).

We might recall here Rhys's remarks concerning her heroine in

Voyage in the Dark: "there's no more time for her as we think of time. That's how she feels, I'm certain." Similarly, in describing her second dream, when Antoinette tells us she "will not go any further" with "the man who is with me" and clings to the tree to preclude going further, she writes, "Still I cling and the seconds pass and each one is a thousand years. 'Here, in here,' a strange voice said, and the tree stopped swaying and jerking" (p. 50). The "strange voice" becomes her own in the "simultaneity in time" that marks a dream-text, the narrating voice of the dream that rescues her from Brontë's text and from Brontë's dream, just as recognition of the "fire red" of her signature signals the beginning of the remembering, which we can see as a re-membering of her self (her selves). She will *now* make an effort to save herself—unlike her refusal of the second dream when, "sick with fear," she tells us, "I follow him [. . .] but I make no effort to save myself; if anyone were to try to save me, I would refuse. This must happen" (p. 50). She is remembering her own dream, and Brontë's dream is coming to its end. Antoinette "let the dress fall to the floor, and looked from the fire [which Grace Poole had set; Grace's making of a fire is the first of her actions described by Antoinette when she takes up the final narrative] to the dress and from the dress to the fire" (p. 152). When Antoinette looks at the dress on the floor, "it was as if the fire had spread across the room. It was beautiful and it reminded me of something that I must do. I will remember I thought. I will remember quite soon now" (p. 153).   ∩

The next sentence recalls the serial nature of the dreams, recording their progress and Antoinette's. She tells us, after telling herself that she would "remember quite soon now": "That was the third time I had my dream, and *it ended*" (my emphasis). "I know now," she emphasizes, "that the flight of steps leads to this room where I lie watching the woman asleep with her head on her arms." She herself is now watching over a sleeper and dreamer. The "flight of steps," or a "wall" as she calls it also in her second dream, is the wall that leads Jane Eyre, in her dream, to a view of the receding figure of Rochester. For Antoinette, the steps lead to a room "where I lie watching the woman asleep with her head on her arms." Not Rochester, certainly, and not any man—the sleeper is instead a woman, another dreamer. Soon, when she calls to Christophine for help, Christophine doesn't answer. Rather, Antoinette looks behind her and sees that she has been "helped" by the fire, emblem of signature, of the writing of self.

Antoinette's caretakers had been concerned to take care of the "cold" she felt, her "shivering"; even Grace Poole remarks, just prior to Antoinette's looking back and forth between dress and fire, "Well don't stand there shivering," "quite kindly for her," as Antoinette observes (p. 152). In the final case it would seem the warming fire is "self-starting."

The narration now carries us through what we know is the "end" of the dream and the "end" of the text that Antoinette—Brontë's Bertha—is narrating for us. But Rhys has given us a dream within a dream. We reach the end of the dream as we know it from *Jane Eyre*, as we knew it from the beginning, just as Antoinette does, from the inception of her dreaming; however, at its climax, Antoinette wakes up: "I called 'Tia!' and jumped and woke" (p. 155). Fully awake, she then "lay still, breathing evenly with my eyes shut," and it is Grace Poole who says, "I must have been dreaming." After Grace goes back to sleep, Antoinette gets up, takes the keys, unlocks the door, and is, we know, on her way to making the dream "reality," as Brontë's script has written it *and* as she herself will open and expand it.

IN ANTOINETTE'S final dream, the outline of whose events we know from Brontë's prior text and which Antoinette is soon to enact, she sees an overview of the context of her life in the fire that she herself has already set and *will* set:

> out on the battlements it was cool and I could hardly hear them.
> [. . .] Then I turned round and saw the sky. It was red and all
> my life was in it. I saw the grandfather clock and Aunt Cora's
> patchwork, all colours, I saw the orchids and the stephanotis
> and the jasmine and the tree of life in flames. I saw the chande-
> lier and the red carpet downstairs and the bamboos and the
> tree ferns, the gold ferns and the silver, and the soft green vel-
> vet of the moss on the garden wall. I saw my doll's house and
> the books and the picture of the Miller's Daughter. I heard the
> parrot call as he did when he saw a stranger, *Qui est là? Qui est
> là?* and the man who hated me was calling too, Bertha! Bertha!
> The wind caught my hair and it streamed out like wings. It
> might bear me up, I thought, if I jumped to those hard stones.
> [. . .] Tia was there. She beckoned to me and when I hesitated,
> she laughed. I heard her say, You frightened? And I heard the

> man's voice, Bertha! Bertha! All this I saw and heard in a frac-
> tion of a second. And the sky so red. Someone screamed and I
> thought, *Why did I scream?* I called "Tia!" and jumped and woke.
> (p. 155)

The "strange voice" Antoinette hears in her second dream is identified here. It is her own, the voice of one who had been a "stranger"
to her but is no longer. The "someone" of her first dream—identified with Rochester—has become herself, a woman, the one that she
seeks; unlike Jane Eyre, who, in her dreams, seeks Rochester. A
woman speaks when Jane returns to her childhood and turns to a
rewriting of the "light" that visited her and became the human form
she identifies with the mother. Here the two texts—Rhys's and Brontë's—do coincide, for it is also here that Antoinette returns to the
"mother-text" in answering her own question.

Antoinette's last words are to Tia; indeed, the child's name is the
only word in this passage indicated as being spoken or called aloud.
Even "Rochester's" calling Bertha! Bertha! remains "unvoiced"
within our conventions of the printed text. Rhys/Antoinette marks
the subtext and her use of it at this culminating moment: Tia, her
"mirror-image," an image that she, Antoinette, claims for the writing
of her text, " 'Tia!' "—"like in a looking-glass," the looking-glass of
the fire, written in red, like her own name, *her* signature.

"There is no looking-glass here," Antoinette tells us earlier in the
narrative, "and I don't know what I am like now. I remember watching myself brush my hair and how my eyes looked back at me. The
girl I saw was myself yet not quite myself. Long ago when I was a
child and very lonely I tried to kiss her. But the glass was between
us—hard, cold and misted over with my breath. Now they have taken
everything away. What am I doing in this place and who am I?" (p.
147). Antoinette does not claim "that ghost of a woman whom they
say haunts this place" (p. 153). Of course she will not claim "her"—
especially as "they say" she is; moreover, "this place," "England," is
not *her* place. Antoinette cannot "see" herself here, in *his* place,
Rochester's England. She doesn't want to see, to encounter, "that
ghost of a woman." In this she is like Brontë's Jane, who cannot or
will not recognize the figure of the woman, Bertha, who is leaning
over her bed and looking at her, *except* as she sees Bertha's features

in the looking glass as the woman contemplates her own reflection. What Antoinette wants to see—with some pathos—is "herself."

In one of Antoinette's forays into the house, she goes out into the hall, as she is used to doing; "it was then I saw her—the ghost"— Brontë's version of her, of "Bertha": "The woman with streaming hair. She was surrounded by a gilt frame but I knew her. I dropped the candle I was carrying and it caught the end of a tablecloth and I saw flames shoot up. As I ran or perhaps floated or flew I called help me Christophine help me and looking behind me I saw that I had been helped. There was a wall of fire protecting me" (p. 154). This is the incident that we are first given to believe results in the fire that ends her life, within the framework of Brontë's text, before Antoinette wakes up from the dream. The "woman with streaming hair" can be identified as Antoinette's mother, particularly as her sexuality is emphasized; but it also—because of Antoinette's own identification and bond with her mother—all the more Antoinette. She "knew her." This recognition "takes her back to herself," as the phrase has it, "recalls" her to herself. In a logical process of association she calls to Christophine, who "answers" her—allows her to answer herself—in the "wall of fire protecting me." In her "life" that she sees in the fire, her mother's question and the parrot Coco's question upon seeing a "stranger" becomes central to her life and to the dream's culmination: *Qui est là? Who is there?* Recognition of the image of Tia allows her to answer; the *use*, the naming of the name, allows her to wake and *continue* her narrative, her text, even when the dream—Brontë's dream of her—is ended. The subtext marked by the use of Tia's name remains unwritten; it is the salient strand in the weave of a tapestry that is not closed and that demands a reweaving.

Rhys's use of the dream, doubled in the last segment of this final narration—itself the "end" of the external description of events from Brontë's text—tripled, multiplied, with the inclusion of the dream(s) Antoinette records for us in Part I of the novel (pp. 23, 50), becomes the place where all the strands of the dream-text are brought together. Rochester's England, Brontë's dream—the wrong context— ends.

Christophine arranged for Tia to fill the gap in the child Antoinette's life. Tia's image calls up all the images of Coulibri, the events during the fire there, and what they represent for Antoinette. Just as

Christophine provided the opportunity for Antoinette to find her own image in the child who was "like a looking-glass" for her, so *this* fire, provided by the unvoiced calling of Christophine's name, is the larger "looking-glass" in which a whole "life" can be seen. Seeing the life, however, focuses finally on that figure who fills the gap in Antoinette's life, who completes her recognition of "self" and enables her to answer her mother's question, *Who is there?* In effect, Rhys/ Antoinette completes the desire of her text here by using Tia, just as Rochester uses Antoinette to complete the desires of his text. The difference is in the opening out, the seeing of oneself in another. As is clear from the closing of Rochester's narration, he sees "Nothing" (p. 142), having tried to accomplish his "seeing" exclusively in words. Antoinette sees Tia, another woman, another girl-child, and, in seeing her, sees herself. It was the mother-text that seemed originally to offer safety. In answering the question posed by that text, Antoinette/ Rhys reaches the end of the journey, the destination toward which her own text, as well as Brontë's, had set her.

ANTOINETTE'S MOTHER, Annette, is the original care-taker, the first woman we see standing by her bedside, the woman who provides comfort after the "bad dream." Of all the women to whom she wakes, Antoinette's mother seems to provide a partial key to the genesis of the dream, to the motor force that precipitates the incipient text seeded by Brontë's. Antoinette's relationship with her mother seems to exacerbate the uncertainty in Antoinette that allows the dream-text to surface, the mother's role in this sense confirming the ontological uncertainty that is the result of, as well as a central fixing place for, the interracial incident with Tia: the hurtful, per-haps truthful, name-calling. Nevertheless, in the child's mind, she remains in her mother's keeping, "safe" from strangers. She is not safe, however, from her bond with her mother, from an identifica-tion with her for good or ill, just as she cannot and does not want to deny her bond and her desire for identification with Tia.

In the culminating moments of the dream in Part III, the dream from which Antoinette awakes to complete her task, she answers her mother's question, the parrot Coco's question, *Qui est là?* After her "bad dream," the child Antoinette is concerned solely that her mother be there, that she feel "safe," that the space they share re-main inviolate. I have already described the immediate framework and points of reference for that dream, as I have also described how the child's dream is the beginning of the dream that is the framework for Rhys's novel, the beginning of an explicit response to Brontë's text. But another "dream," the mother-text, encompasses Brontë's text as well as Rhys's and our own. This text, in which Antoinette's mother serves as the protagonist, is a "dream" that is rooted in what the novel presents as reality, a part of Antoinette's life, indissolubly woven into and from the context of that life.

The mother-text begins with a fire that serves as the object and the starting point for rewriting in the last dream-narrative, the burning of the house at Coulibri. The family members have made their way outside, where a crowd of blacks is waiting:

> It was very hot on the *glacis* too[. . . .] I saw tall flames shooting up to the sky, for the bamboos had caught. There were some tree ferns near, green and damp, one of them was smoldering too.
>
> "Come quickly," said Aunt Cora, and she went first, holding my hand. Christophine followed, carrying Pierre[. . . .] But when I looked round for my mother I saw that Mr Mason [. . .] seemed to be dragging her along and she was holding back, struggling. I heard him say, "It's impossible, too late now."
>
> "Wants her jewel case?" Aunt Cora said.
>
> "Jewel case? Nothing so sensible," bawled Mr Mason. "She wanted to go back for her damned parrot. I won't allow it." She did not answer, only fought him silently, twisting like a cat and showing her teeth.
>
> The parrot was called Coco, a green parrot. He didn't talk very well, he could say *Qui est là? Qui est là?* and answer himself *Ché Coco, Ché Coco.* [. . .]
>
> "Annette," said Aunt Cora. "They are laughing at you, do not allow them to laugh at you." She stopped fighting then and he half supported, half pulled her after us, cursing loudly. (pp. 34–35)

When the family comes outside, there is a "roar" in front of them, of the crowd's voices, and a "roar" behind them (p. 34). They are caught between the voice of the crowd and the voice of the fire. Annette is already like an animal, like Coco, who, protective and "bad tempered" after his wings had been clipped, "darted at everyone who came near her" (p. 35). The struggling woman is "caught," not only between the roar of the fire and of the crowd who set the fire, but in the arms of the Englishman, Mason, who "half supported, half pulled" her when she "stopped fighting."

Later we shall see Annette as her daughter sees and describes her, in the arms of the black (or colored) "man who is in charge of her" (the text is ambiguous) (p. 130): "she seemed to grow tired [. . .] and the man lift[ed] her up out of the chair and kiss[ed] her [. . .] and she went all soft and limp in his arms and he laughed" (p. 111). The struggling, fighting woman becomes "limp," in the arms of the "cursing" white man, the Englishman, and then, reiteratively, in the arms of the "laughing" black man. Then "somebody yelled," breaking the silence, " 'But look the black Englishman! Look the white niggers!' and then they were all yelling, 'Look the white niggers! Look the damn white niggers!' " (p. 35). The "somebody" in the crowd who breaks the silence emphasizes the reversing of images between which the Creole family is caught, but especially between which Annette and her daughter are caught, as Tia's assertions to Antoinette had earlier identified them.

Coco is first mentioned and described in this account of the fire in a specific interruption of the account of Annette's struggles with Mr. Mason. The interjection proceeds as if in fact a fire weren't raging: "Our parrot was called Coco[. . . .] After Mr Mason clipped his wings he grew very bad tempered, and though he would sit quietly on my mother's shoulder, he darted at everyone who came near her and pecked their feet" (p. 35).

Coco, the parrot with "clipped wings," causes the crowd to become silent again: "The yells stopped."

> I opened my eyes, everybody was looking up and pointing at Coco on the *glacis* railings with his feathers alight. He made an effort to fly down but his clipped wings failed him and he fell screeching. He was all on fire.
>
> [. . .] I heard someone say something about bad luck and remembered that it was very unlucky to kill a parrot, or even to see a parrot die. They began to go then, quickly, silently, and those that were left drew aside and watched us as we trailed across the grass. They were not laughing any more. (p. 36)

Because of an island superstition, because of the sacrifice of Annette's parrot, the family is saved. Had the parrot's wings not been
clipped, he might have saved himself, perhaps with other consequences for the family. The parrot, who couldn't "talk very well,"
could, as a result of his own survival instincts and the very restraints
that had been inflicted on him, effect the escape of the woman to
whom he belonged and whom he tried to defend while he was alive.
The collaboration between the constraints delivered by an outsider,
the Englishman Mr. Mason, and the beliefs of the islanders—that
coming together—that saves Annette and her family. Coco's worth to
her, then, is implicit in his death: in that death, his question becomes
her own. Annette could not, like the parrot, answer the question,
"Who is there?" Her daughter can.

Antoinette is enabled to answer in part through the very strength
of the "spirit" of the place where she was born and raised. The same
spirit allows the parrot's imminent death to invoke a belief that
causes the island's black people to turn away from watching that
death—in contradistinction to the reaction of the bystanders who
watch Charlotte Brontë's "Bertha" fall to her death from the battlements of Thornfield Hall. From this same spirit Antoinette derives
whatever strength she does have, whatever sense of "self" she retains
under the seeming mutations that Rochester has forced upon her.
Grace Poole "knows" that spirit, as she notes in her last observations
before Antoinette's voice takes over the final narrative: *"I'll say one
thing for her, she hasn't lost her spirit. She's still fierce"* (p. 146).

"Who is there?" is the question invoked following the aftermath of
the fire in an auditory image of Antoinette's mother as the child
describes it. Antoinette awakens to the next of her female caretakers,
her Aunt Cora, who tells her, "You've been very ill, my darling." [. . .]
"But you are safe with me now. We are all safe" (p. 38). These reas-
surances are spoken in almost the same words Aunt Cora uses in the
midst of the fire itself: "Don't be afraid, you are quite safe. We are all
quite safe" (p. 33). When her Aunt Cora tells Antoinette that her
mother is "in the country. Resting," Antoinette observes, "What was
the use of telling her that I'd been awake before and heard my
mother screaming *'Qui est là? Qui est là?'* then 'Don't touch me. I'll kill
you if you touch me. Coward. Hypocrite. I'll kill you.' I'd put my
hands over my ears, her screams were so loud and terrible. I slept
and when I woke up everything was quiet" (p. 39).

Later in the novel, two descriptions of Annette's life "in the country" reveal that her "rest" is permanent; her "self" has seemingly "died," even as her parrot did. Antoinette describes her mother as she saw her in her last visit; Christophine's remarks concerning Annette, also addressed to Rochester, occur in her critical dialogue with him. Both accounts are made to Rochester as a direct result of his charges against Antoinette after he has received the incriminating "evidence" of the letter from Daniel Cosway.

This is Antoinette's account, as she speaks to Rochester:

> "Pierre died [. . .] and my mother hated Mr Mason. She would not let him go near her or touch her. She said she would kill him, she tried to, I think. So he bought her a house and hired a coloured man and woman to look after her. For a while he was sad but he often left Jamaica and spent a lot of time in Trinidad. He almost forgot her."
>
> "And you forgot her too," I could not help saying.
>
> "I am not a forgetting person," said Antoinette. "But she—she didn't want me. She pushed me away and cried when I went to see her. They told me I made her worse. [. . .] One day I made up my mind to go to her, by myself. Before I reached her house I heard her crying. I thought I will kill anyone who is hurting my mother. I dismounted and ran quickly on to the veranda where I could look into the room. I remember the dress she was wearing—an evening dress cut very low, and she was barefooted. There was a fat black man with a glass of rum in his hand. He said, 'Drink it and you will forget.' She drank it without stopping. He poured her some more and she took the glass and laughed and threw it over her shoulder. It smashed to pieces. 'Clean it up,' the man said to the woman, 'or she'll walk in it.'
>
> "[. . .] My mother did not look at them. She walked up and down and said, 'But this is a very pleasant surprise, Mr Luttrell. Godfrey, take Mr Luttrell's horse.' Then she seemed to grow tired and sat down in the rocking-chair. I saw the man lift her up out of the chair and kiss her. I saw his mouth fasten on hers and she went all soft and limp in his arms and he laughed. The woman laughed too, but she was angry. When I saw that I ran away." (pp. 110–11)

At this point Antoinette says to Rochester, "I have said all I want to say. I have tried to make you understand. But nothing has changed." (Conversely, in relation to the dream-text, the circuit among the women, we recall Antoinette's remark following her first dream: "I woke next morning knowing that nothing would be the same. It would change and go on changing" [p. 23].) She laughs, and Rochester replies, "Don't laugh like that, Bertha." "My name is not Bertha," she responds, "why do you call me Bertha?" "Because it is a name I'm particularly fond of," he answers her. "I think of you as Bertha" (p. 111). Of course we know, because Antoinette told us before, when she visited Christophine, that this is not the first time he has called her Bertha: "He hates me now. [. . .] When he passes my door he says, 'Goodnight, Bertha.' He never calls me Antoinette now. He has found out it was my mother's name. 'I hope you sleep well, Bertha'— It cannot be worse" (pp. 93–94).

Antoinette's realization that "I have said all I want to say" in relation to Rochester is a different kind of lesson from that of the dream-text, of what she wants to say, and how to say it, in relation to women. Hers is a realization that reaffirms, finally, the positive bond with her mother, with the mother-text in the achievement of her own text, when she names herself in recognition of herself.

"It doesn't matter," she replies to Rochester. "I will tell you anything you wish to know, but in a few words because words are no use, I know that now" (p. 111). (Again, we can recall that after her mother's death, in relation to her and to the dream, she has already observed that "the words fell to the ground meaning nothing" [p. 51].) Any attempt at conversation with Rochester, of a dialogue between them, is at an end. He has named her, finally re-named her, and she knows that words are "no use" anymore: "I know that now." That form or aspect of the struggle is at an end. She has, for Rochester, "become" her mother—a "drunken, lying lunatic." He will see to it. Antoinette, finally, will use that identification just as Rhys has used it, to expand the "meaning" of "Bertha's" name in her struggle with Rochester for the maintenance and achievement of her self, her own text of self.

The question Antoinette's mother's parrot asks, the question her mother Annette asks, *Qui est là?*, has been answered by Rochester: you are your mother, you are like your mother. See, your name is now your mother's—but especially your mother's as I choose it,

"Bertha," not Annette, the name *she* used. Hence, on the battlements of Thornfield Hall, when Antoinette hears the parrot call as he did when he saw a stranger, *Qui est là? Qui est là?*, she also hears "the man who hated me" calling Bertha! Bertha!—that part of her mother's "self" that Rochester chose to name, an identification that is not Antoinette's except as she chooses to find it in her mother. The voice of the man gives *his* answer to the question of *her* existence. The recollection of the parrot gives Antoinette the idea that she can, perhaps, fly. Of course, the notion is suicidal even as a memory, for the parrot with its clipped wings could not be expected to escape the burning house. On the other hand, Antoinette can answer the dare of her chosen mirror-image, Tia, and it is this choice that makes the decision for her in the context of her own "naming," written in the red sky—the screen on which the final dream-text is seen, is dreamt for us, before Antoinette "wakes."

Christophine's account of Antoinette's mother is given us in her critical dialogue with Rochester. She has told him, "It's lies all that yellow bastard tell you." Referring to her assertion, he says—he isn't "asking," despite the question mark—"And that her mother was mad. Another lie?" Christophine explains:

> "They drive her to it. When she lose her son she lose herself
> for a while and they shut her away. They tell her she is mad,
> they act like she is mad. Question, question. But no kind word,
> no friends, and her husban' he go off, he leave her. They won't
> let me see her. I try, but no. They won't let Antoinette see her.
> In the end—mad I don't know—she give up, she care for noth-
> ing. That man who is in charge of her he take her whenever he
> want and his woman talk. That man, and others. Then they
> have her. Ah there is no God." (pp. 129–30)

Rochester "reminds her," "Only your spirits." " 'Only my spirits,' she said steadily" (p. 130), the "spirit" that Rochester perceives as fear, a fear of the "spirit of a place." The same spirit gives Antoinette the center and the strength to be unafraid; it is a "spirit" that has not left her, as Grace Poole notes. "In your Bible," Christophine continues, " 'it say God is a spirit—it don't say no others. Not at all. It grieve me what happen to her mother, and I can't see it happen again. You call her a doll? She don't satisfy you? Try her once more, I think she satisfy you now. If you forsake her they will tear her in pieces—like they did her mother'" (p. 130). Rochester has, of course, already set that process in motion. But in remembering, in "re-membering" herself and the women who have helped her reach the end of her dream-text, Antoinette effects the wholeness that the process of re-membering, through the dream-text, implies. In the vision of the child, Rhys, we remember that "God" is a book. But there are two versions of this book—a father-book and a mother-book, the mother-text. Plainly, she chooses the mother-text for her expression of self and for her model of aesthetic re-presentation. Rochester, just as plainly, can only follow the father-text. Antoinette/Rhys knows, however, that the *two* texts make up this "strange thing or person," God, the concept—a "spirit" (for Christophine, "spirit*s*"). Antoinette tries to explain, in another context, what this "thing or person" might be. Rochester has said, "I feel very much a stranger here[. . . .] I feel that this place is my enemy and on your side." Antoinette replies: "'You are quite mistaken[. . . .] It is not for you and not for me. It has nothing to do with either of us. That is why you are afraid of it, because it is something else. I found that out long ago when I was a child. I loved it because I had nothing else to love, but it is as indifferent as this God you call on so often'" (p. 107). She is talking about her island, but also about her mother, for the mother's "indifference" to the child is part of the context for recognition of self that both offer. However, it is in the holding two in one—the island, her mother—and in the safety in recognizing the indifference of both, as in her conception of God, that one can "love" this "indifference." Antoinette/Rhys, as a woman caught in the dilemma of relationships, "sees" and "knows" this spirit. It is not in acting antagonistically *against* difference, against "strangers," that human beings can achieve this "indifference," as Rochester seems to think. Rather it comes through noting the difference and then crossing the gap or blending it in, as Antoinette attempts to do.

In the closing moments of Antoinette's dream-narrative, Rhys disposes of the hard-won and insisted-upon identities—with mother *and* with mirror-image—that have carried the heroine-narrator this far. At the same time she completes Brontë's text even in its own terms, allowing us to see the figure of the mad "Bertha" jumping to her death from the battlements of Thornfield Hall, just as it was reported by the male eyewitness of Brontë's story. Obviously, Antoinette identifies herself momentarily with her mother's parrot, which in turn is identified, as we see, with her mother's attempt to escape the "man who hated me," the "stranger." The parrot's call is the question asked upon a stranger's approach: "Who's there?" The stranger, as it turns out, is herself, just as the "answer" to the question is "herself."

Antoinette's dream-narrative effectively displaces the locus of Antoinette's identity and then, seemingly, for the contemplation of the space of her own, manifest text, rids her of the consequences of that displacement. In the movement from mother to parrot, the question of the one already the central question of the other, Antoinette moves from the parrot's *call* to the image of Tia, to whose gestures she responds, whose *voice* she hears. "All this," Antoinette tells us, "I saw and heard in a fraction of a second" (p. 155). The further displacement occurs in another split second in terms of the writing, a rapid movement not only representative of the "simultaneity in time" proper to a dream-text, but also reminiscent of, learned from, the kind of displacement that has proven its own efficacy in the masculine text.

"Someone screamed," she writes, "and I thought, *Why did I scream? I called 'Tia!' and jumped and woke*" (p. 155). From the parrot's "call," through her mother's question, to Tia's voice, which she hears, to "someone's" scream—her own: this is the line of movement that accomplishes the maneuver. (Do *we* repeat the reading of the text and recall the "someone" who "hated" her in her earliest dream? Do *we* equate the two to provide us with another kind of mirror-image, that of Rochester as a distorting mirror-image of Antoinette? Do *we* begin yet another circular reading, another kind of repetition, another kind of dream-text?) We move to the single word that Antoinette's narrative describes as *voiced*—a woman's name, a little black girl's name, the name of her alleged "mirror-image": *Tia!* Although Tia has not appeared in the novel except as a child, we can say that, as Antoinette's alter ego, she has grown with her. Conversely, the adults are gone, and to effect her achievement of self, Antoinette returns to the time and the place in which the image of her alter ego was originally fixed. She awakes by means of this talisman, this magic. Antoinette's accomplishment of self, of knowing "what I have to do," is achieved by the fixing in place of the black child, her "looking-glass," whom Antoinette/Rhys has used to secure her own image. The saving grace, if we may call it that, the *difference*, is in the original attempt, which was a desire for a fusion, a melding of self and self.

In rendering a woman's text, a collectively woven text, the writer ultimately jettisons the most salient subtext(s) to assert her own. Yet, since she retains the weave, she reopens the text, at its formal closure, to a repetition and a rewriting. The adult Christophine and the adult Amélie are missing here. Only the child Tia is used to bolster the white Creole woman's assertion of self. As she has "grown with" Antoinette as her alter ego, Tia, whose subtext is the most salient in the story, has also been repressed in the text. The subtexts of the two adult women, Christophine and Amélie, would perhaps unbalance, if not overwhelm, the mechanism at this point in a culminating narrative, since Antoinette's use of Tia here can be said to constitute a return of the repressed. For if the text is dependent on the subtext, the mark of the subtext must be deep, its absence felt and signaled in the writing so as to mark the possibilities of the continuation that is implicit in a dream-text. The censored material in effect completes the manifest text. This may be a lesson that the woman's text will help us to "unlearn"; such a lesson may be a "necessity" we wish ultimately to discard. And Rhys does at least make what we may call a notation of the even more recessive subtexts of her novel. These subtexts, a single subtext in the sense that I will describe them, are those of Amélie and Sandi.

Antoinette's description of her mother's dilemma is a pointer to this subtext. Her ambivalence in designating the "color" of the man who "is in charge of" Antoinette's mother, Annette, calls our attention to this submerged, almost hidden text. At one point he is identified as "coloured"; at another as "black." In fact, "he" may be more than one man, as Christophine's description of the situation suggests. This ambivalence points us to the two figures who seem to have some independence from the manipulations of the societies in which they live. Sandi is the successful, light-colored cousin of Antoinette, with whom, in another story, she might have lived "happily ever after," the single male figure who offers her care, tenderness, and safety (pp. 42, 141–52). Amélie is the only figure who "goes her own way" within the framework of the story, who is able to "feel sorry" for both Rochester and Antoinette, saying to Rochester, "Yes [. . .] I am sorry for you. But I find it in my heart to be sorry for her too" (p. 116).

The two of them—female and male—seem to represent for Rhys a possibility closed to the other characters, and they remain shadowy figures, only partially formed, not fully integrated into the text. Their shared characteristics are two: their color (not black, not white, but a blend of the two) and their independence. Neither has made a pact with the white culture in a way that constrains their actions, as, for example, Daniel Cosway has. They remain the subtext of an ideal, just as Tia—the desired object for fusion and Antoinette's alter ego—represents the "mix" that the two of them, a little black girl and a little white girl, might be seen to make into an "ideal." The difference is that Rhys wrote one of these subtexts—Tia's—into the story; the other—Amélie and Sandi's—remains a notation or mere registering of Rhys's own ultimately ambivalent attitude toward race. It is to Rhys's credit, at least from the point of view of our reading, that she marks her own censorship in this way.

The salient subtext, then, is unambiguously marked. The "mother-text," however, remains the most ambiguous text of all in its seemingly overt presentation, overarching as it does both text and subtext (including Brontë's), encompassing both, offering the original locus for anxiety and identification. The mother-text is made central to both from the opening lines of the novel and woven tightly into the black/white dichotomy: the "Jamaican ladies" in whose "ranks," those of the "white people," Antoinette and her mother do not belong, "never approved of" her mother, "because she pretty like pretty self," as Christophine explained (p. 15). A point of Rochester's text, seemingly taken from Brontë, makes the mother-daughter bond the thematic crux, interwoven as it is with all the texts. The mark of this thematic crux is his renaming, rechristening, his wife Antoinette with her mother's alleged name. Significantly for our view of Rhys's text as a response to Brontë's, Antoinette's name in relation to her mother's is a point of Brontë's text from which Rhys makes a deliberate break, a break that involves a telling inversion.

In Brontë's novel, the formal document of Rochester's marriage to Richard Mason's sister "Bertha" includes the names of her mother and father as well as her own name. Her father (not a stepfather as in *Wide Sargasso Sea*, but her natural father) is Jonas Mason. Her *mother* is named Antoinetta and *her* daughter, Rhys's Antoinette, is named Bertha Antoinetta Mason. The mother's name in Rhys's text is here given as the daughter's, Bertha, and the mother in *Jane Eyre*'s text is designated solely by the name—or a near equivalent—that is her daughter's alone in Rhys's—"Antoinetta" (*Jane Eyre*, p. 255). The nature of the revision marks a curious, compelling insistence in the matter of names and naming. Rhys's inversion of the names of mother and daughter suggests an "identification" of the daughter with the mother even more pointedly than does Rhys's text itself. (Rhys does give us a direct textual cue in Rochester's final emotional monologue. Antoinette, who has become "silence itself," is addressed cynically: "Sing, Antoinetta. I can hear you now" [p. 138].) Rhys's avowal, spoken by Antoinette, that "He has found out it [Bertha] was my mother's name" (p. 94), is a seeming collusion with Rochester's text, if not with Brontë's. On the other hand, with some irony Rhys's acting "for" Antoinette makes an early claim to the identification that both Brontë's Rochester and Rhys's Rochester seem to "force" upon Antoinette against her will.

Names are thematically important here; they are important stylistically as well, in Antoinette's final naming of herself through calling the name of her alter ego Tia in the last dream-narrative. However, again the more crucial story is acted out in the subtext. Naming is a symbolic act: naming of self is an accession to self through the distancing of language, as in "THIS *is my* DIARY"; naming of others is a means of appropriating their qualities for one's own purposes. The subtextual movement and its genesis are again a key to the transcription at work in the production of the manifest dream-text. It is the mother-text and *its* subtext that are basic to the weave of Rhys's text and to Antoinette's dream-text. Antoinette answers her mother's question here by appropriating the subtext of her alter ego, Tia. In doing so, she can be said to return not only to a repression of her own, but to the even more profound repression in her mother's text. It is not that the mother-text gives the text its meaning in this way. Rather, the mother-text provides the direction(s) of its movement, which in turn provides for its full display of release and repression.[23]

In posing the question of the mother-text, *Qui est là? Who is there?*, Rhys also anticipates what Judith Kegan Gardiner calls "a central question of feminist literary criticism"—"Who is there when a woman says 'I am?'"[24] Rhys takes up this question in *Wide Sargasso Sea*, posing and answering it within the text's own literary and historical framework, while at the same time attempting to suggest the way to an answer for us in our "real lives." The suggestion is that we attend to that "book" of our mother's, as Rhys did in her writing, rather than to the other book, the "large book standing upright and half open" that "made no sense to me."

The dream-text, then, is embedded in the mother-text, in the mother's story. In examining the story of Antoinette's mother and Rhys's use of it, we encounter the dream-mother of one of the other young women with whom we have previously been concerned— Freud's Dora. So wide-reaching is the net of the mother-text in any woman's story.

FREUD'S ACCOUNT of Dora's dreams is an important part of what was meant to be not only a showpiece for the analysis of a typical case of hysteria, but also an early example of the use of dream analysis. "A periodically recurrent dream," Freud wrote, "was by its very nature particularly well calculated to arouse my curiosity." The first of Dora's dreams had recurred on at least three successive previous occasions and then again more recently when she was under Freud's treatment. He "determined to make an especially careful investigation of it."

> Here is the dream as related by Dora: "*A house was on fire. My father was standing beside my bed and woke me up. I dressed myself quickly. Mother wanted to stop and save her jewel-case; but Father said: 'I refuse to let myself and my two children be burnt for the sake of your jewel-case.' We hurried downstairs, and as soon as I was outside I woke up.*"[25]

A comparable capsule version of Antoinette's account of the fire at Coulibri is as follows:

> I woke up and it was still night and my mother was there. She said, "Get up and dress yourself, and come downstairs quickly." [. . .] "There is no reason to be alarmed," my stepfather was saying as I came in. [. . .] "Come quickly," said Aunt Cora[. . . .] But when I looked round for my mother I saw [. . .] she was holding back, struggling. I heard [my stepfather] say, "It's impossible, too late now." [. . .] "Wants her jewel case?" Aunt Cora said. "Jewel case? Nothing so sensible"[. . . .] "She wanted to go back for her damned parrot. I won't allow it." (pp. 32–35)

Reading these two accounts juxtaposed, it is difficult not to believe that Rhys is deliberately using and refuting Freud's reading of Dora's dream, but no reliable published source verifies the suspicion.[26] Rhys may or may not have consciously included Dora's "rescue" in her effort to "rescue" Brontë's Bertha. There is sufficient textual evidence, however, for us to compare the two accounts and the use to which they are each put by their separate authors—Freud and Dora in the one case, as co-authors, and Rhys in the other. I will not here discuss Freud's reading of Dora's first or second dream in all of their particulars, although the second, too, could be drawn fully into the framework I want to suggest. My intention is to point to those parts of Rhys's novel and of Dora's dream that are held in common and to suggest how they seem to interact.[27]

One of the pivotal questions Freud asks Dora concerns the "jewel-case," a central element both in Dora's dream and in Antoinette's account of the fire at Coulibri. Concerning Dora's mother and the jewel-case, Freud presses Dora with a leading question: "I daresay you thought to yourself that you would accept [jewelry from her father that her mother was not "very fond of"] with pleasure?" She replies, "I don't know. I don't in the least know how Mother comes into the dream." Freud's footnote here is that this reply—"I don't know"—was "the regular formula with which she confessed to anything that had been repressed."[28] We might recall the words of the "interrogator" in "The Trial of Jean Rhys": *The phrase is not 'I do not know' but I have nothing to say.* Rhys's reply, as we might also recall, is that *she* had "plenty to say. Not only that, but I am bound to say it."[29]

Freud asks Dora, with some delicacy, "Perhaps you do not know that 'jewel-case' [*Schmuck-kästchen*] [along with "box" in the second dream: the words are used similarly in English] is a favourite expression for the same thing that you alluded to not long ago by means of the reticule you were wearing—for the female genitals, I mean."

"I knew you would say that," Dora replies. Freud's footnote here, as we might expect, is that this is "a very common way of putting aside a piece of knowledge that emerges from the repressed." "That is to say," Freud continues, "you knew that it *was* so,—. . . You said to yourself:

> "This man is persecuting me; he wants to force his way into my
> room. My 'jewel-case' is in danger, and if anything happens it

will be Father's fault." For that reason in the dream you chose a situation which expresses the opposite—a danger from which your father is saving you. In this part of the dream everything is turned into its opposite; you will soon discover why. As you say, the mystery turns upon your mother. You ask how she comes into the dream? She is, as you know, your former rival in your father's affections. In the incident of the bracelet, you would have been glad to accept what your mother had rejected. . . . Then it means that you were ready to give your father what your mother withheld from him. . . . Now bring your mind back to the jewel-case which Herr K. gave you. You have there the starting-point for a parallel line of thoughts, in which Herr K. is to be put in the place of your father just as he was in the matter of standing beside your bed. . . . In this line of thoughts your mother must be replaced by Frau K. . . . So you are ready to give Herr K. what his wife withholds from him. That is the thought which has had to be repressed with so much energy, and which has made it necessary for every one of its elements to be turned into its opposite. . . . Not only that you are afraid of Herr K., but that you are still more afraid of yourself, and of the temptation you feel to yield to him. In short, these efforts prove once more how deeply you loved him."[30]

"Naturally," Freud observes, "Dora would not follow me in this part of the interpretation."[31]

Rhys might have considered and rejected Freud's interpretation in her presentation of events at Coulibri, in her use of the "jewel case" and the significance it might hold for her and for the readers of *her* "dream." In Dora's dream, it is understood that her mother wanted "to stop and save her jewel-case" and that her father would not allow it. In Antoinette's account of events, her Aunt Cora suggests that the jewel case is a proper object to be saved. Indeed, Cora's question, "Wants her jewel case?" seems almost too pointed and abrupt in its interjection in the account, and Mason's reply, "Nothing so sensible[. . . .] She wanted to go back for her damned parrot. I won't allow it," draws our attention back to the parrot, the seemingly central element in the account.

The significance of Aunt Cora's question, however, becomes clear much later in the book, in Antoinette's nine-page interruption of

Rochester's narration. Rhys's return of the narrative to Antoinette at this point is a strategic placing of material essential to the dialogue that the novel enacts, as is the specific dialogue that will soon take place between Rochester and Christophine. This portion of Antoinette's narrative clarifies the extent of her unwitting complicity with Rochester's as yet unfocused manipulations. In talking with Christophine, trying to think of whom she can "trust," she recalls her Aunt Cora. In this recollection the significance of a woman's "jewel case" in a nineteenth-century marriage (in a class in which a woman might expect to have jewelry of any value) becomes unequivocally clear to her readers, if not thoroughly clear to Antoinette. She describes a quarrel overheard prior to her marriage, a quarrel between her Aunt Cora and her stepbrother, Richard Mason:

> "It's disgraceful," [Cora] said. "It's shameful. You are handing over everything the child owns to a perfect stranger. Your father would never have allowed it. She should be protected, legally. A settlement can be arranged[. . . .] That was his intention."
>
> "You are talking about an honourable gentleman, not a rascal," Richard said. "I am not in a position to make conditions, as you know very well. She is damn lucky to get him, all things considered. Why should I insist on a lawyer's settlement when I trust him? I would trust him with my life," he went on in an affected voice.
>
> "You are trusting him with her life, not yours," she said[. . . .]
>
> [. . .] She [Aunt Cora] was too ill to come to my wedding and I went to say good-bye, I was excited and happy thinking now it is my honeymoon. I kissed her and she gave me a little silk bag. "My rings. Two are valuable. Don't show it to him. Hide it away. Promise me."
>
> I promised, but when I opened it, one of the rings was plain gold. I thought I might sell another yesterday but who will buy what I have to sell here? . . . (pp. 95–96)

Antoinette's Aunt Cora knows the value of a woman's "jewel case." It was the only economic recourse, under the law, that she might have if she found herself in extremity, her only independence of means. This resource was what Antoinette's Aunt Cora tried to provide her by the gift of her rings. However, we may also see "independence"—

and violation—in terms of both sex and money. The two are often integral to the same social transactions and cultural valuations.

We have then, in Rhys's novel, two specific instances of a "denial" of Freud's interpretation of Dora's dream. Antoinette's mother does not want to save her "jewel-case" as Dora's mother did; instead, Annette wants to save "herself" figuratively, her parrot, *Ché* (which might also be read, if inaccurately, as a corrupt form of that self-accession through language-distancing: "C'est") *Coco,* dear Coco, a treasured self. And it is another woman, Aunt Cora, who introduces the significant object, the jewel case, into a heightened discussion at the moment of the fire, for reasons eminently practical from a woman's point of view.

The furious Antoinette later demonstrates her own knowledge of how important legal and economic resources—access to legal and economic systems—can be. In fact, not until the final narrative does Antoinette demonstrate the antagonism toward this dual "power," which she might well have felt earlier, perhaps as a child. Then, it was her mother alone who seemed to feel, and to suffer, the consequences of a lack of those resources. "It was when he said 'legally' that you flew at him [Richard Mason, her stepbrother, who, as Aunt Cora points out, had "trusted" Rochester with Antoinette's "life"]," Grace Poole tells her (p. 150). Later, when she is in the room that we recognize as Rochester's from Brontë's text, Antoinette remarks, observing that the room is "like a church" but "without an altar," "Gold is the idol they worship" (p. 154). In this room she "felt very miserable" despite the "softness" of the couch upon which she was sitting (p. 154).

Another Freudian psychoanalytical tool whose efficacy Freud hoped to demonstrate in this case study, along with a close interpretation of dreams, was "transference," especially in the relationship between analyst and patient. Freud was, he tells us, "obliged to speak of transference, for it is only by means of this factor that I can elucidate the peculiarities of Dora's analysis. Its great merit, namely . . . unusual clarity . . . is closely bound up with its great defect, which led to its being broken off prematurely. I did not succeed," he confesses, "in mastering the transference in good time." "For how," Freud asks the reader, "could the patient take a more effective revenge than by demonstrating upon her own person the helplessness and incapacity of the physician?"[32]

Later in his life, Freud introduced a revision of his discussion of Dora's case, in juxtaposition to his discussion of transference:

> The longer the interval of time that separates me from the end of this analysis, the more probable it seems to me that the fault in my techniques lay in this omission: I failed to discover in time and to inform the patient that her homosexual (gynae-cophilic) love for Frau K. was the strongest unconscious current in her mental life. I ought to have guessed that the main source of her knowledge of sexual matters could have been no one but Frau K.—the very person who later on charged her with being interested in those same subjects. Her knowing all about such things and, at the same time, her always pretending not to know where her knowledge came from was really too remarkable. I ought to have attacked this riddle and looked for the motive of such an extraordinary piece of repression. . . . Before I had learnt the importance of the homosexual current of feeling in psychoneurotics, I was often brought to a standstill in the treatment of my cases or found myself in complete perplexity.[33]

Let us note the "gynaecophilic" love that Freud emphasizes as the "strongest current in [Dora's] mental life." It is not female homosexuality that I would emphasize, unless we speak in terms of a "lesbian continuum," as Adrienne Rich has done, meaning a primary bonding, rather than the sexual interest or focus between and among women.[34] Rather, it is literally "gynaecophilia," love of women. Just as the passionate or sensual love between Rochester and Antoinette is not the point at issue in *Wide Sargasso Sea*, so the love among or between women that I emphasize as a key to Rhys's text is not one of sensual passion. It is instead a feeling founded in kinship, recognition, and mutuality, whose genesis is to be found in the mother-text, the bond with the mother.

In Antoinette's account of the fire at Coulibri, Rhys is in one sense revising Dora's dream. She brings some of the dream's latent content to the surface so that, as Freud calls it, "such an extraordinary piece of repression" becomes manifest in the written framework of Rhys's novel.

When Antoinette awakes, not only from her first childhood dream but also during the fire at Coulibri, her mother is there—not, as in Dora's dream, her father. Throughout the events of the novel, when

Antoinette wakes, a woman caretaker is standing by. Antoinette, as we have seen, watches over another woman sleeping and dreaming near the end of her narrative. When Antoinette "finishes" the dream(s) of which she had given us earlier accounts (the first dream in inchoate form, the second in a more complete, more formal account, as well as the "dream," the mother-text, that her mother's drama represents), the several dreams come together: her text and Brontë's, her dream(s) and Brontë's, her narrative and Brontë's. The dreamed events of Part Three complete the events narrated in Part One, culminating in the rewriting of the burning of the house at Coulibri and especially her mother's part in her dream-text. In a sense, this completion of her own text completes *one* aspect of Dora's dream as well, that "part" of Dora's "pathogenic material"—the "current of feeling" that she withheld from Freud, "a part of which," he confesses, "I was in ignorance." This "part" of Dora's material for dreaming, pathogenic or not, is the mother-text. Its significance in any woman's life is that it is the "strongest current in her mental life," as Rhys's text demonstrates by displaying the structure and the elements of a woman's "dream-text."

The question central to the dream and to feminist literary criticism is also the question central to Rhys's *Wide Sargasso Sea*. The parrot, after his wings were clipped, persisted in defending Annette even as he had done throughout his life: *Qui est là?* Who's there? *Who is there?* The answer is to be found in responding to one's "mirror-image," even if one sees in the looking-glass the negative of herself, the other, not oneself; one answers in speaking to that other in return. " 'Tia!' " Antoinette responds, calling her name, not misnaming her, acting in response to that recognition, to "write" her own name. Rhys recognized her own life in that of Brontë's Bertha. So might Charlotte Brontë and her Jane Eyre in a different time and place. Rhys also binds her earlier heroines to her last, especially her heroine-narrators, and especially the young Anna Morgan of *Voyage in the Dark*.

Among the many women here, kinship moves in several directions and through several mediums, through race and class, even through hostility, mistrust, and envy. Our common text is indissoluble. It admits of no final allegiance but the acting out of our common "dream," which may be found in our waking lives, our common waking lives, as well as in the dreams and dream-work of our "sleep." We wake to the women who make and reinforce this context of our lives, that life of ours that we "dream" when we "sleep." Rhys is one of these women; her model, the book of her mother's; her knowledge, that there is more than one book that makes up that "strange thing or person" called God: there is no such thing as *a* book, one book, one *text*. Rhys's heroine-narrator replies to Rochester—firmly, passionately—when he asks, "Is there another side?": "There is always the other side, always" (p. 106).

CHAPTER EIGHT.

THE OTHER SIDE:

"ROCHESTER'S" NARRATIVE

IN *WIDE SARGASSO SEA*

*As for my confused impressions they will never be written.
There are blanks in my mind that cannot be filled up.*
  —Rochester, *Wide Sargasso Sea*

IN the previous chapter I suggested that Rhys's novel
poses and answers the question that Judith Gardiner
construes as central to feminist criticism: "Who is there
when a woman says 'I am'?" In considering Rochester's narrative we
can ask a similar question: "Who is there when a man says 'I am'?"
How a person tells his or her story can itself provide an answer to the
question as it is made historically possible. Rhys chose the first-person point of view and the narrative mode to show how answers to
these questions are revealed and to emphasize the difference, as well
as the relationship, between the man's text and the woman's. In the
interweaving of the narrative strategies of each, Rhys not only demonstrates the predominant pattern of the woman's dream-text but
also further emphasizes the importance of our reading of ourselves
and others on which the difference between the two texts turns. Rhys
has here used the first-person narrative in such a way that it flushes
our quarry—the "I" who says "I am"—into the open.

The salient subtext of Rochester's narrative is the mother-text. In
his strenuous rejection of it as a present influence in his life, in his
forced and unsuccessful reiteration of its absence, its presence is all
the more emphasized, and the pattern of it in his narrative becomes
less and less opaque. The further he attempts to thrust the mother-
text from him, the closer he comes to an identification with it. Within
this subtextual framework, we can also see "Rochester" and Antoi-

nette as distorting and distorted mirror-images of one another.[1] The novel may be about the relationship between "Rochester" and Antoinette, and its consequences, but the man's narrative provides a testing ground for the real combatants, the mother-text and the father-text. His narrative is consistently poised between mother and father, and he tries again and again to opt for the father-text, the "view" he has "always accepted" (p. 85). In his incomplete attempts at emotional and literary transvestism—dressing up in mother's clothes as well as father's—"Rochester's" narrative finally raises more questions than it answers, at least insofar as his own sense of identity is concerned. Unlike Antoinette, Rochester does not find his mirror-image. His text remains, as it begins, without a name.

I will often refer to "Rochester" as "the man," for in strict adherence to Rhys's presentation of him, he is not Rochester; he is never named, and it is only with recourse to Charlotte Brontë's *Jane Eyre* that we presume to call him by that name. We do so "naturally," so compelling is the designation of a name once we think we know it. We cannot think of him any other way, and I will eventually omit the quotation marks. I cite Brontë's novel because Rhys's patterning of the dream-text inevitably weaves the character of Brontë's Rochester into the narrative identity of the man in her own novel. As we see in the interweaving of Jane Eyre's dreams into Antoinette's, so we see the character—indeed, some of the very words and ideas of the fictionally and chronologically older Rochester—in the young man Rhys presents. An outline of the young "Rochester's" narrative can be found in that of Brontë's Rochester in *Jane Eyre*. As we might expect, the latter events described in this narrative furnish part of the structure of events in Antoinette's final narrative as well, since her text and Brontë's coincide at that point in *Wide Sargasso Sea*. Brontë and her protagonist give the floor to Rochester for the express purpose of allowing him to tell "his side of the story" to Jane (*Jane Eyre*, pp. 268–78). The young "Rochester" whom we read in Rhys's novel is a creature of Brontë's Rochester, of his chronological "later" narrative in the fiction, in combination with Rhys's actually later narration. The line of descent of the man's narrative moves backward retroactively, from Rhys's presentation of it to Brontë's; the line of literary descent, meanwhile, moves forward, and the man's text becomes irretrievably woven into Rhys's dream-text through the medium of the two women who are writing him. Both women know, however, that the appropriate vehicle for the man is his own statement of the case, a conscious telling of his tale, which is to say, a traditional narrative. Hence they both allow him his form and give him the space in which he is used to perform.

"Rochester's" narrative can be interwoven firmly into the dream-text as the warp of the weave in part because of its apparent conservatism, its fixity. When the selvage of a fabric is loosened, the threads that one can peel away are those of the weft, the threads carried by the women's shuttle. The ghostly imprint of the whole pattern can be seen only in the absence of the threads which, in their absence, already suggest the possibility of recombination elsewhere. The warp is abandoned or orphaned.

In his attempts to adhere to the dictates of the father-text, "Rochester," and his text, are fixed in the confines of its definition. In the writing of such a text there is only one author, one narrator, the father, until the son accedes to his place, in contrast to the woman's text, in which the narration is shared. The mother-text offers a direction for movement, for an opening out and expansion, the obverse of confinement. "Rochester" can repeat the text of the father, but, since that text cannot be shared, he cannot find in it even a reflection of himself. The result is his ultimate discovery that he has no text of his own. In disallowing the name that might be derived from the already set text of Brontë's novel, Rhys points up this lack in his text. She underscores his attempts and his failure to resolve the dilemma in which she places him by confronting him with the text represented by Antoinette.

The inhibited movement of "Rochester's" narrative itself provides focal points for discussion and an indication of the ambivalence at work in the narrative: his basic childlike ambivalence toward the mother-text (in behavioral psychology, an attitude usually labeled "approach-avoidance"); his preference for the father; his attempt to find the secret of the mother-text, to join with it; and his return to the father-text. These focal points roughly parallel the chronological presentation of events, a fact that emphasizes the basic linearity of the classifiably masculine text. Elements at work here are those that emphasize the means by which the man attempts to maintain the structure of his world and the placing of himself in that world. These elements present themselves to our notice in similarly chronological fashion. First is his willed dependence on the law and on his father, the conflation of the two into what Christophine calls "Letter of the Law." Second is the feminization, especially the "hysterization,"[2] of the man as he goes on the journey into the forest in his attempt to discover the "secret" that the women and all the islanders know. This feminization works in concert with Rhys's use of the fixed quality reflected in the traditionalism of the masculine narrative. Feminization of a typical, and therefore representative, man becomes analogous to the use of "Woman"—women—fixed in the iconography of hysteria that we have seen epitomized in the narrative attempts of M. Charcot's *Iconographie photographique.*

Similarly, Rhys's use of "the uncanny" here both exploits Freud's reading of it, which is based on the Oedipal configuration, and inverts the object or prop used in acting out the drama into an opportunity for the woman's text to show itself, as the doll Olympia is used by the male characters and readers of E. T. A. Hoffmann's story. We can here invert Xavière Gauthier's dictum, and restore its logic, at least for Rhys's novel: *If there is a madman, then it's definitely the Man.* Rhys achieves this inversion of the question of the madwoman, the hysteric, the immobile woman who cannot "see herself," as I earlier described the position in which many young women of the nineteenth century found themselves. The feminization of the male text within this framework is a strategy for which Rhys receives her cue from Brontë, as I will describe.

The third element concerns "Rochester's" displacement of Antoinette as he plots it after his failure to learn the "secret" of the place. He doesn't recognize himself in what he sees; he becomes frightened, but he doesn't learn. He becomes his own object (of fear: he might, after all, have learned something), so he looks for another: Antoinette. His plan solidifies then and he sets out to displace her, to make her like the place and the people who have frightened him into almost seeing himself. His text, unlike Antoinette's, unlike the woman's text, must stop movement at all costs, lest he see or recognize himself in what he is doing. In his manliness, his apparent control, he is at his most hysterical. He is hysterical because he can't find a mirror-image. He can only look "inward," that is to say at his father, the father-text.

This demonstration, the culmination of his narrative, involves the futile conversations with Antoinette and Christophine during which both women attempt to explain their side of the story to him and come to realize, as Antoinette puts it, that "words are no use" anymore (p. 111). His "sanity" is displayed at the last with a pathetic return, not to the specific father-text, but to literary father-texts, ironically and significantly including Brontë's, a feminine text, a "mother-text." He has not escaped the mother-text, but he cannot admit or recognize it. Thus he cannot recognize himself either.

"Rochester" recites the father-texts, and he sees nothing, finally. He refuses the "looking-glass." He will not or cannot recognize himself in another. His text remains the father-book, that single book; and his own text, his "looking-glass" of self, remains empty and without a name of its own. One of the books "Rochester" finds in the "refuge" of his dressing-room at Granbois can be seen as an emblem for the nameless man, "Rochester," and even that book is inherited from another man. On the last shelf of a "crude bookshelf" over a small writing desk, he finds *"Life and Letters of . . . The rest was eaten away"* (p. 63).

 In "Writing Like a Woman," Peggy Kamuf asks us to consider Freud's restatement of "a fundamental assumption of what we know as culture: that the movement away from the unmediated maternal bond toward the mediated (or hypothetical) paternal bond is the motor of cultural advance."[3] Despite his determination to join in the "fundamental attempt," Rochester has difficulty taking the "momentous step," as Freud describes this "turning," thus "taking sides."[4] "The authority of patriarchy," Kamuf points out, "relies on our failing to ask the question which Freud implicitly poses, on our refusing to think the absence, at the origin, of an origin."[5]

Before continuing our examination of "Rochester's" attempts, let us consider one of Kamuf's concluding suggestions: "Reading a text as written by a woman will be reading it *as if* it had no (determined) father, *as if*, in other words, it were illegitimate, recognized by its mother who can only give it a borrowed name."[6] The dream-text of Rhys's novel does not refuse the "question which Freud implicitly poses"; Rhys does not refuse to "think the absence, at the origin, of an origin." The movement of her text may be generated by the mother-text, but, as I suggest, the mother-text provides a model for movement outward. Her text, the woman's dream-text, is specifically written as if it had no (determined) father. Rochester's problem is that he fears the "illegitimacy" of his narrative; the mark of this near-illegitimacy, of his sensed betrayal of the father-text, is that the only name he and his text have is "borrowed." Betrayal works both ways: he is afraid of betraying the father and also of being betrayed by him.

At the same time, Rochester is placed in this position by Rhys's inclusion of his text in her own, despite the apparent authenticity of her reading of the man as it is presented in "his" narration. Indeed, to my knowledge there has not been a single critical charge against her on the point of the authenticity of the male narrative. On the contrary, she is praised for her sympathetic rendering of the man.[7] What her dual strategy achieves is insistence on inclusion of the man, as revealed in the masculine narrative, in the net of the mother-text, suggesting its preeminence for all of us, despite the "cultural advance," the "momentous step" that Kamuf rightly observes to be founded in, "lost in," an "aporia."[8] In Rhys's use of Rochester's text, his text of self as it is revealed in his narrative, she asks an even more fundamental question than those with which we started: "Who is there when a woman (or a man) says 'I am'?" As Hélène Cixous observes, the answer to such questions is not to be found in asking "who," but in posing the question in terms of "how":

> The quest for origins, illustrated by Oedipus, doesn't haunt a feminine unconscious. Rather it's the beginning, or beginning*s*, the manner of beginning . . . starting on all sides at once, that makes a feminine writing. A feminine text starts on all sides at once, starts twenty times, thirty times, over. . . .
> A feminine textual body is recognized by the fact that it is always endless, without ending: there's no closure, it doesn't stop, and it's this that very often makes the feminine text difficult to read. For we've learned to read books that basically pose the word "end." But this one doesn't finish, a feminine text goes on and on and at a certain moment the volume comes to an end but the writing continues and for the reader this means being thrust into the void. These are texts that work on the beginning but not on the origin.[9]

We can use this as a description of Rhys's novel. While allowing the confrontation of the mother-text and the father-text, Rhys valorizes the bastard text, the text that proceeds "as if it had never known its father." This kind of text writes itself in the space of the mother-text, which, as Julia Kristeva points out, Plato in the *Timeus* 52 recognized as "unnameable": "'Indefinitely a place . . . perceptible . . . by means of a sort of bastard reasoning; . . . it is precisely that which makes us dream when we perceive it."[10]

"Rochester's" narrative clearly goes for the "end," which is unsatis-factory even for him, the narrator. The man sees "nothing" finally, in contrast to his wife, who sees her entire life, and herself, in the look-ing-glass of another woman. "Rochester" is offered, and refuses, the same kind of looking-glass. His own reading, of self and others, moti-vates his attempt and structures, almost literally dictates, his narrative progress. It displays for us how a man answers the question "Who is there when a man says 'I am,'" just as the feminine text answers the woman's question in its narrative processes.

The further question, however—one that, as Kamuf observes, Freud implicitly posed—is also one that "Rochester" cannot bring himself finally to ask of his text. His narrative senses the question, draws near, retreats, retrenches, and then "goes mad." It is his re-fusal "to think the absence, at the origin, of an origin," the question that is insured by the continuing presence of the mother-text in his own strategies of approach and avoidance, that might have answered his more basic question: Who is here, in this narrative, trying to say "I am"? The answer might have been "his mother's child."

Caught between the two seemingly opposed systems of identifica-tion, "Rochester" cannot fully take the "momentous step," but nei-ther can he endure the bastardization that choosing the·mother-text would imply. He remains used by both mother- and father-texts. Rhys used him as his text by writing him *into* her woman's dream-text, catching him in the net of the mother-text as his own narrative reveals him to be. In the story that Rhys's novel tells, he is used by the father-text, whose dupe he remains at the expense of any achieved sense of self. The counter-balance of the two in his narra-tion is what shapes the narrative itself. Rochester's narrative is thor-oughly haunted by the quest for origins; he is afraid of writing his narrative "as if it had never known its father," which is to say, finally, even if in a kind of shorthand, "like a woman."[11]

THE NAMELESS MAN who begins the narration of Part Two of *Wide Sargasso Sea* may be, as one commentator describes him, the "most complex and fully drawn male she [Rhys] has ever accom-plished."[12] Another writes, he is "more than a type; he is as complex as Antoinette, treated with understanding Rhys earlier extended only to female characters."[13] However, as Rhys presents "Rochester" initially, we can know him only in his reading of himself and others, *as* his text and in his manner of narration. Commentators often refer to "Rochester" familiarly and, as if to suggest his parity with Antoinette, as "Edward." In *Wide Sargasso Sea*, however, even in Grace Poole's introduction to Part Three (when, if we have read *Jane Eyre*, we know with a certainty that we are "in" Brontë's novel and that the two novels meet here), "he" is not named. He remains an individual representative of the generic: "*'They knew that he was in Jamaica when his father and his brother died,' Grace Poole said*" (p. 145).

Rhys names Grace Poole; Grace Poole names Mrs. Eff and Leah; and Antoinette has already been named (indeed, her name is a major textual problematic) in an extensive departure from the texts of Brontë and "Rochester." The women are named by one another. Neither Rhys nor Grace Poole (nor even "Mrs. Eff," who defends him) names the man, and Grace Poole places him in relation to an equally unspecified father and brother. Early in his own narrative he identifies himself as "a younger son" (p. 59). In both instances he is identified by the circumstances of the relationship with the father under the laws of patrimony: he is a younger son who becomes heir to his father. His text remains nameless and not of his own making, as his narration stresses repeatedly. The only thing worse than being "a younger son" is to be a bastard, and that designation also threatens, at least figuratively.

Clearly, the man is uncertain enough of himself to take careful steps in the beginning of his narrative. He knows he is in alien territory. Concerned to locate himself as quickly as possible in his own personal topography of reaction and response, he juggles his acquired sense of who he is, or who he ought to be, with his feeling of insecurity as to who, in fact, he is. In the beginning of the narrative the man's only initial designation of himself is "myself." In the progress of a narrative that will reveal him, it is not surprising that he places himself in relation to two women—in contrast to Grace Poole's description, which puts him in relation to two men. His own narrative, in a time prior to the events of Brontë's novel, initially places him in relation to the two women, who, in the racially ambiguous context in which he finds himself, figuratively become halves of the same woman: Amélie and Antoinette. If "Rochester" has any identification by name here, it is as Antoinette's husband, or at least as the man whose "wife" is Antoinette: "There we were," he says in the third line of the beginning of the narrative, "myself, my wife Antoinette, and a little half-caste servant who was called Amélie" (p. 55). He possesses something, but it does not give him security or confidence.

After placing himself in relation to the two women, the three of them "sheltering from the heavy rain under a large mango tree," he neatly isolates them from "two porters and a boy," male servants who, along with the luggage, are "under a neighbouring tree" (p. 55). The first person who *speaks* in the frame of this opening is "the girl Amélie," who says, "I hope you will be very happy, sir, in your sweet honeymoon house." "She was," the man tells us, "laughing at me I could see. A lovely little creature but sly, spiteful, malignant perhaps, like much else in this place" (p. 55).

Already we are given the configuration of his response to the place. Within this configuration, we can discern muted and dominant texts, although which is which at this point in the novel is moot. Amélie, like Tia, is an alter ego for Antoinette; she is the almost hidden subtext of Antoinette's narrative. Antoinette does not mention Amélie by name in her own narrative. Only in her climactic, drunken dialogue with her husband—one he reports—does she acknowledge Amélie. Earlier the two women have an altercation in which Amélie's words and actions recall Tia's childhood antagonism (pp. 83, 122); even then Antoinette does not call Amélie by name. Christophine takes up Antoinette's case against "the good-for-nothing" girl; she does not call her by name, either, in her dialogue with Rochester. "Like goes to like," she says to Rochester, tripling the distorting mirror-image of the three of them (p. 123). She does use her name once in direct address and in defense of Antoinette, and the name is isolated: "Amélie" (p. 84). But "Rochester" recognizes her as Antoinette's double in terms of his own text, as does Rhys. In "Rochester's" narrative, Amélie knows from the beginning what's happening; her expression as the man describes it is "so full of delighted malice, so intelligent, above all so intimate that I felt ashamed and looked away" (p. 57). Already she has taken on the "knowledge" that he fears in Antoinette as their story proceeds, and an "intimacy" he will exploit with both women in different ways. Only one of them can "escape" him within the context(s) of the novel's story: the half-caste Amélie, who is not bound by prior texts—by Brontë's actual text or by the cultural text or milieu which has matched the white Englishman and Antoinette, the white Creole woman.

The man then is embarked on his narrative, and Rhys on the weaving of the weft of the woman's text through the warp of the man's. His narrative is a process of identification that demonstrates an acute concern for place—his place, where he is, how or why he got there, and how to maintain himself. A notation of whom he notices (pp. 55–58) and how and in what order he describes them is illuminating. It provides a chart, the topography of responses that he registers to place himself. Seemingly imperative components of this construct are located not in the physical landscape itself, but in the people he sees, especially as he describes them in relation to their sex or gender, their responses to him, and finally by their apparent cultural loyalty as it is signaled by the language they use. Women and male children (there are no female children here) are described in their response to him almost exclusively in their manner of looking at him; men are described by what they say and how they say it. The whole is, of course, suffused by his sense of their racial difference from him. But the topography is indeed more "intimate" than that implied in a seemingly reflexive and generalized response to race and gender, as Amélie discerns. The charting is personal, "intimate" in the extreme, and prefaces his attempt at the maintenance—even if unsuccessful—of a constitution of "self" as he understands it.

"How old was I when I learned to hide what I felt?" he asks himself later in the narrative. "A very small boy," he answers. "Six, five, even earlier. It was necessary, I was told, and that view I have always accepted" (p. 85). After placing himself in relation to the two women, the black male servants isolated from them, the first people he sees in the bleak seaside village (threateningly called Massacre) are three male children. He fixes his attention on one: "three little boys came to stare at us. The smallest wore nothing but a religious medal round his neck and the brim of a large fisherman's hat. When I smiled at him, he began to cry. A woman called from one of the huts and he ran away, still howling" (p. 56). The "smallest" boy presents the emblems of the aspirant, the protected, and the unformed. No wonder the man, who finds himself persistently (though bitterly) supplicant to the text of his father, tries to signal his recognition of the child. The other two little boys are noted, and two more women appear, serially, at their doors.

Antoinette recognizes the third woman who appears. Attentive to Antoinette's recognition of the woman, Carolina, "Caro," the man reconsiders his wife's racial background, her "long, sad, dark, alien eyes." "Creole of pure descent she may be," he observes, "but they are not English or European either." In the first paragraph of her narrative Antoinette already placed herself for us in this racial frame-work, but the lines were more clearly, knowledgeably, and poignantly drawn because she speaks from within the experience. The man's description of Antoinette's conversation with Caro further empha-sizes his identification of Antoinette with the black and colored is-landers: "The two women stood in the doorway of the hut gesticulat-ing, talking not English but the debased French patois they use in this island" (pp. 56–57). He invokes then his father's name and the place of his own origin, thinking "about the letter which should have been written to England a week ago. Dear Father. . . ." He does not continue; the fragment seems a form of prayer. ✔

Turning from the women, the man "went to talk to the porters," placing himself in relation to the men. "The first man," who, like Rochester, "was not a native of the island," remarks conversationally, "This a very wild place—not civilized." "Why you come here?" he asks (p. 57). We have moved away from the women, who speak a debased language, to the men, who speak English with him. We have also moved from the male children, especially the smallest of them, to a young man with a "magnificent body and a foolish conceited face," the "Young Bull" who marks his likeness with the Englishman; finally to an old man, Emile, who does not know his own age, a proof of how "uncivilized" the islanders are.

"Ask him how old he is," the Young Bull suggests, knowing the joke. "Fourteen? Yes, I have fourteen years master," Emile answers. "Impossible," the Englishman says. "Fifty-six years perhaps," Emile offers. "He seemed anxious to please," Rochester notes. The Young Bull interjects his reiteration that "these people are not civilized." But Emile asserts his own source of authority: he "muttered, 'My mother she know, but she dead'" (p. 58).

Rochester's narrative here invokes and dismisses the mother-text.

His own mother is not mentioned in his account in Rhys's novel, in Brontë's account of him, or in his account of himself to Jane when he is describing his marriage to "Bertha." Emile, native to Antoinette's island, seems to adhere to the mother-text in his brief account of himself. He cannot make a tabulated response to Rochester's question, but he knows where the answer might accurately be found, echoing Rhys's story of the little girl in catechism class who, in response to the question "Who made you?," steadfastly answered "My mother."

Unerring in his topography of self, the man then notices "the women," who were "looking at us but without smiling" (p. 58). "Some of the men were going to their boats," and when "Emile shouted, two of them came towards him. He sang in a deep voice" and "they answered," presumably in the same "debased patois" that the women use. By contrast, the "Young Bull," Rochester notes, "sang to himself in English," glancing up at Rochester "sideways" and "boastfully."

When Antoinette emerges from Caro's hut, she takes off her shoes and "balanced her small basket on her head and swung away as easily as the porters," breaking the isolation from them which Rochester earlier established. She allies herself with the black men as well as with the women, especially with Emile, who, after muttering "My mother she know," "produced a blue rag which he twisted into a pad and put on his head."

The last details of the map the man draws for us are introduced by a recollection of the night before, a recollection precipitated by his hearing "a cock [that] crowed loudly." This motif, the betrayal sign in Christian mythology, reappears as the man's narrative proceeds and outlines its own kind of internecine betrayal. He recalls that he "lay awake listening to cocks crowing all night." When he arose early, he saw "the women with trays [. . .] on their heads going to the kitchen" and he heard the women in the streets selling "small hot loaves" and "sweets."

The introductory section of the man's narrative ends with the sight and sound of women speaking the "debased patois" the man has intimated he finds objectionable because it is not his own. The concluding words of the account, however, belie the alliances and identifications he has attempted. Against a background of the sight and sound of the island's women, a people and a language he does not *claim* as his own, he nevertheless describes himself finally in this way: "In the street another [woman] called *Bon sirop, Bon sirop,* and I felt peaceful."

In the next set passage of his narrative (pp. 58–64), the road turns upward into the mountains. The place seems to the man "not only wild but menacing" (p. 58), and his wife "a stranger" (p. 59). He does not even call her his wife: "the woman is a stranger," whose "pleading expression" annoys him. He now addresses his father bitterly; he continues his prayer, in a letter that he composes as he rides after the woman. Bitter, weary in its expression of what is obviously a long battle with himself, and poignant in its specificity, the spoken letter is also a directly antagonistic response toward himself in relation to his father. He turns that antagonism against Antoinette, reviling himself in her, in the pleading expression he thinks he sees in her face. He turns the mirror-image there against her and speaks through her to his father, about himself. "I have not bought her, she has bought me, or so she thinks," he prefaces the spoken letter:

> . . . Dear Father. The thirty thousand pounds have been paid to me without question or condition [This is the exact amount given in Rochester's narrative in *Jane Eyre*]. No provision made for her (that must be seen to). I have a modest competence now. I will never be a disgrace to you or to my dear brother the son you love. No begging letters, no mean requests. None of the furtive shabby manoeuvres of a younger son. (p. 59)

At Granbois he meets Christophine, who was, Antoinette tells him, "my da, my nurse long ago" (p. 61). He "looked at her sharply but she seemed insignificant"; "she looked at me," he says, "steadily, not with approval, I thought. We stared at each other for quite a minute. I looked away first and she smiled to herself." Despite his claim that she looks "insignificant," Rochester apparently cannot help asking Antoinette, "That old woman who was your nurse? Are you afraid of her?" "If she were taller," he says, "one of these strapping women dressed up to the nines, I might be afraid of her," he admits. The childishness of this confession is appealing, and we understand that he is "afraid of her." In drawing his narrative into the dream-text, we can note that among these "strapping women" are "Bertha" and Jane Eyre's erstwhile rival, Blanche Ingram, as Brontë's Rochester describes them: "I found her ["Bertha"] a fine woman, in the style of

Blanche Ingram; tall, dark, and majestic. . . . [Her family] showed her to me in parties, splendidly dressed" (*Jane Eyre*, p. 268). The "little boy" is made plain, as naked here as the "smallest" boy in whom Rochester saw himself earlier, and who reacted with fear against him. In reply to Rochester's question, Antoinette laughs and says, "That door leads into your dressing-room." Rochester's only response is that "I shut it gently after me" (p. 62). Do we read him here as a small boy being sent to his room, and gratefully?

Here, in the dressing-room that he recognizes as "a refuge," he finds the book *The Life and Letters of* . . . that is his emblem. Immediately, reflexively, he begins the first letter to his father that is actually written. Now, as at the last, he speaks a letter that he does not write, or send, before he writes the formal letter that is intended to speak for him. He never finds the voice he might use to speak in direct response to others, especially in direct response to his father. He can only speak, finally, and find a voice, in writing and in the "Letter of the Law."

He concludes the postscript to the letter, "I feel better already and my next letter will be longer and more explicit." The "small" boy has located himself again in reference to the father; in doing so, he "feels better." However, the last brief paragraph of the section concludes: "As for my confused impressions they will never be written. There are blanks in my mind that cannot be filled up" (p. 64). His use of the passive voice here suggests that he knows he cannot find his voice, not even in writing. And, in his passivity, he also knows that he lacks the means even to place himself finally where he might not have to be "written," which is to say, in relation to the mother-text where a single voice, or author, does not confer authority. He cannot bastard-ize himself; he cannot give himself up to the mother-text, and he mourns its loss. He is still "haunted" by the quest for origins. He has appealed to the father-text at the writing-desk in his "refuge" in the only way he knows how, and it is not enough; he remains poised between the mother-text and the father. It is Rhys who finally "writes" him into her woman's text, using the inhibitions of his own manner of narration to do so.

In light of my earlier observation that Rochester's narrative is presented chronologically and linearly as a representative masculine narrative, I must comment on the seemingly minor displacement of chronological sequence represented by the first three sections of the narrative, the first two of which I have just described. This displacement reveals much of Rochester's character, in the colloquial as well as in the literary sense. The purpose of this displacement I have already intimated: he needs to establish a personal topography to place himself in a new context, and, in particular, to take a reading, as it were, of himself in the balance between mother- and father-texts. His manner of transition to the third section of the narrative, the logical beginning of his story in relationship to Antoinette, supports the reading of insecurity manifested in the topography of the first-placed narrative section ("I am not myself yet," the man observes defensively [p. 57]), and introduces his more specific need for refuge and re-identification with his father in the second. He is "afraid" of the women who know something he cannot admit to himself, that he cannot know as long as he places himself within the "view" that he "has always accepted." His responses and reactions to the women of the novel early in the narrative represent the approach-avoidance pattern in relation to the mother-text I have already suggested. Rochester's own ontological uneasiness, the dis-ease he manifests in his tightrope walking in this place where as old Emile says, "My mother she know, but she dead," might be summed up in that same phrase, although with a different emphasis.

The mother-text is dead for him; he long ago gave it up, in allegiance to his father, for a placing of himself in the text of his father. He is still "haunted" by it, however, and since he cannot think the "absence, at the origin, of an origin" that would allow him to acknowledge a bond with the mother as well as with the father, he tries repeatedly to deny the mother-text and return, absolutely, to the father, to the single text that offers the seeming certainty of "an origin." Such a view, however, is at best tautological, as Peggy Kamuf's analysis points out. Looked at in this way, it is logical that what Rochester discerns, at the first and at the last, is "nothing." This is the word, and the concept, crucial to Rochester's text, to its development and to its shaping as he presents it to himself.

Repetition of the word "nothing" and the patterning that turns on it is certainly the core, the literal ending and the figurative beginning of the narrative. This patterning at the heart of the narrative is responsible for the restructured chronology that is Rochester's only departure from a strictly chronological linear representation. The third section of the narrative (pp. 64–66) returns us to the chronological beginning, moving from the description of the "confused impressions" that cannot be written, the "blanks" in his mind that cannot be "filled up," to an explicit statement that molds his response.

Rochester's description of his sojourn on the island begins with the word "it"—the indefinite and impersonal pronoun that takes the entire context of the place and rapidly moves to "the girl," Antoinette, by way of the word "nothing": "It was all very brightly coloured, very strange, but it meant nothing to me. Nor did she, the girl I was to marry" (p. 64). Like Rhys's response to the father-book when she was a child, "it meant nothing to me," he says. The mother-book, of course, did make sense to Rhys, and to Antoinette; "it meant" something to her, it was something that could be used. The whole book, we can remember, is made up of both books, and of our recognition that there is never only one book, one text. Rochester's remarks demonstrate his lack of this knowledge and his rejection of the mother-book—the "it," the island and what it represents, which he finally represents in *his* text by Antoinette herself. The mother-text, which is "brightly coloured" and "very strange."

Throughout his narrative, despite Antoinette's attempts to teach him about her "book" and about the mother-text represented by the island with its heightened colors, even the fire-red signature of herself as we know it from her own narrative (including the sexuality that he finds repugnant precisely to the extent that he is drawn to it), Rochester attempts to return to the single text, the father-text, with its concomitant lack. He attempts, finally, to displace the mother-text represented by Antoinette into the "madness" that proves his "sanity."

In his description of meeting and marrying the girl his father had "bought" for him, or, as he corrects himself, who "bought" him (for it is her money, not his father's, that is to provide for him), he tells us, "I played the part I was expected to play." His "performance," he surmises, was "faultless" (p. 64). Rochester makes himself a marionette, unlike Antoinette, who at first refuses to "go through with it," as her stepbrother puts it (p. 65).

In Rochester's description of his persuasion of Antoinette, two moments are especially important. The first is Antoinette's initial response to Rochester's questioning of her to ascertain why she doesn't want to marry him. "What have I done?" he asks. "She said nothing," he reports. He speaks more plainly: "You don't wish to marry me?"

"No," she answers, but "in a very low voice." We are given a recapitulation of the muted—more, the silenced—half of the dialogue to which Rhys gave voice in the "unspoken" portions of the "fundamental conversation" in *Voyage in the Dark*. Her final reply to his last question concerning whether or not he can tell her stepbrother Richard that they are proceeding with the wedding returns her to silence, to the gesture of the muted text: "She did not answer me. Only nodded" (p. 66).

We have moved in these two pages from what, to Rochester, "means nothing" to Antoinette's acquiescence to his proposed desires. He has transferred what means nothing to him, what he prefers to see as "nothing," to the girl's demonstrated capitulation: her silent speech. Antoinette is placed now, by him, by Rhys, in the immobility of the living doll that Rochester thinks he has made of "Bertha" at the last. This interchange represents Antoinette's only attempt to break out of Brontë's text; it is a gesture that all the more firmly places her in the nineteenth-century context of Brontë's novel, out of which Rhys finally delivers her.

The directly chronological narration of events is now under way. In the next section (pp. 66–70), the conversation between the two of them establishes Antoinette's island as a "dream" for Rochester and his England as a "dream" for her (p. 67). In this section, too, the mother-text is introduced and again rejected. Antoinette tells him, in an overtly sexual context, a story of her sleeping in the moonlight "too long," as Christophine told her (p. 69). "Do you think that too," she said, "that I have slept too long in the moonlight?" (p. 70). This marks a patent interweaving of Antoinette's dream-text and Jane Eyre's dreams and childhood experience with their central image of the mother, the Moon, into the dialogue between the man and the woman. Here Rochester admits the mother-text—in relation to Antoinette, if not in relation to himself—and accedes to the "mother's" place. He will not do so again:

> Her mouth was set in a fixed smile but her eyes were so withdrawn and lonely that I put my arms round her, rocked her like a child and sang to her. An old song I thought I had forgotten:
>
> > "Hail to the queen of the silent night,
> > Shine bright, shine bright Robin as you die."

"She listened, then sang with me," and they repeat the last line of the couplet together (p. 70). The Elizabethan pun on "dying" is not lost here, even if (or perhaps especially) in its connection with the mother-text. They drink to their "happiness, to our love and the day without end which would be tomorrow." As he so often does, however, Rochester abruptly, even violently, undercuts the movement of the narrative passage he has just written. In this case the undercutting is especially brutal, even in its syntax: "I was young then. A short youth mine was" (p. 70). We know that the Rochester of *Jane Eyre* is about to develop in this young man; we know, even if we don't know *Jane Eyre*, that this true and ringing note sets the tone for the story and for the narrative already accomplished in the man's mind when he begins: "So it was all over[. . . .] Everything finished[. . . .]" (p. 55).

Rochester awakens the next morning to find a woman watching over him. His reaction, however, is quite different from that of the woman dreamer when she wakes: "I woke [. . .] feeling uneasy as though someone were watching me" (p. 70). The watcher, the caretaker whom he will not admit, is of course Antoinette, who, he observes, "must have been awake for some time."

As the narrative proceeds, the threads of the tapestry are drawn together ever more tightly, with each narrative section offering its precise detail for the *progression d'effet* that Ford Madox Ford emphasized was so much a part of Rhys's craft. As the effect and the pattern of the weave intensify—both vertically and horizontally—Rochester reveals himself more, discovering, as we do, "who he is," whether he likes it or not. Questions of trust and betrayal have begun to intermingle with the others: in Rochester's early dishonest presentation of himself to persuade Antoinette to marry him (p. 66) and in his later notation to himself, "She trusted them and I did not. But I could hardly say so. Not yet" (p. 75).

Another related thread is introduced into the narrative as his text attempts to shape itself: Rochester's hope that he can discover the "secret" of the "place," with its "alien, disturbing, secret loveliness." "I'd find myself thinking," he says, "what I see is nothing—I want what it *hides*—that is not nothing" (p. 73). He has begun his journey into the delusion that he can make "something" out of "nothing." The secret is offered by the mother-text, which he has already rejected, and his text is on the way to betraying itself.

Rochester betrays himself and Antoinette in describing his sexual passion for her, demonstrating his contempt for himself through her denigration. The word, the unlucky but compulsively chosen verbal talisman for this betrayal is, of course, "nothing": "'You are safe,' I'd say. She'd like that—to be told 'You are safe.' Or I'd touch her face gently and touch tears. Tears—nothing! Words—less than nothing. As for the happiness I gave her, that was worse than nothing. [. . .] she was a stranger to me, a stranger who did not think or feel as I did" (p. 78). In his sweeping negation he observes, "Nothing that I told her influenced her at all" (p. 78). Palpably, he is unable to influence even himself, especially himself, at least not with the spoken word. The written word is another matter. After the betrayal of himself, of Antoinette, of the act of sex itself as he describes it, Rochester listens to the rain. Unlike the women who dream, he learns nothing, he finds nothing in his kind of sleep: "Drown me in sleep," he says. "And soon." He knows there is nothing to which he can wake (p. 79). Rochester's response to his dilemma begins to take its final shape as a result of "words," which, in contemptuous familiarity, he can call "less than nothing." These words, however, are between man and man and they are written down. With the receipt of the letter from Daniel Cosway, Rochester's narrative begins to assume a textual shape that he can recognize, a shape in which he can locate himself, as he tried earlier and more tentatively to do. Eagerly he embraces the father-text in the form of the "Letter of the Law" as it is recalled to him by another man, a colored man who also identifies himself in relation to the white father-text.

IN CONTRAST TO Rochester, Antoinette conspicuously lacks a father in the time of her narrative: "My father, visitors, horses, feeling safe in bed—all belonged to the past" (p. 15); "They were all the people in my life—my mother and Pierre, Christophine, Godfrey, and Sass who had left us" (p. 19); as for the stepfather, as Rochester accurately observes, "she always called [him] Mr Mason" (p. 75). This lack seems to concern her little in her own narration, except for the protection her father's presence might have afforded her and her mother. In the context of Rochester's narration, Antoinette speaks specifically of this protection, and of more compelling concerns: "If my father, my real father, was alive you wouldn't come back here in a hurry after he'd finished with you. If he was alive.

[. . .] I loved this place and you have made it into a place I hate" (p. 121).

As her signature, "Antoinette Mason, née Cosway, Mount Calvary Convent, Spanish Town, Jamaica, 1839," suggests, Antoinette places herself—who she is, where she is—with the formality of the names of the two men. But place is preeminent in her conception of herself, and time is not excluded, either; all are inseparable from her signature, the naming of herself. The color in which she writes her signature ("fire-red") oversees and blends them all. Just as she accepts her colored "cousins," also children of her father, so she accepts her father as part of the context of her recognition of herself; he is party to the illegitimate mixing that, rather than frightening her, helps her to place herself. The father is one aspect of her identification; she is not, like Rochester, locked into recognition of a single, legitimate text of self. Granbois, her property and the place she loves, came to her from her mother; it had belonged to her mother, not her father. Rochester, tabulator of such accounts, notes this for us.

Rochester is compelled to seek means to reinforce his own sense of legitimacy, to prevent his text as "a younger son" from tipping over into that mother-space where it would be not only tenuous but bastardized. His own sense of urgency is answered by the "bulky envelope addressed in careful copperplate" that is delivered to him the morning after he has asked to be "drown[ed] . . . in sleep." " '*By hand. Urgent*' was written in the corner" of the envelope. Rochester succumbs gladly, although bitterly, to Daniel Cosway's impugning of his wife's character and background; after reading the letter he remarks, "I felt no surprise. It was as if I'd expected it, been waiting for it" (p. 82). Rochester's dependency on the idea of formality, the protocol of law, is exacerbated by his recognition of the way it works around him in this colonial society (doubly colonized: by the French—the Creoles—then by the English), thrown into relief by the "strangeness" of the place, the working out of such laws against a lush, alien background. He readily grasps at and believes the evidence of a breach of this protocol of law and custom, as he understands it, when such evidence is presented by his doubles, his mentors and shadows: authorities, officials, other men of some honor or standing, even Richard Mason, "Richard the fool," who, he suspects, "knows something he doesn't; even, or especially, Daniel Cosway; even, finally, the unnamed author of *The Glittering Coronet of the Isles*. His father overshadows all of these. "Unforeseen circumstances," Rochester writes in his last letter to him, "at least unforeseen by me, have forced me to make this decision. I am certain that you know or can guess what has happened" (p. 133).

Daniel Cosway's letter is extremely effective rhetorically; he knows his reader, the Englishman. He appeals to that structure of seeming indifference in which Rochester can believe: "God," and the "truth" of propriety represented by the rigors of reading and writing, and the laws, written and unwritten, of the society to which they both owe whatever position they have, Daniel as the bastard son of a white landowner (Antoinette's father, he claims) and Rochester as the second son who has a "modest competence now," his father having "sold" him, having sold his "soul" by arranging for Antoinette to "buy him."

In describing himself, however, Daniel makes an even stronger emotional appeal. In a conflation and parody of Rochester's own fears about himself, Daniel writes, "of all his illegitimates I am the most unfortunate and poverty stricken. [. . .]" He continues, "My momma die when I was quite small and my godmother take care of me. The old miser hand out some money for that though he don't like me. No, that old devil don't like me at all, and when I grow older I see it and I think, Let him wait my day will come" (p. 80). Daniel has, in effect, written the letter that Rochester could only think to himself. Daniel may claim to be Antoinette's brother; he here claims Rochester as his double, although he cannot know that. He does know the kind of man to whom he speaks, however, especially in writing.

The laboriously detailed letter begins: "Dear Sir. I take up my pen after long thought and meditation but in the end the truth is better than a lie." Daniel's letter is given in full (pp. 79–82); as it reaches its peroration, Daniel again reminds Rochester that he is "telling the truth." In effect, he is giving Rochester his ultimate credentials:

> Sir ask yourself how I can make up this story and for what
> reason. When I leave Jamaica I can read write and cypher a lit-
> tle. The good man in Barbados teach me more, he give me
> books, he tell me read the Bible every day and I pick up knowl-
> edge without effort. He is surprise how quick I am. Still I re-

main an ignorant man and I do not make up this story. I cannot. It is true.

I sit at my window and the words fly past me like birds—with God's help I catch some. (p. 81)

The "pen" that Daniel "takes up" and dutifully "lay[s] down" with one last request, is not his, he implies. (Just as Anna Morgan in *Voyage in the Dark* recognizes when she writes her last letter to Walter Jeffries.) Like Rochester, he cannot "make up" a text of his own. It is "with God's help" that he will try to "catch" some of the "words [that] fly past him like birds." He does not "make up this story. It is true." Poor instrument that he is, Daniel reminds Rochester forcefully that to speak the truth is to adhere to the given text. His own evident investment in the white father-text is itself a kind of reassurance to which Rochester can respond and condescend.

In a kind of postscript, however, Daniel insinuates the ideas that keep Rochester consciously bound for a time to his need to continue the search for his own "truth," for the "secret" whose text he is still trying to thrust from him. "Ask the girl Amélie where I live," Daniel writes. "She knows, and she knows me. She belongs to this island" (p. 82). Shortly after receiving this letter, Rochester goes on his search for truth into the forest, where he becomes "lost." The journey is foreshadowed by Amélie's remark, soon after he has "folded the letter carefully" and put it in his pocket, that "he look like he see zombi" (p. 83).

After this journey, and while his wife is still on her journey to Christophine to ask for her help, Rochester receives the second letter from Daniel. It is an angry complaint because the first letter has not been answered. This letter applies the pressure that Antoinette and other Rhys heroines know so well, the pressure of what "everyone says." Daniel's original pose of one reading-and-writing man to another is gone: "Why don't you answer? You don't believe me? Then ask someone else—everybody in Spanish Town know. Why you think they bring you to this place? You want me to come to your house and bawl out your business before everybody? You come to me or I come—" (p. 98). "At this point I stopped reading," Rochester informs us. He consults Amélie, as Daniel originally suggested he do, to verify what Daniel intimates is common knowledge. Daniel wants money if he is to keep his mouth shut. After this incident Rochester has the only conversation with Antoinette in which she attempts to explain what "they say." Rochester asks, "Is there another side?" and she answers, "There is always the other side, always" (p. 106).

↵"The other side" in their conversation is specifically about the literal "mother-text" of the novel, the story of Antoinette's mother as she tries to tell it, in contradiction to the story elaborated upon by Daniel Cosway in Rochester's visit to him (pp. 100–104). In their discussion Antoinette corrects Daniel's name, among other things: "He has no right to that name [Daniel Cosway]. His real name, if he has one, is Daniel Boyd" (p. 106). When Rochester does not want to talk about the "truth" as Antoinette might tell it to him, she says, "fiercely," "You have no right [. . .] You have no right to ask questions about my mother and then refuse to listen to my answer." "Of course I will listen," he replies, "of course we can talk now, if that's what you wish." To himself he says, "But the feeling of something unknown and hostile was very strong." Aloud he says, "I feel very much a stranger here[. . . .] I feel that this place is my enemy and on your side" (p. 107). Antoinette's answer is a description of the quality of the mother-text, the "other side" of the father-text, the two together making up "God, this strange thing or person"—the whole text, the context, within which we can build our lives: "'You are quite mistaken,' she said. 'It is not for you and not for me. It has nothing to do with either of us. That is why you are afraid of it, because it is something else. I found that out long ago when I was a child. I loved it because I had nothing else to love, but it is as indifferent as this God you call on so often'" (p. 107). The last conscious possibility for a capitulation to a text of self that would include the mother-text is recorded in Rochester's narration of the final moments he recalls when he goes to bed with Antoinette, after she has given him the obeah potion that Christophine, against her better judgment, gave Antoinette: "She need not have done what she did to me," he says. "I will always swear that, she need not have done it" (p. 113). ↵

At first and at last, Rochester speaks or imagines a letter he might write to his father but does not. He speaks one letter, then writes another, the formal letter that he sends to his father. After the first such letter(s), he wonders—in the innocence of his text and in the irony of Rhys's—"how they got their letters posted" (p. 64). As Rochester's narrative continues, it is clear that he has learned precisely how they do so. The letters in the text of his narrative are symbolically as well as structurally and thematically important: they are given in full, and Rochester's first act upon gaining the "refuge" of his dressing-room with its "small writing-desk" is to complete the formal act of letter-writing.

As a kind of postscript to the initial letter-writing episode, Rochester makes the declaration that constitutes a description of the remainder of his narrative: "As for my confused impressions they will never be written." What is left out of the letters, what Rochester cannot write, or collaborate in allowing to be written, especially to his father, are those "confused impressions," the "blanks" in his mind that cannot be filled up. The rest of his narration is a demonstration of all those impressions that he does not, cannot, write to his father. Rochester's letter-writing, both literal and imagined, is a way of keeping in mind his own place of certifying it and himself, just as Anna Morgan's unwritten letters to Walter Jeffries in *Voyage in the Dark* allowed her to keep intact an idea of the context in which she wanted to place herself.

While Antoinette is gone on her second journey to Christophine's, where Christophine helps her "sleep," Rochester writes on the third day "a cautious letter to Mr Fraser," the retired magistrate in Spanish Town. He pretends to be interested in writing a book on obeah in order to elicit information on Christophine (p. 117). "This letter was sent down by the twice weekly messenger and he must have answered at once for I had his reply in a few days," Rochester tells us, demonstrating that familiarity with "how they got their letters posted" that is essential to the construct he is attempting to put in place. Christophine's "case" is one that Fraser had insisted on telling Rochester about "at length" during the latter's original stay with the Frasers before his marriage, as Rochester reported to his father in his first letter to him. Fraser tells Rochester, "I had often thought of your wife and yourself. And was on the point of writing to you. Indeed I have not forgotten the case. The woman in question was called Josephine or Christophine Dubois, some such name." (Like the men in *Voyage in the Dark* and like Rochester in this novel, Fraser cannot keep "their" names straight—they might as well remain nameless.) Fraser "did not like the look of her at all, and consider[s] her a most dangerous person." Fraser continues the chain of letters that Rochester has begun, a chain that, presumably, his father actually began. "I have," he assures Rochester, "written very discreetly to Hill, the white in-spector of police in your town. If she lives near you and gets up to any of her nonsense let him know at once. He'll send a couple of policemen up to your place and she won't get off lightly this time. I'll make sure of that" (p. 118). "So much for you, Josephine or Chris-tophine, [Rochester] thought. So much for you, Pheena" (p. 118). "Pheena" is, as we know, Antoinette's childhood name for Chris-tophine.

After Antoinette and Christophine's return, the dialogue between Christophine and Rochester takes place. Rochester finally plays his trump card in showing Christophine the letter from Fraser. He threatens her with the police, after she has told him the truth as she sees it, in her "judge's voice." When she "drew herself up" and said, "Who you to tell me to go? This house belong to Miss Antoinette's mother, now it belong to her. Who you tell me to go?" Rochester assures her that the house is his and that he will have the men put her off. Christophine replies, "They not damn fool like you to put their hand on me." When he threatens her with the police, she dis-dains them as well. It is then that Rochester tells her that he wrote to Fraser: "I wrote to him about you. Would you like to hear what he answered?" He reads "the end of Fraser's letter" aloud: "*I have written very discreetly to Hill*[. . . .]" (pp. 131–32).

When, "against his will," Rochester asks Christophine if she wants to say good-bye to Antoinette, Christophine says, "I don't wake her up to no misery. I leave that to you." "You can write to her," Rochester replies "stiffly." We know Christophine's reply: "Read and write I don't know. Other things I know" (p. 133). Christophine does not participate in that destructive possibility.

Having taken the "momentous step" represented by the "turning from the mother to the father," the "triumph of patriarchy over ma-triarchy,"[14] Rochester realizes the full significance of what he has accomplished. He feels he is no longer drugged by the pull of the mother-text toward "that which makes us dream when we perceive it," as Plato describes it.

> All wish to sleep had left me. I walked up and down the room and felt the blood tingle in my finger-tips. It ran up my arms and reached my heart, which began to beat very fast. I spoke aloud as I walked. I spoke the letter I meant to write.

"I know now that you planned this because you wanted to be rid of me. You had no love at all for me. Nor had my brother. Your plan succeeded because I was young, conceited, foolish, trusting [all adjectives—except for the first—that he has applied to others, practicing, as it were, minimal and consistent displacements before taking on his final task: Antoinette]. Above all because I was young. You were able to do this to me. . . ." (p. 133)

He breaks off, registering the "momentous step": "But I am not young now, I thought, stopped pacing and drank. Indeed this rum is mild as mother's milk or father's blessing" (p. 133). Inadvertently, he has betrayed the flaw in his reckless construct of himself as he now perceives it. He has effectively orphaned himself, or so he thinks, but one cannot orphan oneself, because the texts of self remain, mother- and father-text. One can no more escape them than one can escape oneself, even if they ("it," as Antoinette tries to explain to him) seem "indifferent."

Rochester's pose of maturity, of accession to independence of mother or father, is just as quickly revealed. "I could imagine his expression if I sent that letter and he read it," he says, and immediately he gives us the text of the formal letter that he does write. The paragraph that initiates the text is the bald, the naked, the little "I wrote":

I wrote

Dear Father,
We are leaving this island for Jamaica very shortly. Unforeseen circumstances, at least unforeseen by me, have forced me to make this decision. I am certain that you know or can guess what has happened, and I am certain you will believe that the less you talk to anyone about my affairs, especially my marriage, the better. This is in your interest as well as mine. You will hear from me again. Soon I hope. (p. 133)

In his triumph is his failure. He has written it, again, both in the actual letter to his father and in his narratives; he places the letter he writes side by side with the letter he wants to write but can only speak to himself. He remains within the father-text, his father's marionette, echoing its voice even as he thinks he has found his own.

Within the letter he explains his failure: "Unforeseen circumstances, at least unforeseen by me, have forced me to make this decision." Like Daniel Cosway, he claims not to be responsible for what he does. He continues the chain of letters, still posing as a man who has taken control of his life in the world he has chosen: "Then I wrote to the firm of lawyers I had dealt with in Spanish Town" (p. 134).

The betrayal sign appears. "What's that damn cock crowing about?" Rochester asks the servant Baptiste. The cock's crow signals Rochester's betrayal—of himself, of his wife, Antoinette, as well as the attempted betrayal of the father-text, the one desired betrayal he cannot manage to accomplish.

With his wife asleep in the other room ("*dormi, dormi,*" as he tells Baptiste), using the "debased patois" of the island, the language that is not his, the man makes a drawing, "a child's scribble" as he himself describes it: "I drew a house surrounded by trees. A large house. I divided the third floor into rooms and in one room I drew a standing woman—a child's scribble, a dot for a head, a larger one for the body, a triangle for a skirt, slanting lines for arms and feet. But it was an English house" (pp. 134–35). The "smallest boy" has appeared again, and the specific detail of the "child's scribble" is that of "a standing woman." No matter that she is, in advance, isolated in that third-floor room. She stands, and it is to her that the child returns, even as the man thinks of England and wonders "if I ever should see England again" (p. 135), even while he has already made plans to do so.

In the novel's last section, in Grace Poole's introduction to Antoinette's narrative, Rochester is designated by the pronoun "he." His words are reported as they are written in a letter to Mrs. Eff. She reads them to Grace Poole. They concern money and the disposition of his own responsibility into the hands of the women. Significantly, his written words are shared by the two women disparately. Mrs. Eff reads half a line to Grace; Grace sees the words on the next page that complete the line. In effect, they speak him to one another in the whole of their conversation, and Grace Poole completes the view of him by spying out the rest: " '[. . .] *If Mrs Poole is satisfactory why not give her double, treble the money,' she* [Mrs. Eff] *read, and folded the letter away but not before I had seen the words on the next page, 'but for God's sake let me hear no more of it'* " (p. 145). In her narrative Antoinette calls the England to which Rochester wishes to return "this cardboard house where I walk at night." By means of the "English house," the "cardboard house," which he draws in a "child's scribble," Rochester acknowledges and confines the mother-text. He does so in the only way he knows how, on paper, the pen in his hand no more his own than the pen that Daniel Cosway takes up to write the "truth," and just as dutifully lays down.

The man's narrative construct of himself remains as insubstantial as the paper he writes it on, and the man, the "smallest boy." The "child's scribble" of the mother-text is his last inscription, his only letter to her.

IN THIS SECTION I examine what is perhaps the core of Rhys's presentation of Rochester's narrative, if not the core of the character's attempt to structure that narrative. The metaphor for the masculine text in Rhys's novel—the warp of the woman's dream-text—is a particularly apt tool for describing the point in the novel where the radical intertextuality of Rhys's presentation surfaces the most boldly and prolifically. To adhere closely to the metaphor, we can say that the interweaving of warp and weft has gained such a thickness and a tightness that it is bound by ambivalence; indeed, by multivalence. We are offered so many textual strands thus bound that, in untangling them, we could lose sight of the most expansive, and the most exquisite, patterns of the weave.

The multivalence operative here is actually founded in a basic ambivalence. This ambivalence is the result of the man's text being poised between mother-text and father-text in Rochester's own narrative presentation, while the shared text(s) of the women involved in the weave—Antoinette, Brontë, Amélie, Jane Eyre—pass against the substantive portions of his text and through the interstices of it as the narrative's own ambivalence allows. Christophine remains aloof from this aspect of the patterning, except insofar as she serves Antoinette as continuing caretaker and spokeswoman: she is preeminently Rochester's formal antagonist. As such, Christophine retains a place in the overall pattern conspicuously aside from any ambivalence.

Rhys, too, has stepped back from the text to direct its movement. In doing so she joins her understanding of her specific, personal text as a woman to the novel that gives it form, allowing her to step back into the weave after she has completed the task at hand. Rochester himself locates for us the vantage point from which he perceives the possibility that Rhys exploits. The revealing episode is Rochester's journey into the forest. From the window in his dressing-room, he sees "the path" he decides to follow. It is Rhys's wit perhaps, learned from the "real-life" model of Maudie in *Voyage in the Dark*, to "turn the tables" on a man bent on his own kind of exploitation. The turned tables are the two configurations or "complexes" that have been at issue from the beginning of Rochester's narrative and that are at odds throughout the novel. They are the neurotic, misused, and distorted versions of the mother- and the father-texts: the classic Oedipal complex, unresolved, and its correlative, the Olympia complex, which Rhys allows Antoinette to break out of and in which Rochester tries to confine her.

Rhys's perspicacity allows her to put the man in the place of the woman, exchanging her text of hysteria, of the terror of immobility, for his text of the legitimacy of manhood (the ruse of reason) and the mobility of action. The inverse mirror-imaging involved here is highlighted in several ways. First it cuts across all textual boundaries, beginning with a leap from Brontë's text, suggested by the episode in *Jane Eyre* in which Rochester dresses up as the old gypsy woman who tells Jane Eyre's fortune. He speaks in intimate detail and in disguise in order to reveal himself to her, to speak to her as a man, but not as he might have done in his own shape, or even as his own sex (*Jane Eyre*, pp. 172–80). The discovery is Jane Eyre's recognition of herself in him—not so surprising on reflection, but startling nevertheless in its initial context:

> "I think I rave in a kind of exquisite delirium ["The old woman," Rochester says]. I should wish now to protract this moment *ad infinitum*; but I dare not. So far I have governed myself thoroughly. I have acted as I inwardly swore I would act; but farther might try me beyond my strength. . . ."
>
> Where was I? [Jane responds] Did I wake or sleep? Had I been dreaming? Did I dream still? The old woman's voice had changed: her accent, her gesture, and all were familiar to me as my own face in a glass—as the speech of my own tongue. . . .
> And Mr. Rochester stepped out of his disguise. (*Jane Eyre*, p. 177)

Similarly, Rhys presents Rochester in the part of a heroine from a Gothic novel for the space of time he is lost in the forest, before he is rescued by Baptiste. ("It's a long time I've been looking for you,"

Baptiste says. "Miss Antoinette frightened you come to harm" [p. 88].) Rhys's use of the classic response of effeminacy (or any other parodied inversion) in a man in an extreme and uncomfortable situation is, of course, reminiscent of the way she presents Walter Jeffries in *Voyage in the Dark*, when she shows Jeffries acting like, and talking like, a stereotypical woman. The implications of this conventional inversion are profoundly explanatory of the relationship not only between the woman's and the man's text, but also of the kinds of exploitation that any dominant text or culture is likely to exercise over a muted cultural text. Rochester's dilemma and his mechanisms of response to that dilemma are by no means restricted to an individual neurotic man's confused intentions and desires. They are indicative of the impulses and the neuroses of that culture whose advance has been dependent on the "momentous step" that Freud described. As she does with Dora's dream, Rhys is here undoing several pieces of man's work for her own purposes and to make her own point.

Finally, we note that Rochester's journey, and Antoinette's (the nine-page description of which is given over to her narration), carry us to what is very nearly a midpoint in Rochester's narrative. Their journeys are synchronous; each represents the last, unsuccessful attempt of each to capitulate to the other's dream, the other's text. After that, the collision course is set. The second half of Rochester's narrative, of "his" section of the book, consolidates his position and his displacement of Antoinette into the text of madness, the making of her into the doll. He replaces her in the confinement of the woman's text that he himself attempted to engage. Like the disguised Rochester in *Jane Eyre*, he fears that "farther might try me beyond my strength." As he found, he might lose himself in the woman's text, in the "spirit of the place."

Rochester's responses and reactions can be illuminated by some of Freud's observations in his discussion of the "uncanny." "The German word '*unheimlich*' is obviously the opposite of '*heimlich*' . . . the opposite of what is familiar; and we are tempted to conclude that what is 'uncanny' is frightening precisely because it is *not* known and familiar. Naturally not everything that is new and unfamiliar is frightening, however; . . . Something has to be added to what is novel and unfamiliar in order to make it uncanny."[15] "It is not difficult,"

Freud observes, "to see that this definition is incomplete, and we will therefore try to proceed beyond the equation 'uncanny' = 'unfamiliar.'"[16] "What interests us," he concludes,

> . . . is to find that among its different shades of meaning the word "*heimlich*" exhibits one which is identical with its opposite, "*unheimlich*." What is *heimlich* thus comes to be *unheimlich*. . . . In general we are reminded that the word "*heimlich*" is not unambiguous, but belongs to two sets of ideas, which, without being contradictory, are yet very different: on the one hand it means what is familiar and agreeable, and on the other, what is concealed and kept out of sight. . . . Schelling says something which throws quite a new light on the concept of the *Unheimlich*. . . . According to him, everything is *unheimlich* that ought to have remained secret and hidden but has come to light.[17]

Grimm's dictionary further corroborated this seemingly contradictory movement:

> *From the idea of "homelike," "belonging to the house," the further idea is developed of something withdrawn from the eyes of strangers, something concealed, secret. . . .*
>
> *The notion of something hidden and dangerous . . . is still further developed, so that "heimlich" comes to have the meaning usually ascribed to "unheimlich."*[18]

Freud's conclusion, as I noted earlier in an analysis of Freud's reading of E. T. A. Hoffmann's story, "The Sand-Man," is that "*Unheimlich* is in some way or other a sub-species of *heimlich*. Let us bear this discovery in mind, though we cannot yet rightly understand it, alongside of Schelling's definition of the *Unheimlich*. If we go on to examine individual instances of uncanniness, these hints will become intelligible to us."[19]

Freud's discussion can be useful in examining the episode in Rhys's novel in which Rochester encounters the "uncanny," and her use of it in relation to the project of her text overall. I would bear in mind (as Freud does) that, along with our knowing that *unheimlich* is in some way or other a subspecies of *heimlich*, we remember Schelling's definition: "'*Unheimlich*' is the name for everything that ought to have remained . . . secret and hidden but has come to light." What Rochester attempts to keep "secret and hidden" from himself is the "malignant" influence of the mother-text in his narrative construction of self. At the same time, because of his projection of that influence onto the island and its people, the mother-text also becomes the "secret" that is hidden from him and that he wants, contradictorily, to uncover. "I looked out of the window," he says. "The silence was disturbing, absolute." What he sees is "Nothing"; what he hears is "Silence" (p. 86). As he has told us, "What I see is nothing—I want what it *hides*—that is not nothing" (p. 73).

Rochester becomes emboldened enough to essay a collusion with the mother-text, to discover the "secret" and, simultaneously, to keep his discovery from ever "com[ing] to light." The failure of the attempt is implicit in the meaning of the word *heimlich*. The episode itself acts out the meaning of the word, which, as Freud notes, develops in the direction of ambivalence until it finally coincides with its opposite, *unheimlich*. The man does not find the secret of the mother-text in the space at the heart of his journey, and at the end of the path he follows impulsively. The difficulty lies in the "disguise" of which he cannot rid himself, because he cannot *exchange* it for another: the concept of "father's time," the linear concept of his narrative of self. He cannot accept what he experiences as the continued ambivalence of "Father's time, mother's space." Instead, he feels himself in the uncanny, the *unheimlich*, position of someone who has revealed, or has had revealed to him, "something that ought to have remained . . . secret and hidden but has come to light." "Father's time, mother's species" is James Joyce's phrase, the shape of which I have borrowed. It serves as the alerting flag for Julia Kristeva's essay, "Women's Time." "[A]nd indeed," Kristeva observes, "when evoking the name and destiny of women, one thinks more of the *space* generating and forming the human species than of *time*, becoming, or history."[20] Joyce's aphorism serves to describe a masculine narrative and the masculine presentation of self as the man writes it. The man attempts to place himself within the aporia at the base of that contradictory conjunction. It is little wonder that he loses himself, that he gets "lost."

Knowing that he is drawn to the space of the mother-text, Rochester also knows that he cannot depart from "father's time," the linear presentation of himself, and his own place in the lineage, if he is to take the "momentous step" he feels bound to make. His concerns—and Rhys's—collaborate to stop his narrative's progress, allowing time, and space, for him to explore the secret of the text that has been haunting him. At the same time—in the same fictional time— Antoinette picks up the narrative to describe her own journey. The synchronicity of the two narratives in the story's time represents a juncture, however, not a joining. The space each occupies and the time each is allotted are discrete units. The juncture is a kind of pivoting, the turning of the "looking-glass" on its metaphorical hinges. In the dual presentation Rochester and Antoinette exchange concerns and focus. Unlike Antoinette's narrative in Part III, how- ever, where her text and Brontë's cohabit the same textual space, these two do not; appropriately, Antoinette's is the second rendered. The return of the narrative to Rochester is a figurative capitulation signaling his superficial control for the remainder of the space allot- ted for his narration.

Despite the dual presentation, Rochester's journey is the center- piece here, and at the center of the interweaving of his text into the defining pattern of the woman's text is another explicit inversion. This inversion pivots on the detail of a passage from Brontë's novel; it centrally interweaves the text of one of Jane Eyre's dreams into the warp of Rochester's narration. Like a prism, the looking-glass turns many times in the weave of Rhys's novel. In the turning, the ambiva- lence that results from the interweaving of warp and weft in the radical intertextuality of the novel can be seen to assume the multi- valence that binds the final weave and reveals its patterns. Just as Brontë's Rochester steps out of his disguise, admitting that "farther might try me beyond my strength," and as Jane Eyre sees in the "old woman," as if she dreamed, what was "familiar to me as my own face in a glass—as the speech of my own tongue" (*Jane Eyre*, p. 177), so we have here an initial turning of the looking-glass that reveals Roches- ter to be "like a woman." When he steps out of that disguise, we see him revealed again as a child—but this time, through the looking- glass, as a girl. The final disguise is that to which he is compelled to return—the little boy in this father's clothes; his father's doll, the marionette.

Recall here Alice James's observations as she contemplated the "head of the benignant pater."[21] So may we see Rochester, confined in the text of the "immutable laws" of the father-text, attempting to keep himself and his narrative construction of that self within the bounds of the proprieties that define it. Like Alice James, he fears "that if you let yourself go for a moment your mechanism will fall into pie."[22] When one stops to consider, it is surprising that the conception of "hysteria" was not applied in the first place to the struggles of men and shaped to their form, as it were, to reflect their "never-ending fight" to keep to the "paved road" of their predecessors, taking momentous step after momentous step.

Rochester's fairy-tale mission is cast in the "green light" of the forest, a light that is "different." Even if the light is a reflection of the "hostile" forest, it nevertheless guides the fearful man to the "large clear space" at the end of the path. Here he finds "the ruins of a stone house and round the ruins rose trees that had grown to an incredible height" (p. 86). He has reached the place he had glimpsed before, a "beautiful place—wild, untouched, above all untouched, with an alien, disturbing, secret loveliness" (p. 73)—the bathing pool, the place toward which Antoinette jumps in response to her mirror-image—" 'Tia!' " This place is also "A beautiful place. And calm—so calm that it seemed foolish to think or plan. What had I to think about and how could I plan?" Rochester asks (pp. 86–87).[23] He had begun to change in mood and attitude even as he walked along the path ("How can one discover truth I thought and that thought led me nowhere. No one would tell me the truth" [p. 86].) Following the track which was "just visible," he arrives at the place almost inadvertently. It is given to him: "I stubbed my foot on a stone and nearly fell."

Brontë's Jane Eyre had also glimpsed her vision of another place that is more fatefully "his." Like Rochester's, her vision precedes the later sight of the actual place. The image of the place Jane Eyre had seen before can be compared to that upon which Rochester finally literally stumbles—the house that occupies, in its ruined state, the large, clear space of the mother-text. This is Jane Eyre's description of the ruins of Thornfield Hall as she, who becomes for a time the "eyes" of the blinded Rochester, sees them: "The front was, as I had once seen it in a dream, but a shell-like wall, very high and very fragile-looking. . . . And there was the silence of death about it: the solitude of a lonesome wild. No wonder that letters addressed to people here never received an answer" (*Jane Eyre*, p. 374). (The last remark rings the note of its own irony, given Rochester's "writing" of letters he never sends.) Her description of the dream to which she refers incorporates the very words she uses above to describe the actual ruin of Thornfield Hall. The full text of the dream is worth requoting here for its resemblance to, and inversion of, Rochester's account of his stumbling walk through the forest. We see how Rhys combines and intertwines here the stories of both Rochester and Antoinette with Jane Eyre's dream and foreshadows the conclusion of the stories told by each of their narratives:

> "I dreamt . . . that Thornfield Hall was a dreary ruin. . . . I thought that of all the stately front nothing remained but a shell-like wall, very high, and very fragile-looking. I wandered, on a moonlight night, through the grass-grown enclosure within: here I stumbled over a marble hearth, and there over a fallen fragment of cornice. Wrapped up in a shawl, I still carried the unknown little child: I might not lay it down anywhere, however tired were my arms—however much its weight impeded my progress, I must retain it. I heard the gallop of a horse at a distance on the road: I was sure it was you; and you were departing for many years, and for a distant country. I climbed the thin wall with frantic, perilous haste, eager to catch one glimpse of you from the top: the stones rolled from under my feet, the ivy branches I grasped gave way, the child clung round my neck in terror, and almost strangled me: at last I gained the summit. I saw you like a speck on a white track, lessening every moment. The blast blew so strong I could not stand. I sat down on the narrow ledge; I hushed the scared infant in my lap; you turned an angle of the road; I bent forward to take a last look; the wall crumbled; I was shaken; the child rolled from my knee, I lost my balance, fell and woke." (*Jane Eyre*, pp. 248–49)

The reverberations among the several texts, the points of their interweaving, are perceptible at a glance. Among them, "the wild blast" that initiates Rochester's litany of father-texts in the culminating passages of his narrative (pp. 135ff.) is foreshadowed here, as is the culmination of Antoinette's dream, "I [. . .] jumped and woke" (p. 155). The child, however (as Jane Eyre earlier describes it, a "very small creature, too young and feeble to walk . . . which shivered in my cold arms and wailed piteously in my ear" [*Jane Eyre*, p. 247]) is an image whose inversion is worth special note. "The child rolled from my knee," Jane says. In the inverting interchange between the

texts, the child who represents Jane herself in Brontë's text joins the
image of the man Rochester, whom Jane sees "like a speck on a white
track, lessening every moment," with that of the "smallest boy" of
"Rochester's" narrative. The child we read in the texture of the
weave here is Rhys's Rochester, a child who has indeed rolled from its
mother's knee. In so doing he is also the figure who "fell, and woke."

When Rochester realizes that the "light," the magical light of the
forest that had allowed him to see the "large clear space," "had
changed," he sees "a little girl carrying a large basket on her head." "I
met her eyes," he says, "and to my astonishment she screamed loudly,
threw up her arms and ran. [. . .] I called after her, but she screamed
again and ran faster. She sobbed as she ran, a small frightened
sound. Then she disappeared" (p. 87). At the beginning of his narration, it is a boy from whom he seeks a response; here it is a girl.
Ultimately it will be a boy again, not the "smallest" but an appropriately older child, who offers him a looking-glass for his recognition
of self. This time he will refuse the child; he will refuse the looking-
glass.

With this refusal Rochester also refuses the return to a possibility
of space—calm, beautiful, clear, unconfining—in which he doesn't
have to think and plan in order to "know." The "secret," in fact, has
been offered to him; he found in that large, clear space the ability to
"think the absence, at the origin, of an origin," to think, to "write"
himself, "like a woman." By being able to see himself in the looking-
glass of an "other," he could thereby recognize himself—at once like
and different from the other.

In this instance the other is a female, a girl-child, and presumably
black or colored as well. Antoinette is not the one who "constantly
needs to be reassured of her identity" and is thus "linked" to "the
looking-glass motif," as one commentator has suggested.[24] On the
contrary, it is Rochester who needs such reassurance, and when the
little girl whose eyes he "met" responds in terror, he turns from the
looking-glass, unable to accept what it reveals, or what his own attempt to look into it implies. He re-commits himself to the path
which will return him to the house and to his refuge, where he will
have to "think" and "plan" a self. Having almost been lost in the
mother-text, he has not retained its secret or learned its lesson.

The questions Rochester brings back with him out of the forest are
matters about which Baptiste refuses to satisfy him. About the zombi,

Baptiste knows "nothing"; and he "repeated obstinately," "No road."
Rochester seeks to find the only knowledge he can of the place in the
only source to which he has access—a book, *The Glittering Coronet of
the Isles*. The "negroes," the book tells him, will "refuse to discuss the
black magic in which so many believe. [. . .] They confuse matters by
telling lies if pressed" (p. 89). At the end of the journey Rochester
knows only what his own senses tell him, dulled and disturbed as they
are by fear. What he has seen, where he has been, is confirmed by the
book, not by what he himself might have made of it. He turns to the
chapter "Obeah": " 'A zombi is a dead person who seems to be alive
or a living person who is dead. A zombi can also be the spirit of a
place, usually malignant but sometimes to be propitiated with sacri-
fices or offerings of flowers and fruit.' [I thought at once of the
bunches of flowers at the priest's ruined house.]" (pp. 88–89; brackets in original). He has seen both of these spirits: the spirit of the
place which was "calm" and "beautiful" that allowed him to realize
that "it seemed foolish to think or plan"—the secret he forgets as
soon as he becomes frightened; and the other spirit, the figure of the
zombi. He has seen himself in the looking-glass of the little girl's eyes.
That is what he recalls: the fear of what he has become, if not of
what he is.

There is nothing "uncanny" about Rhys's presentation of the literal episode of Rochester's journey into the forest except for Rochester's own exposition of his response. His use of what he learns in the
forest is demonstrated in his next expression of "calm." He turns the
experience to account in his siege against his wife's identity:

> "Will you listen to me for God's sake," Antoinette said. She
> had said this before and I had not answered, now I told her,
> "Of course. I'd be the brute you doubtless think me if I did not
> do that."
> "Why do you hate me?" she said.
> "I do not hate you, I am most distressed about you, I am
> distraught," I said. But this was untrue. I was not distraught. I
> was calm, it was the first time I had felt calm or self-possessed
> for many a long day. (pp. 104–5)

The gothic overtones of Rochester's journey into the forest overcome any real feelings of the uncanny as they might be brought to
bear on the reader's response. Rhys's presentation of the episode

very nearly parodies the conventionalized use of the "uncanny" that attaches itself to that genre.[25] The uncanny aspect of Rochester's narration is revealed in the intertextuality that compels our reading of it—the ambivalence between mother- and father-texts that forces the shape of his narrative attempts to identify himself. Our interest, of course, is that starting point of Freud's exploration of the "uncanny": how our literature can reveal its workings, and ours, in our attention to our own responses to it. The Oedipal complex is one explanation of how we understand "who is there when a man says 'I am,'" or, to put it another way, 'who is there when he looks in a mirror.'"[26] Which or whose mirror is the next question.

Rhys allows Rochester's narrative to answer those questions to our satisfaction, if not to his. The father may stand behind the man, looking over his shoulder into the mirror, but it is the mother-text that offers the mirror and the possibility for answering the question without recourse to the man who stands behind and is, in effect, the censor. The woman's text is not only illegitimate; it is also uncensored in a way that a man's text apparently cannot be. The uncanny thing about Rochester's presentation is the transvestism of his text, the near illegitimacy of the act that allows him dress up in mother's clothes for the time that he inhabits the large clear space in the forest, even as he discovers that he cannot see himself without father looking over his shoulder. He cannot brazen through the discovery that, even in mother's clothes, he is seen to be what he has already tried to make of himself: the "zombi" that the little girl thinks she sees in the ruins of the priest's house. Rochester cannot hold onto the image of himself that he has uncovered. He looks into the girl's mirror, accepts her terror, and moves quickly to cover this new nakedness. He accepts himself as the creature of his father, the zombi the little girl thinks she sees.

Rochester has served to represent the man who is a typical case of the unresolved Oedipal complex. At the same time he shows that the lack of such resolution is founded in a dual allegiance that it is not in his best interest to resolve in favor of the father. The woman in the man is freeing, not inhibiting. The inhibition lies in acceptance of the father-text as the only mark of legitimate identity. In accepting this premise the man, in effect, loses himself. The uncanny and not surprising aspect of this loss is that the terms of its negation, the mark of full acceptance, is to become the marionette, the doll, that each man, in acceding to his father's text, is pleased to consider the mark of the woman. To better the woman in her obedience to the confinement imposed by the father-text becomes the mark of the man. He betters her in his more willing acceptance of the role, a "faultless performance" of the kind Rochester shows himself capable in his early presentation of himself to his bride and her family. At the time he marveled at his "own voice [. . .] calm, correct but toneless, surely" (p. 64). The man displaces the woman, perhaps more completely than he knows or intends. He finds himself in her place, in a space marked out for her (and by her?) more readily than he or his explanations of himself can bear, "farther" indeed, as Brontë's Rochester explains, than his "strength" might allow.

If we compare the description of a "zombi" given to us, and to Rochester, in *The Glittering Coronet of the Isles* with Freud's description of the "uncanny effect of automata," of seeming "living dolls" like Olympia, we note an almost "uncanny" resemblance: A "zombi" is "a dead person who seems to be alive or a living person who is dead"; the "uncanny" effect of automata or dolls like Olympia arises from our doubts "whether an apparently animate being is really alive; or conversely, whether a lifeless object might not be in fact animate." The lines of intersection and conjunction make for a reading that emphasizes the absence of firm grounding for the kind of speculation that men like Freud and his predecessor in the study of the "uncanny," Jentsch, the physician-in-charge of the Salpêtrière, Charcot, or, for us here, Rochester, appear to accept in "placing" women and other muted cultural groups, but not in placing themselves: that the effect of the "doll" is similar to the effect of the epileptic "fit," which is much "quieter" than the "hysterical fit," as Charcot pointed out; that the manifestations of "insanity" are similar to the effect of the doll. All of these effects draw the "spectator's" attention to the "automatic, mechanical processes at work behind the ordinary appearance of mental activity," as Freud observed. The "spectator" is, of course, at the center of any such speculation. Her eyes or his make for the point of view that recognizes, and places, such "manifestations" and registers their "effects."

In a climactic moment in the dialogue between Rochester and Christophine, which Rochester is narrating, the following exchange takes place:

I said loudly and wildly, "And do you think that I wanted all this? I would give my life to undo it. I would give my eyes never to have seen this abominable place."

She laughed. "And that's the first damn word of truth you speak." (p. 132)

After this outburst, and Christophine's response, Rochester turns away: "She's as mad as the other, I thought, and turned to the window" (p. 132). The fixing place, the summation of the final arguments in the emotional exchange between Rochester and Christophine, is indicated in Rochester's wild and loud lament that he *would* give his eyes to undo what he never wanted in the first place.

We are returned to Freud's reading of Hoffmann's story, "The Sand-Man." Rochester's fate, as we know it from Brontë's text, is to receive that "punishment," the fear of which forms the basis for Hoffmann's story: the boy-child's fear of castration by the father, represented by the loss of his eyes. Rochester's punishment is exactly that: he is blinded, although, in the domestic epilogue to *Jane Eyre*, Brontë recants and his sight is restored. Only through the humbling experience of figurative castration are Rochester and Jane Eyre able to overcome the oppositional and contextual clashes within which *their* story is cast. Both Rhys and Brontë insist on this failure of Rochester's, a rendering of the man who is conflicted precisely because of his inability to perceive, to know, to *see*, and to act upon the knowledge that is seemingly available to the female protagonists, to their authors, and to men of another culture. The positing of the Olympia complex in Rhys's novel is integral to the imagining of her heroine-narrator's possibilities as well as those of her text. And, in its inversion and application to the masculine text, the Olympia complex offers the structure through which Rhys reveals the man's motivations and constructions.

Rochester has, then, found a kind of truth—the truth that Christophine calls "the first damn word of truth you speak." He would give "his eyes," the mark of his manhood; he would submit to figurative castration by the father to resolve the masculine complex and allow him, by implication, to enter as fully as he might into the mother-text. But he has seen himself in the girl's eyes. What she saw is what he has become, and she/he does well to be frightened by it. Naturally, he "would give his life to undo it. [. . .] never to have seen" it. He is his father's creature, just as Olympia was the creature of her two fathers, Spalanzani and Coppola. Like her, he does not have "his own eyes."

In his own madness, as the culminating passages of his narrative reveal, Rochester tries to take on the voice of indifference, a distorted retrieval of the "spirit of the place." These "spirits," as *The Glittering Coronet of the Isles* describes them, "cry out in the wind that is their voice, they rage in the sea that is their anger" (p. 89). The child has rolled off the woman's knee; it is alone with the father. The man who is still the child can do nothing except take on the disguise of the father, the voice that is the spirit of the father's space, where he is imprisoned. When he is offered the looking-glass, again, at the close of the events he has described, he sees the "nothing" with which he started.

"[A]ll my life would be thirst and longing for what I had lost before I found it," he says near the end of his narrative (p. 141). "I hated the place. [. . .] I hated its beauty and its magic and the secret I would never know. [. . .] its indifference" (p. 141), that indifference which Antoinette tried to explain to him. He was not able to learn the lesson of the place in which his "fever weakness" and "all misgiving" left him, in which the "weather," as he puts it, "was fine" and "lasted all that week and the next and the next and the next" (p. 73). The modality of mother's time, the repetition and recurrence of it, is what he had lost before he found it, a possibility that resides in that large clear space. In mother's time and in mother's space, the man might have been able to find his own voice if, indeed, he had learned how to write himself *as if* he were a woman.

IN THE return to "the other side of the looking-glass," Rochester shows all the manifestations of madness, an exaggerated manliness that is the sign of the man who has seen himself and cannot bear to look upon what he sees. Like Jane Eyre, who cannot look her mad double in her fiery eye, Rochester retreats from his own image, assuming the mantle of "indifference" that he thinks he finds in the remnants of the classic father-texts of his culture, especially in Shakespeare, the father of them all for white anglophones. With the assumption of these grand paper figures he thinks he can assume a shape worthy of his own specific, familiar father-text. But he is caught in the woman's dream-text, just as Jane Eyre and Charlotte

Brontë are caught, in part, in the father-text. Of all the characters
central to Rhys's novel and to the dream-text, the man is the only one
who is an object in the dream, rather than a participant in its shared
narration. He is being dreamed; he is not a dreamer. His role is the
passive one that needs to be "written" for him; he cannot write it
himself. He serves in this capacity as the hinge or copula between
and among the texts of the women, Brontë's and Rhys's preeminently. In Brontë's text he also serves as object—the destination of
Jane Eyre's desires. In both capacities he serves to complete the
"woman's sentence" that I earlier described.[27] His service as warp of
the dream-text is the expansion of that metaphor. The aspect of Jane
Eyre that mirrors Rochester is the aspect that oils the hinge of the
pivoting looking-glass and facilitates the interweave of the texts of
the two women's novels. The conjunction, Jane Eyre/Rochester, allows the most basic inversions and the pivoting in place that firmly
binds the warp of the man's narrative into the women's weave.

The first swing of Rochester's return is to the parent-text of his
original creator, Charlotte Brontë, to the point in Brontë's novel at
which Jane Eyre refuses to live with Rochester. The words she uses
to describe the reasons for her refusal might have come from the
mouth of Rhys's young "Rochester":

> "I will keep the law given by God; sanctioned by man. I will
> hold to the principles received by me when I was sane, and not
> mad—as I am now. Laws and principles are not for the times
> when there is no temptation: they are for such moments as this,
> when body and soul rise in mutiny against their rigour; strin-
> gent are they; inviolate they shall be. If at my individual conve-
> nience I might break them, what would be their worth? They
> have a worth—so I have always believed; and if I cannot believe
> it now, it is because I am insane—quite insane: with my veins
> running fire, and my heart beating faster than I can count its
> throbs. Preconceived opinions, foregone determinations, are all
> I have at this hour to stand by: there I plant my foot." (*Jane
> Eyre*, p. 279)

Her "madness" is met with his own:

> Mr. Rochester, reading my countenance, saw I had done so. His
> fury was wrought to the highest: he must yield to it for a mo-

ment, whatever followed; he crossed the floor and seized my arm, and grasped my waist. He seemed to devour me with his flaming glance: physically, I felt, at the moment, powerless as stubble exposed to the draught and glow of a furnace—mentally, I still possessed my soul, and with it the certainty of ultimate safety. The soul, fortunately, has an interpreter—often an unconscious, but still a truthful interpreter—in the eye. My eye rose to his; and while I looked in his fierce face, I gave an involuntary sigh: his grip was painful, and my overtasked strength almost exhausted.

"Never," said he, as he ground his teeth, "never was anything at once so frail and so indomitable. A mere reed she feels in my hand!" (And he shook me with the force of his hold.) "I could bend her with my finger and thumb: and what good would it do if I bent, if I uptore, if I crushed her? Consider that eye: consider the resolute, wild, free thing looking out of it, defying me, with more than courage—with a stern triumph. Whatever I do with its cage, I cannot get at it—the savage, beautiful creature! If I tear, if I rend the slight prison, my outrage will only let the captive loose. Conqueror I might be of the house; but the inmate would escape to heaven before I could call myself possessor of its clay dwelling-place. And it is you, spirit . . . that I want: not alone your brittle frame." (*Jane Eyre*, pp. 279–80)

If Jane Eyre's statement of her stance seems to mirror the young "Rochester's" conscious motivations, the response of Brontë's Rochester offers a model—one of the father-texts—for the young Rochester's assumed attitude in the opening pages of his culminating narrative in Rhys's novel. The immediate cue for his opening is the narrative description in *Jane Eyre* of the night when Rochester makes the decision to return to England and bury his wife, her identity, and her connection to him "in oblivion" (*Jane Eyre*, p. 272): "it was a fiery West Indian night; one of the description that frequently precede the hurricanes of those climates . . ." (*Jane Eyre*, pp. 270–71). In *Wide Sargasso Sea*, his narrative reads:

The hurricane months are not so far away, I thought, and saw that tree strike its roots deeper, making ready to fight the wind. [. . .] The bamboos take an easier way, they bend to the earth, and lie there, creaking, groaning, crying for mercy. The contemptuous wind passes, not caring for these abject things. (*Let them live.*) Howling, shrieking, laughing the wild blast passes.

But all that's some months away. It's an English summer now[. . . .] Yet I think of my revenge and hurricanes. Words rush through my head (deeds too). Words. Pity is one of them. It gives me no rest. ["Words," Antoinette had said, fall "to the ground meaning nothing."]

Pity like a naked new-born babe striding the blast.

I read that long ago when I was young—I hate poets now and poetry. [. . .]

[We know, as other of his comments have made us aware, that this is the "older" Rochester, Brontë's Rochester, who has been writing his younger self in the narrative of the man in Rhys's novel. The younger has always been implicit in the older man, and inversely, the younger in the older, despite "Mrs. Eff's" defense of him, as both older and younger sons are implicit in the father, and the father in the sons.]

Pity. Is there none for me? Tied to a lunatic for life—a drunken lying lunatic—gone her mother's way. [. . .]

[. . .] I could not touch her. Excepting as the hurricane will touch that tree—and break it. You say I did? No. That was love's fierce play. Now I'll do it. [. . .]

The tree shivers. Shivers and gathers all its strength. And waits.

(There is a cool wind blowing now—a cold wind. Does it carry the babe born to stride the blast of hurricanes?) (pp. 135–36; italics in original)

The interweaving of Brontë's text into Rochester's narration, as well as Rhys's continuation of the detail of the weave here, are too numerous to trace exhaustively. I will indicate some that can be recalled in the framing contexts that Brontë sets both before and soon after Rochester's narration. His narration is designed in the hope of eliciting "pity," which she proffers: "—Jane, you don't like my narrative . . .—shall I defer the rest to another day?" "No sir," she answers, "finish it now: I pity you—I do earnestly pity you" (*Jane Eyre*, p. 270). Her refusal—not to pity, but to marry—follows the continuation of his narrative; it is upon the refusal that he enacts the "madness" demonstrated in the passage quoted above. The continuation of the narrative by means of which he hopes to gain her pity provides a lengthy section that could be inserted almost verbatim into Rhys's novel at this point:

"One night I had been awakened by her yells—(since the medical men had pronounced her mad, she had of course been shut up)—it was a fiery West Indian night; one of the description that frequently precedes the hurricanes of those climates; being unable to sleep in bed, I got up and opened the window. The air was like sulphur-steams—I could find no refreshment anywhere. Mosquitoes came buzzing in and hummed sullenly round the room; the sea, which I could hear from thence, rumbled dull like an earthquake—black clouds were casting up over it; the moon was setting in the waves, broad and red, like a hot cannon-ball—she threw her last bloody glance over a world quivering with the ferment of tempest. I was physically influenced by the atmosphere and scene, and my ears were filled with the curses the maniac still shrieked out; wherein she momentarily mingled my name with such a tone of demon-hate, with such language!—no professed harlot ever had a fouler vocabulary than she: though two rooms off, I heard every word— the thin partitions of the West India house opposing but slight obstruction to her wolfish cries.

"'This life,' said I at last, 'is hell! this is the air—those are the sounds of the bottomless pit! I have a right to deliver myself from it if I can. The sufferings of this mortal state will leave me with the heavy flesh that now cumbers my soul. Of the fanatic's burning eternity I have no fear: there is not a future state worse than this present one—let me break away and go home to God!'

"I said this whilst I knelt down at and unlocked a trunk which contained a brace of loaded pistols: I meant to shoot myself. I only entertained the intention for a moment; for, not being insane, the crisis of exquisite and unalloyed despair which had originated the wish and design of self-destruction was past in a second.

"A wind fresh from Europe blew over the ocean and rushed through the the open casement: the storm broke, streamed, thundered, blazed, and the air grew pure. I then framed and fixed a resolution. While I walked under the dripping orange-trees of my wet garden, and amongst its drenched pomegranates and pine-apples, and while the refulgent dawn of the tropics kindled round me—I reasoned thus, Jane:—and now listen; for it was true Wisdom that consoled me in that hour, and showed me the right path to follow.

"The sweet wind from Europe was still whispering in the refreshed leaves, and the Atlantic was thundering in glorious liberty; my heart, dried up and scorched for a long time, swelled to the tone, and filled with living blood—my being longed for renewal—my soul thirsted for a pure draught. I saw Hope revive—and felt Regeneration possible. From a flowery arch at the bottom of my garden I gazed over the sea—bluer than the sky: the old world was beyond; clear prospects opened thus:—

" 'Go,' said Hope, 'and live again in Europe: there it is not known what a sullied name you bear, nor what a filthy burden is bound to you. You may take the maniac with you to England; confine her with due attendance and precautions at Thornfield: then travel yourself to what clime you will, and form what new tie you like. That woman, who has so abused your long-suffering—so sullied your name; so outraged your honour; so blighted your youth—is not your wife; nor are you her husband. See that she is cared for as her condition demands, and you have done all that God and Humanity require of you. Let her identity, her connection with yourself, be buried in oblivion: you are bound to impart them to no living being. Place her in safety and comfort: shelter her degradation with secrecy, and leave her.' " (*Jane Eyre*, pp. 270–72)

Antoinette's ("Bertha's") life with Rochester, as his narrative in *Jane Eyre* depicts it, is the life from which Rhys wanted to rescue her by "writing a life" for her—and for Brontë and Jane Eyre in part as well, since Brontë's treatment of Bertha does not vary in its particulars from those provided by Rochester's self-serving and ethnocentric narrative. In contrast, Rhys's writing of "Rochester's" narrative in *Wide Sargasso Sea* is very much the life that had already been written for him by another woman, Charlotte Brontë, especially as his story of his life, the narrative that Brontë allows Rochester originally, reflects herself to some extent—the woman Brontë within her own historical context. This context, of necessity, compelled Brontë to locate some important aspects of her own constitution of self within the confines of the father-text. Brontë's novel is remarkable, however, and continues forcefully to engage us to the degree that she and it transgress the borders of the father-text. Rochester's text, both then and now, is not capable of such a transgression. Rhys's Rochester consciously constructs his narrative to reflect the "spirit of the place" described by *The Glittering Coronet of the Isles*, the spirits that "cry out in the wind" and "rage in the sea." But Rochester's description of himself in the parent-text of *Jane Eyre* has already given him the image that is confirmed in his youthful experience of himself: "A wind fresh from Europe blew over the ocean and rushed through the open casement: the storm broke, streamed, thundered, blazed, and the air grew pure. I then framed and fixed a resolution" (*Jane Eyre*, p. 271).

In the overt return to the parent-text of *Jane Eyre* we see the dependency of "Rochester's" narrative on that of his "older brother," the Rochester of *Jane Eyre*. Rhys does not depend on the single authority of such an "origin," however. The man's overt return to literary father-texts, especially Shakespeare, signals not only his allegiance to "England," "his" place, but also his place in Antoinette's dream, and *her* break from his narrative as well as from Brontë's text. Rhys also gives her Rochester a specificity and a simplicity in his longing for "England"; Brontë's Rochester puts it more encompassingly in his reiteration of the "Europe" to which he longed to return. He opposes the old world to the new more sweepingly than does his "younger brother," Rhys's Rochester. (Lesser known literary father-texts are also invoked here, but they are almost "hidden" in his general invocation and offer, in at least two instances, what amounts to a clue to the name of the man who has remained without one throughout his narrative.)[28] Rochester invokes the father-text, but he places himself first of all in Brontë's dream of him, a dream that Rhys has already opposed in a single detail of her interweaving of Antoinette's dream with Brontë's. In so doing, she opposes the literary father-texts as well.

The "wild blast" that figures so prominently in Jane Eyre's dreams, in Rochester's narrative in *Jane Eyre*, and in Shakespeare's *King Lear* (in whose story the unlucky talisman "nothing" serves in a capacity similar to its use here and in which the mother is similarly and conspicuously absent; in which legitimacy, loyalty, and betrayal are all at issue, as are the brutal bonds of patrimony) is negated in a single phrase, a half-sentence, in Antoinette's description of her second dream: "[. . .] and there is no wind."

> [. . .] Now we have reached the forest. We are under the tall dark trees and there is no wind. "Here?" He turns and looks at me, his face black with hatred, and when I see this I begin to cry. He smiles slyly. "Not here, not yet," he says, and I follow him, weeping. [. . .] We are no longer in the forest but in an enclosed garden surrounded by a stone wall and the trees are different trees. [. . .] I touch a tree and my arms hold on to it. "Here, here." But I think I will not go any further. The tree sways and jerks as if it is trying to throw me off. Still I cling and the seconds pass and each one is a thousand years. "Here, in here," a strange voice said, and the tree stopped swaying and jerking. (p. 50)

The route of escape from Brontë's text, and from Rochester's, lies in the half-sentence "and there is no wind." The other intersections are plain here. We see Antoinette encounter the mother-space as Rochester saw it in the forest. We see her climb the wall of the ruin that Jane Eyre climbed in her attempt to catch a glimpse of Rochester's departing figure; all three of them have "stumbled." Like Jane Eyre, she hears the mother's voice, but it is Antoinette alone who finally wakes from the dream in which they have all been interwoven. Rather than Antoinette's being broken by the "hurricane" that Rochester claims "will touch that tree—and break it," "a strange voice" speaks to her, even as the mother, the Moon, speaks to Jane Eyre, and Antoinette makes her escape to "write" a text, her narrative, that opens itself to others. She does not "weep" here, at the last, as in the early dream; Rochester assures us of that (p. 137).

In contrast, Rochester retreats into the paper figures of the father-texts, including the "father"-text that is his ultimate authority, the "mother"-text of *Jane Eyre*. In the interweave of the novel's narratives, Rhys allows him to take up the voice of the man in Antoinette's dream. The words the man speaks in the dream elide into and are regenerated in the mother's voice as Antoinette looks for her escape in her version of the dream, indeterminate though it is. But here Rochester picks up where the man in the dream left off. "Not here, not yet," the man in the dream says. "Now I'll do it," Rochester says here in his final narrative, as if he has made up his mind.[29]

The patterning of Rochester's final narrative is very nearly the "word salad" of schizophrenics. He assumes numerous disguises and roles and his verbal presentation is composed of "the poets" he "hates now," their characters and figures (Lear, Macbeth, Hamlet, even the "mad" Ophelia); the previous arguments and conversations he has had with himself, with Antoinette, and with Christophine; his review of his experiences of near-capitulation to Antoinette and to the space of the mother-text; the songs and music of the island, which he also "hates" now. Even "swaggering pirates" are enlisted in his attempt to stave off the effects of his continued vacillation and to prepare him for the final disguise of "sanity," whose veil he rends in the closing paragraphs of the narrative.

The most brutal and brutalizing of the roles is derived from one of the almost "hidden" father-texts, a reference that amounts to a kind of coded footnote to his text. Rhys may not have intended to mark Rochester's identity—his name—as explicitly as it may be construed; however, if the role and the reference find themselves here in Rochester's narrative through Rhys's "intuition" alone, they nevertheless are in keeping with the tone of rage that the narrative attempts to present. I include the reference here in order not to evade the vein of coarseness that is as much a part of the character as his more sympathetic aspects.

A "Song" by John Wilmot, Earl of Rochester, is not unlike the ribald verse and limericks of other men, many of them nameless, that might serve to substantiate Jane Eyre's response to Rochester's narrative in Brontë's novel. Rochester says, "But, Jane, I see by your face you are not forming a very favourable opinion of me just now. You think me an unfeeling, loose-principled rake: don't you?" "I don't like you so well as I have done sometimes, indeed, sir," she replies (*Jane Eyre*, p. 274). It has been suggested that Rochester's name in *Jane Eyre* is "apparently an allusion to the dissolute Earl of Rochester," an allusion associated with the man's feelings of "male sexual guilt"[30]; so Rhys would seem to have identified one aspect of Rochester's confused feelings of guilt and envy, as well as one of his borrowed attitudes. One of the Earl of Rochester's "Songs," bowdlerized in some editions (the last stanza omitted) but found entire in others, is composed of these unpleasantly misogynistic and "classist" stanzas:

Love a woman? You're an ass!
'Tis a most insipid passion
To choose out for your happiness
The silliest part of God's creation.

Let the porter and the groom,
Things designed for dirty slaves,
Drudge in fair Aurelia's womb
To get supplies for age and graves.

Farewell, woman! I intend
Henceforth every night to sit
With my lewd, well-natured friend,
Drinking to engender wit.

Then give me health, wealth, mirth, and wine,
And, if busy love entrenches,
There's a sweet, soft page of mine
Does the trick worth forty wenches.[31]

This reference coincides too neatly with the other "hidden" reference to Rochester's name to be dismissed or ignored, although Rhys's own wit in this instance is so attenuated as to be the joke that counters the ill will of the masculine attitude just delineated. In Shakespeare's *Henry IV, Part One* (Act II, Scene 1), two "carriers" exchange observations in a setting designated as "Rochester. An inn yard." The first carrier replies to Gadshill's "I prithee lend me thy lantern to see my gelding in the stable" with "Nay, by God, soft! I know a trick worth two of that, i' faith."[32]

We may put these references with two of Rochester's observations to himself, the first in connection with the carrier's remark: "she's drunk so deep, played her games so often that the lowest shrug and jeer at her. And I'm to know it—I? No, I've a trick worth two of that" (p. 136). The second, only a few lines removed from the first, continues the envy and attempt at degradation implicit in the first:

[. . .] She'll not dress up and smile at herself in that damnable looking-glass. So pleased, so satisfied.

Vain, silly creature. Made for loving? Yes, but she'll have no lover, for I don't want her and she'll see no other. (p. 136)

In a sense, the man has been named here, but it is a poverty of naming, offering little scope for generosity toward the character, the reader, or the writer. It is not a joke at which we can laugh with any pleasure, nor is the discovery of the place of his naming an occasion for any sort of congratulation, as, one expects, Rhys knows. The next line of his narrative reads, "The tree shivers. Shivers and gathers all of its strength. And waits."

In the later moments of the narration, when, according to Rochester, Antoinette is "waiting" to "join all the others who know the secret and will not tell it" (pp. 141–42), Rochester adds himself to the list of the mad, those "who know the secret and will not tell it. Or cannot. Or try and fail because they do not know enough." "They can be recognized," he says: "White faces, dazed eyes, aimless gesture, high-pitched laughter. The way they walk and talk and scream or try to kill (themselves or you) if you laugh back at them. Yes, they've got to be watched. For the time comes when they try to kill, then disappear. But others are waiting to take their places, it's a long, long line. She's one of them. I too can wait—for the day when she is only a memory to be avoided, locked away, and like all memories a legend. Or a lie. . . ." (p. 142). He might be describing himself and the verbal display he has offered in the introductory passages of his closing narrative. He does, finally, settle into what he calls "sanity" out of sheer exhaustion. His sensibility has seesawed wildly as if to find the balance that has been missing in his presentation from the beginning. These passages represent the crisis of ambivalence between mother-text and father-text, a crisis that the man tries to resolve by the most extreme measures.

Baptiste speaks to him "in his careful English" about the servant Hilda leaving, a matter of no importance. But Rochester feels the "same contempt" in Baptiste's voice that he had in Christophine's offering to him: " 'Taste my bull's blood.' Meaning that will make you a man. Perhaps. Much I cared for what they thought of me! As for her [Antoinette], I'd forgotten her for the moment. So I shall never understand why, suddenly, bewilderingly, I was certain that everything I had imagined to be truth was false. False. Only the magic and the dream are true—all the rest's a lie. Let it go. Here is the secret. Here" (p. 138). The words that Rochester uses echo those of Antoinette's dream, in yet another continuation of the voice in that dream.

But this time he speaks in the mother's voice, the voice that is later revealed to Antoinette as her own, that "strange voice" of the dream, in which the man's voice was originally subsumed. He repeats the answer, in the voice, that saves Antoinette: "Here, in here." His own ambivalence offers him the "secret" once again. But Rochester can no longer be "saved." In recollecting the possibility he refuses it again: "*(it is lost, that secret, and those who know it cannot tell it)*" (p. 138; italics in original). Again he counters himself, swinging back and forth in his continued ambivalence: "Not lost. I had found it in a hidden place and I'd keep it, hold it fast. As I'd hold her." He looks to Antoinette, as if she could still tell him something.

> I looked at her.[. . .] She was silence itself.[. . .]
> [. . .]—I knew what I would say, "I have made a terrible mistake. Forgive me."
> I said it, looking at her, seeing the hatred in her eyes—and feeling my own hate spring up to meet it. Again the giddy change, the remembering, the sickening swing back to hate.
> (pp. 138–39)

The giddy change, the remembering—the ambivalence he cannot control. What he can control is his wife; he is legally empowered to do so. Mobility, action, and law are plainly his. What are usually called humanity, sanity, a responsible and responsive attitude toward others are just as plainly Antoinette's, even as he calls her a "ghost": "She lifted her eyes. Blank lovely eyes. Mad eyes. A mad girl. I don't know what I would have said or done. In the balance—everything. But at this moment the nameless boy leaned his head against the clove tree and sobbed. Loud heartbreaking sobs. I could have strangled him with pleasure. But I managed to control myself, walk up to them and say coldly, 'What is the matter with him? What is he crying about?'" (p. 140).

Antoinette had followed him, to give him his answer. She is not too "mad" to explain to Rochester why the boy is crying. Rochester, however, "scarcely recognized her voice. No warmth, no sweetness. The doll had a doll's voice, a breathless but curiously indifferent voice" (p. 140). The "doll" is certainly sane enough to make this explanation, to pity someone else: "'He asked me when we first came if we— if you—would take him with you when we left. He doesn't want any money. Just to be with you. Because—' she stopped and ran her tongue over her lips, 'he loves you very much. So I said you would. Take him. Baptiste has told him that you will not. So he is crying.' "

The "indifference" in her voice is not, we may note, the same indifference that Rochester displays toward the boy. The "nameless boy" loves Rochester despite Rochester's indifference—his disguise—in much the way that Antoinette explained such possibilities to Rochester early in their relationship. Rochester cannot, however, recognize the success of the disguise he has assumed. He refuses to consider taking the boy with him. "He knows English," Antoinette says pointedly, although "still indifferently." "He has tried very hard to learn English." "He hasn't learned any English that I can understand," Rochester replies. "What right have you to make promises in my name? Or to speak for me at all?" (pp. 140–41). His "name," his language: Antoinette does well to reply: "No, I had no right. [. . .] I don't understand you, I know nothing about you, and I cannot speak for you. . . ." (p. 141). After Antoinette's good-byes to those who stand there, the man thinks *she* "would cry then," but "No, the doll's smile came back—nailed to her face."

Rochester has shifted the burden of his emptiness, his lack, the "nothing" that he sees in himself onto the woman: "You will have nothing." "Nothing left but hopelessness," he says of the "ghost," the "doll" who speaks in her voice of indifference. He leaves off his present disguise for a few moments, for the formal closure of his narrative: "I was exhausted. All the mad conflicting emotions had gone and left me wearied and empty. Sane" (p. 141). Then follows a litany of hate, a child's list of externally located objects upon which to project his own dissatisfaction: "I was tired [. . .] I disliked [. . .] I hated [. . .] I hated [. . .] I hated [. . .] I hated [. . .] Above all I hated her." What he is "tired of" is "these people." What he dislikes is "their laughter [. . .] their tears, their flattery and envy, conceit and deceit." He hates "the place [. . .] the mountains and the hills, the rivers and the rain [. . .] the sunsets of whatever colour [. . .] its beauty and its magic and the secret I would never know [. . .] its indifference and the cruelty which was part of its loveliness." The child has not been left behind; he peeps out from the assumed mantle of the exhausted man.

"S o w e rode away and left it—the hidden place. Not for me and not for her. I'd look after that. She's far along the road now" (p. 141). The man echoes and inverts Antoinette's words, her attempt to help him learn, in his habitual mode of expression: the echo and the displacing inversion. "It is not for you and not for me," she had told him. "It has nothing to do with either of us. That is why you are afraid of it, because it is something else" (p. 107).

They rode away, bound for Massacre, where Rochester began his story, where a "carriage was to meet us [. . .]. I'd seen to everything, arranged everything," Rochester tells us (p. 137), affecting the tidiness of the traditional narrative ending. But there is a break in the neat package of the "sanity" of his narrative closure.

The break is that passage to which I have already alluded, the passage whose description includes Rochester but in which he attempts to set himself apart from "them"—from Antoinette, who is "one of them"; from all the "others who are waiting to take their places," the terrifying "they" who have to "be watched," the "long, long line" of them. The man is demonstrating the "terrified consciousness" of the "colonizer."[33] However, Rochester's terror is compounded of more, or less, than that, as he made clear in the beginning of his narrative. It is seeing the image of himself there that terrifies him and his narrative returns to the intimate, individual text of his own masculinity. He both emphasizes and rejects the alliance of the several texts of difference that he has attempted to condense into one (the black, the colored men; the black, the colored, the white women—crucially, for his concerns, the women) even as he had just surrendered to it. The "nameless boy"—black or colored; it is never specified—offers the mirror to the white Englishman. It is the looking-glass of likeness, as well as of difference.

The white Englishman, "Rochester," has already uttered "the first damn word of truth" that he speaks aloud and crucially in the whole of his narrative. He returns to its corollary, his one-word evaluation of himself, which he speaks again, twice, at its closing: "That stupid boy followed us, the basket balanced on his head. He used the back of his hand to wipe away his tears. Who would have thought that any boy would cry like that. For nothing. Nothing. . . ." (p. 142).

"Who would have thought that any boy would cry like that." We know the boy who would, if he were able. Rhys has shown him to us in the man.

POSTSCRIPT.

THE LESSON OF

THE TEXT: WHY

LITERATURE?

THE TITLE OF this "Postscript" is purposefully sententious. Its subject and context are themselves framed in terms that are unavoidably moralistic, not a fashionable stance in a discussion of literature in the late twentieth century.[1] On the other hand, as Kenneth Burke reminds us in *A Grammar of Motives*, "our word 'morality' comes from a Latin word for 'custom.'"[2] If we look at the word that way, buffered by the more commonplace aura of "custom," we are relieved of some of the burden of explanation, and excuse, for its use. Rhys's point of view can itself be considered a moral one, as it is given voice in the character of Antoinette and also as it is presented in the aesthetic stance demonstrated in the structure of *Wide Sargasso Sea*. Likewise, given the weight of the father-text in all its forms in the novel, the institutionalized and religious overtones of such a secular lesson are not inappropriate; nor is such explicitness out of place in an academically oriented discussion, given the origin of the universities in our culture. Furthermore, in the concluding remarks concerning a novel that attempts to answer the kinds of questions that many of us are asking ourselves within such institutionalized formats, to formulate possible answers as a kind of lesson (only one among many that might be taken from the novel, and generalized as well) does not seem out of keeping with the spirit in which the questions themselves are asked. To identify this formulation as a lesson suggests its possible place on an agenda for our future consideration of the ways our culture sees itself and reflects what it sees in our aesthetic productions.

Julia Kristeva asks what is perhaps the most sweeping question of all. As with those questions that we have already posed, the model offered by Rhys's novel helps us answer it as well. Noting that "it is in the aspiration toward artistic and, in particular, literary creation that woman's desire for affirmation now manifests itself," Kristeva asks, "Why literature?"[3]

Kristeva attempts to answer her question by posing a series of others, most of them rhetorical: "Is it because, faced with social norms, literature reveals a certain knowledge and sometimes the truth itself about an otherwise repressed, nocturnal, secret, and unconscious universe? Because it thus redoubles the social contract by exposing the unsaid, the uncanny? And because it makes a game, a space of fantasy and pleasure, out of the abstract and frustrating order of social signs, the words of everyday communication?"[4] An even lengthier series of questions and counter-questions soon follows. In the penultimate paragraph of the essay she posits conditions for an answer to the original question. In answering it, she describes what we can call the "lesson" of the novel *Wide Sargasso Sea*, in much the way that Hélène Cixous describes a novel like Rhys's in posing and answering *her* questions concerning a woman's text. Kristeva writes:

> It seems to me that the role of what is usually called "aesthetic practices" must increase not only to counter-balance the storage and uniformity of information by present-day mass media, data-bank systems, and, in particular, modern communications technology, but also to demystify the identity of the symbolic bond itself,[5] to demystify, therefore, the *community* of language as a universal and unifying tool, one which totalizes and equalizes. In order to bring out—along with the *singularity* of each person, and, even more, along with the multiplicity of every person's possible identifications (with atoms, e.g., stretching from the family to the stars—the *relativity of his/her symbolic as well as biological existence*, according to the variation in his/her specific symbolic capacities. And in order to emphasize the *responsibility* which all will immediately face of putting this fluidity into play against the threats of death which are unavoidable whenever an inside and an outside, a self and an other, one group and another, are constituted. At this level of interiorization with its social as well as individual stakes, what I have called "aesthetic practices" are undoubtedly nothing other than the modern reply to the eternal question of morality.[6]

As I emphasize throughout my discussion of *Wide Sargasso Sea*, it is not only the thematic import of the novel that carries the lesson but also the "aesthetic practice" demonstrated there that makes its most forceful assertion and furnishes the weight of its argument. The model of the woman's text, the dream-text, presents the strongest argument for the morality of the paradigm it offers, as well as providing evidence for our highest evaluation of the distinction of Rhys's literary achievement.

I have used the words "model" and "paradigm" almost interchangeably throughout most of my discussion. Now is the time to make a clear distinction between them. The woman's dream-text does offer a model. We need feminine texts—that is to say, texts consciously founded in the mother-text: novels, fiction, narratives, essays—from both women and men. But the example offered in Rhys's presentation of the dream-text is not simply a "model." It is a paradigm. In explanation I offer a set of "pocket definitions" from *The Pocket Oxford Dictionary of Current English*, less exhaustive than its parent-text, but therefore of more commonplace use. Any of these definitions adhere strictly to the more authoritative parent-text.

A paradigm, defined as "the inflexions of a word tabulated as an example," is an example of how we "modify [words] to express grammatical relationships." "Grammar," defined not only as the "science of the sounds (phonology), inflexions (accidence), and constructions (syntax), used in a language," is also the "study" of that entity described as "the general principles on which existing modes of verbal expression rest," as we are all too (un)comfortably aware. I use the word "grammar" precisely to talk about the expanded "grammar" of our language use as it is expressed in our aesthetic constructions. Kenneth Burke implicitly defines what he means by "grammar" when he asks, "What is involved, when we say what people are doing and why they are doing it?"[7] Adding Burke's reminder that our sense of morality corresponds in some manner or kind with our customs, we observe that a new "paradigm" is what Rhys's dream-text offers, and what she makes plain thematically as well.

The moral of Rhys's story, and the morality of the text it displays, is what the woman's text—here, a woman's novel—can offer. Rhys offers new inflections on the "word of the father," the text that Burke explicates at such length and upon which he rings so many changes without leaving its framework. Rhys offers a new grammar, the general principles on which new modes of verbal expression might rest: that of the woman's idiom. She is, however, using the form or genre called "the novel," which was given to us by the grammar of masculine preoccupation with the written word. She uses some of the customs of that convention, eschewing others, to offer the unconventional: a paradigm that gives us a set of new inflections to "express grammatical relationships," which is to say, the relationships that exist in our culture before we express them in the language we use with one another.

I am not suggesting a structuralist formulation or interpretation as that term has come to be understood and is described by Jonathan Culler, who accurately qualifies the description: "In simplest terms, structuralists take linguistics as a model and attempt to develop 'grammars'—systematic inventories of elements and their possibilities of combination—that would account for the form and meaning of literary works."[8] My reading of Rhys's novel does not depart from the more traditional view that the novel, as a genre, can itself be considered a model for the relationships in the culture that produces it, mirroring, as we like to think a novel does, "real life," the life we lead in the societies of our culture and in our personal—our autobiographical—lives. And I emphasize that in the paradigm Rhys offers, and in the grammar of the idiom through which the paradigm is revealed, her novel concerns itself foremost with the ethics of the community and cultures of which she felt herself a part. My own concerns as a reader are compelled by a similar point of view. If there is a structuralist component here it is in the positing of a positive restructuring of our normative possibilities, of the ways we look at ourselves and others in our society. In short, as Kristeva puts it, the novel can be viewed as one kind of "modern reply to the eternal question of morality."

The novel as an artifact is also an object for, and a tabulation of, the displaying of these new inflections. It shows us the new shape that the "written word" can assume in a woman's hand, in the fixing on the page of a woman's voice in her own idiom, even if the fixing of that voice opens itself in the process of its representation to a modifying repetition and rewriting. A woman's text based on this model cannot be univocal, and it does not make an unequivocal statement. It has many voices, even if its "author" signs her name to it, the publisher affixes her name to it and thereby signs it also, even as

Antoinette ultimately affixes her signature to her dream. But the signature is shared even there, for the place of Antoinette's signing of her name in Rhys's novel is also the space that is occupied in common with Brontë's text. In addition, the place for the fixing of the signature is also the place—the seeming closure—in which is signaled the opening out of her text, the invitation to its rewriting and the beginning of another text of difference.

Just as Rhys reveals to us that "that strange person or thing called God" is not one book, but two, so the vision that Charlotte Brontë reveals, in her own transmuted autobiography, *Villette*, is a figure that she finally recognizes as having "upon her something neither of woman nor of man."[9] The woman's text offers a gender-free paradigm, one preeminently suited for a departure from the confining paradigm of the single book, the father-text, whose grammar indeed is founded in "the general principles on which existing modes of verbal expression rest." Rhys structures her novel to show us how a muted text can be revealed to dominate a formerly "dominant" text.

Such a presentation demonstrates a basically moral concern: how human beings, with our likenesses as well as our differences, can express those differences without the strategies of exclusion and appropriation implicit in the masculine model. The rhetorical performance of Rhys's novel is the demonstration of an answer to Kristeva's question: "Why literature?" The key to a new literature can be found in the model for a woman's rhetoric, a model that we can also call her mother's book—the mother's book, for a woman's rhetoric is not exclusive to women. The mother's book belongs to all women and men.

THE TITLE OF this book is "Jean Rhys and the Novel as Women's Text." As a reader may have noticed, I do not use the plural designation until late in the work, for only upon full realization of the collaborative and collective endeavor that produces an individual woman's novel does the accuracy of calling such a novel a *women's* text become clear. The mutuality of purpose attendant upon the act of women reading women and women writing women is demonstrated in the move from the nineteenth-century woman writer's hidden plot—the "muted" idiom gone underground and presented "slant," while the overt presentation remains couched in the dominant idiom —to the overt display of the two idioms in conflict that Rhys presented in 1934 in *Voyage in the Dark*. Rhys gives the emergent femi-

nine pattern an especial clarity in the structure of the dream-text of
Wide Sargasso Sea, in which we see the collaborative process of wom-
en's reading and writing to yield opportunities for a recognition of
our common text as well as of our individuating, contextually based
texts of difference.

"HOW OLD was I when I smashed the doll's face?" Rhys
begins an anecdote from her childhood. "I remember vividly the
satisfaction of being wicked. The guilt was half triumph."

> Two dolls had arrived from England[. . . .] One was fair, one
> was dark. Both beautiful. But as soon as I saw the dark doll I
> wanted her as I had never wanted anything in my life before.
> While I was still gazing my little sister made a quick grab.
> "Oh, no," I said. "Oh no, I saw her first."
> But when I tried to take the doll away she yelled and my
> mother rushed to her rescue.
> "You must let your little sister have it. You don't want to grow
> up a selfish little girl whom nobody will love, do you?"
> "I don't care."
> "Silly. You ought to be pleased she's so happy." Etc., etc.
> "Now here's the fair one. She's just as pretty. Even prettier.
> And look, her eyes open and shut."
> "I don't like her," I said.
> "Don't be silly. Don't be selfish."
> With the fair doll in my arms I walked away.
> "Where are you going?"
> "Into the garden." I walked out of the sun, into the shadow of
> the big mango tree. I laid the fair doll down. Her eyes were
> shut. Then I searched for a big stone, brought it down with all
> my force on her face and heard the smashing sound with de-
> light. (*Smile Please*, pp. 30–31)

"There was a great fuss about this," Rhys tells us. "Why? Why had I
done such a naughty, a really wicked thing?"

> I didn't know. I was puzzled myself. Only I was sure that I
> must do it and for me it was right. (p. 31)

Indeed, figuratively, to "smash the doll's face" was the "right thing"
for Rhys to do, and in her writing practice she has done just that. She

shows us the woman breaking out of the Olympia complex, out of the constraints that would make her doll-like—silent, immovable, unseeing—even if she does have eyes that "open and shut." When the child Rhys lays the "fair doll" down in the garden, the doll's eyes, she notes, are "shut." She smashes the unseeing mask of the doll's face with a stone, just as in *Wide Sargasso Sea* the heroine-narrator's alterego, Tia, picks up a stone to hurl at the face of the little white girl, Antoinette. And, also "in the garden," the man "Rochester" is almost able to "see" himself as something "other" than himself, only to discover finally that he is the "doll," the manipulated marionette.

Iconoclasm takes on a heightened, near-literal meaning when we look at the interwoven text of Rhys's life and work in the culture(s) of which she is a part. Rhys was a native speaker of more than one muted idiom in a culture controlled by the iconography of the "fair doll" and its putative fathers. In smashing the doll's face, breaking the icon, she gives voice and movement to a women's text. In so doing she shows us how other muted speakers can break the frames of perception in which they have been bound by the constraints of the dominant idiom and its culture. The women's text as Rhys presents it is iconoclastic in more ways than one. It shows the man to be prisoner of his own constructions; he maintains his own prison and tightens his own bonds. The dominant idiom is shown to be caught in its own inflexibility. The women's text, in contrast, moves among its collaborative players in a shared narration that opens out to a continuation of our common story, with the addition of difference—without which there is no collaboration, or finally, and not paradoxically, the possibility for a commonality of understanding.

In smashing the doll's face, a mask not unlike the Carnival masks worn by the black women on Dominica and featured prominently in *Voyage in the Dark*, the mask of the doll that native speakers of all muted idioms have worn so uncomfortably for so long, Rhys shows us our powers of movement, speech, and sight.

After the incident related above, the child Jean, in her Great-Aunt Jane's arms, declares, "They are always expecting me to do things I don't want to do and I won't. I won't. I won't." In those arms, too, she realizes that she might weep for the fair doll as well (p. 31). Rhys's adult comments echo the child's original response to her situation. Concerning her experience as a young woman, Rhys remarked, "I don't speak their language and I never will." In the last years of her life, she wrote, "I have plenty to say. Not only that, but I am bound to say it. [. . .] I must. [. . .] I must write. If I stop writing my life will have been an abject failure. It is that already to other people. But it could be an abject failure to myself. I will not have earned death" (p. 133).

Rhys has given us one answer to the "eternal question of morality," to Kristeva's question "Why literature?" The "wicked thing" she did in smashing the doll's face, like the "low" and "immoral" spectacle of the actress Vashti to which Charlotte Brontë's Lucy Snowe gives witness, was to remove the mask of the muted speaker, to speak her own language in her writing life and to put such a spectacle on display for us. In Brontë's text, Lucy Snowe remains a moment. In Rhys's, the smashing of the doll's face takes center stage. Rhys faced and met the "responsibility," as Kristeva puts it, of putting "into play [the "fluidity" that "brings out" both the "singularity of each person" along with the "multiplicity of that person's possible identifications" and the "relativity" of that person's "symbolic as well as biological existence"] against the threats of death which are unavoidable when there is an inside and an outside, a self and an other, one group and another." In her aesthetic practice, Rhys shows us a way out of the bounds of an oppositional cultural text that attempts to maintain itself by adoption and imposition of the "unifying" tool of a dominant idiom. She smashes the doll's face so that we all might see and, in turn, remove the other masks we wear, masks that have muted and constrained too many of us for too long. Indeed, Rhys has "earned her death," and in doing so, she leaves us in no doubt of the answer to the question, "Why literature?"

NOTES

INTRODUCTION

1. Bitzer, "The Rhetorical Situation," p. 6.

2. Ibid., pp. 6–7.

3. See Kinneavy, *A Theory of Discourse*, pp. 23–24, and "The Relation of the Whole to the Part," p. 17.

4. See Suleiman and Crosman, eds., *The Reader in the Text*, and Tompkins, ed., *Reader-Response Criticism*, for essays, overview, and evaluation, and for annotated bibliographies. A more recent collection, Flynn and Schweickart, *Gender and Reading*, does indeed concentrate on "what will happen to reader-response criticism if feminists enter the conversation" (p. 39). See especially Schweickart, "Reading Ourselves," pp. 31–62.

5. As Schweickart describes the situation, "[F]eminist readings of women's writing opens [*sic*] up space for another, equally important, critical project, namely, the articulation of a model of reading that is centered on a female paradigm. . . . The dialogic aspect of the relationship between the feminist reader and the woman writer suggests the direction that such a theory might take" (*Gender and Reading*, p. 52). My discussion of Rhys and her work offers a description of one such female paradigm.

6. Iser, *The Implied Reader*; Booth, *The Rhetoric of Fiction*, p. 71.

7. Ong, "The Writer's Audience Is Always a Fiction," p. 12.

8. Wilson, "Readers in Texts," p. 860.

9. Gallop, "*Writing and Sexual Difference*."

10. Quoted ibid., p. 803.

11. Ibid.

12. Ibid., p. 804.

13. Fetterley, *The Resisting Reader*.

14. Millett, *Sexual Politics*.

15. Woolf to Hugh Walpole, 1932; *Letters*, p. 142.

16. Brontë, *Jane Eyre*, p. 279. All further page references within the text are to this edition.

17. Rich, "XXI," p. 36.

CHAPTER 1

1. Freedman, *The Lyrical Novel*.

2. Hernadi, "The Erotics of Retrospection," p. 244.

3. For another view of a performative text that focuses on a male novelist, see Wadlington, *Reading Faulknerian Tragedy*. Wadlington examines many of the same concerns that are highlighted in this study, presenting what he calls an "anthropology of rhetoric." The masculine writer I myself would pair with Rhys in this regard is William Faulkner.

4. Miles, "Portrait of the Marxist," p. 31.

5. Woolf, *A Room of One's Own*, p. 52.

6. Cixous, "The Laugh of the Medusa," pp. 245–64.

7. Kolodny, "Some Notes on Defining a 'Feminist Criticism,'" p. 90.

8. Morgan, "Feminism and Literary Study," p. 816.

9. Baym, *Woman's Fiction*, p. 19.

10. Kolodny, "A Map for Rereading," p. 463.

11. Lacan, "Seminar on *The Purloined Letter*," pp. 38–72; orig. written in 1956 as the opening text of *Écrits*. Jacques Derrida, "The Purveyor of Truth," pp. 31–113.

12. Kolodny, "A Map for Rereading," pp. 463–64; emphasis in original.

13. Kolodny, "Dancing through the Minefield," p. 18.

14. Rich, "When We Dead Awaken," p. 35.

15. Gilbert and Gubar, *The Madwoman in the Attic*, p. 73.

16. Showalter, *A Literature of Their Own*, p. 258.

17. Woolf, *A Room of One's Own*, p. 81.

18. Moers, *Literary Women*; Spacks, *The Female Imagination*.

19. Gilbert and Gubar, *The Madwoman in the Attic*, p. 78.

20. Ibid., p. 73.

21. Ibid.

22. Ibid., pp. 75–76; my emphasis.

23. Ibid., p. 76.

24. Ibid.; my emphasis.

25. Just as I explore a single writing practice or paradigm in this study, DuPlessis's *Writing beyond the Ending* identifies and catalogs close to a dozen strategies by which modern women writers have attempted to write beyond a conventionally masculinist aesthetic.

26. Ibid., p. 85.

27. Jehlen, "*The House of Mirth* and *Portrait of a Lady*." See also Jehlen's "Archimedes."

28. Wharton, *The House of Mirth*, p. 5.

29. Ibid.

30. Gilbert and Gubar, *The Madwoman in the Attic*, p. 98.

31. Ibid., p. 101.

32. Arnold, "Lesbians and Literature"; emphasis in original, p. 29.

CHAPTER 2

1. Irigaray, *Ce sexe qui n'en est pas un*, whose title essay appears in translation (tr. Claudia Reeder) in *New French Feminisms*; Irigaray, "When Our Lips Speak Together"; Cixous and Clément, *La jeune née*; and Cixous, "The Laugh of the Medusa."

2. Gielgud, interview on "The Dick Cavett Show," Fall 1981.

3. Russ, *The Female Man*, pp. 213–14.

4. Ibid.; my emphasis.

5. Wharton, *The House of Mirth*, pp. 141–43.

6. Brontë, *Villette*, pp. 179–80.

7. Ibid. In *Sexual Politics*, Millett calls Lucy's description "deliberately philistine" (p. 202).

8. Brontë, *Villette*, pp. 234–35.

9. Wharton, *The House of Mirth*, p. 141.

10. Brontë, *Villette*, p. 234.

11. Gilbert and Gubar, *The Madwoman in the Attic*, p. 424; my emphasis.

12. Strouse, *Alice James*, p. 118.

13. See Heath, "Difference," p. 57. See also Showalter's *The Female Malady*, pp. 147–54, for an incisive discussion of Charcot's practice at the Salpêtrière.

14. Ibid., pp. 57–58; emphasis in original.

15. Ibid., p. 58.

16. Strouse, *Alice James*, p. 118.

17. Freud, "Fragment of an Analysis," p. 39.

18. Ibid., p. 37; my emphasis.

19. Ibid., p. 38.

20. Yeazell, *The Death and Letters of Alice James*, pp. 15–16; emphasis in original.

21. Strouse, *Alice James*, p. 118.

22. Gilbert and Gubar, *The Madwoman in the Attic*, p. 85.

23. Freud, "Some Psychological Consequences" and "Female Sexuality." See also Lacan, "Seminar on *The Purloined Letter*."

24. Millett, *Sexual Politics*, p. 199.

25. Ibid., p. 202.

26. Ibid., p. 204.

27. Brontë, *Villette*, p. 233.

28. Russ, *The Female Man*, p. 159.

29. The entry for St. Teresa (1515–82) in *The Oxford Companion to English Literature*, 3rd ed., reads as follows: "a Spanish saint and author, who entered the Carmelite sisterhood and became famous for her mystic visions. Her works include 'El Camino de la Perfección' and 'El Castillo interior.' She

was great not only as a mystic, but as an energetic reformer of the Carmelite Order and a foundress of new convents. Her 'Book of the Foundations' narrates her ceaseless journeys for this purpose and the continually growing labour of organization."

30. Adams, "Ecstasy," p. 57.

31. Grahn, *The Work of a Common Woman*.

32. Freud, "The 'Uncanny,'" p. 219.

33. Ibid., p. 220.

34. Ibid., p. 227.

35. Hoffmann, "The Sand-Man," pp. 210–11.

36. Freud, "The 'Uncanny,'" p. 226.

37. Hoffmann, p. 205.

38. Russ, *The Female Man*, pp. 158–59; my emphasis.

39. Freud, "The 'Uncanny,'" p. 226.

40. Gilbert and Gubar, *The Madwoman in the Attic*, pp. 15 and passim. For a discussion that adds even greater moral resonance to our questioning of the proprietorship of the gaze, see de Lauretis, *Alice Doesn't*, a collection of essays that treats an overtly visual medium, focusing on women and cinema in that intersecting area defined by the subtitle (*Feminism, Semiotics, Cinema*).

CHAPTER 3

1. Freedman, *The Lyrical Novel*, p. 20.

2. Ibid., p. 21.

3. Scholes and Kellogg, *The Nature of Narrative*; *Critical Inquiry* 7 (1980) and *New Literary History* 13 (1982); Jelinek, ed., *Women's Autobiography*; and James Olney, ed., *Autobiography*.

4. Bruss, *The Autobiographical Act*, p. 14.

5. Jelinek, ed. *Women's Autobiography*, p. 4.

6. See Bloom's *The Anxiety of Influence* for a recent restatement of the masculine point of view concerning the rules governing the "internal development of literature," as René Wellek and Austin Warren call it (*Theory of Literature*, p. 235).

7. Jelinek, ed., *Women's Autobiography*, p. 6.

8. Bunyan's *Grace Abounding to the Chief of Sinners* is, Bruss tells us, "in many ways an act groping for an appropriate form," an "autobiography [that] was at best a side effect of his actual intention to give witness to abounding grace in the place where he had discovered it" (p. 34). About her last exemplar, Vladimir Nabokov, Bruss remarks that in Nabokov's blend of parodic autobiography and fiction, in *Lolita*, "Humbert's confessions parallel in ways too numerous for accident the confessions of Jean

Jacques Rousseau" (p. 129). The masculinist's attitude toward autobiography, his description of it as well as his practice of it, would seem not so different from the emphasis on the "individual" in masculine fiction.

9. Jelinek, ed., *Women's Autobiography*, p. 6.

10. Kolodny, "A Map for Rereading," p. 464.

11. Rich, "XXI"; my emphasis.

12. Miller, "Women's Autobiography in France," p. 260; emphasis in original.

13. Ibid., pp. 270, 271; emphasis in original.

CHAPTER 4

1. Marks and de Courtivron, eds., *New French Feminisms*, p. 6.

2. As Marks and de Courtivron observe, Simone de Beauvoir broke this pattern in theoretical or critical writing in 1949 with *The Second Sex*, because at the time she did not consider herself a feminist. "Her text does not defend, does not answer previous attacks. Although she recapitulates them, the center of her study is elsewhere. . . . The focus of the argument is an analysis of process rather than an enumeration or realignment of categories. *It took eight centuries for this shift to take place*" (p. 7; my emphasis).

3. Gauthier, "Is There Such a Thing as Women's Writing?," p. 163; emphasis in original.

4. Ibid.

5. Ibid., p. 164.

6. Miller, "Emphasis Added," p. 42.

7. Ibid.

8. Gauthier, "Is There Such a Thing as Women's Writing?," p. 162.

9. Ibid.; emphasis in original.

10. Ibid., pp. 162–63; emphasis in original.

11. In "Feminist Criticism in the Wilderness" Elaine Showalter recommends to us an "analysis of female culture . . . carried out by . . . Shirley and Edwin Ardener," who "have tried to outline a model of women's culture which is not historically limited and to provide a terminology for its characteristics" (p. 199). The shift in terminology that Showalter suggests can inform our own analyses is based in a shift or change in our descriptive vocabulary.

12. Ibid., p. 200; my emphasis.

13. Showalter herself dismisses this focus using the very words Gauthier offers: "The holes in discourse, the blanks and gaps and silences, are not the spaces where female consciousness reveals itself but the blinds of a 'prison-house of language'" (p. 193).

14. A brief account of her life forms the first chapter of Thomas Staley's study, *Jean Rhys: A Critical Study*. *Smile Please: An Unfinished Autobiography*, on which Rhys was working at the time of her death on May 14, 1979, contains a corrected chronology of the events in her life. Her birthdate, for example, is often given incorrectly; Staley presents it, for instance, as 1894. The correct date is 1890. Three more recent books update the chronology and presentation of Rhys's life and work. See Angier, *Jean Rhys*, for a usefully brief treatment of Rhys's life and work discussed chronologically and in tandem. Also see Benstock, *Women of the Left Bank*, pp. 437–41, 448–50 and passim, which places Rhys against the context of the literary community of the Left Bank in the Paris of the first four decades of this century, noting that "like the women of her fiction, Jean Rhys did not find a place for herself on the literary Left Bank; she was an outsider among outsiders" (p. 448). Selma James, *Ladies and Mammies*, pp. 57–95, offers a brief but cogent and insightful analysis of Rhys's *Wide Sargasso Sea* in terms of Rhys's identity as a white West Indian woman, always the foreigner, the alien.

15. Wyndham, Introduction to *Wide Sargasso Sea*, p. 9.

16. Alvarez, "The Best Living English Novelist," p. 7.

17. Pritchett, "Displaced Person," pp. 8–10; my emphasis. Pritchett's use of the word *capital* here is precise in the context of a world in which money in the hands of men makes all the difference.

18. Alvarez, "The Best Living English Novelist," p. 7.

19. Naipaul, "Without a Dog's Chance," p. 30.

20. Alvarez, "The Best Living English Novelist," p. 7.

21. Pritchett, "Displaced Person," p. 10.

22. Naipaul, "Without a Dog's Chance," p. 31.

23. Rhys, *Smile Please*, p. 104.

24. Rhys, *Good Morning, Midnight*, p. 9. All further page references in the text are to this edition.

25. Rhys, *Smile Please*, p. 20.

26. See overview and discussion in Gilbert and Gubar, *The Madwoman in the Attic*; Showalter, *A Literature of Their Own*; Moers, *Literary Women*; Baym, *Woman's Fiction*; and Kolodny, "A Map for Rereading."

27. See Showalter, *A Literature of Their Own*, pp. 25, 27, 140–41, and passim.

28. See Bridgman, *Gertrude Stein in Pieces*.

29. It can be argued that such privileging of the "novel" as an art form is precisely what Woolf was working out in the essays and in her later work. See Furman, "*A Room of One's Own*: Reading and Absence." She writes: "*A Room of One's Own* . . . investigates the topic of women and fiction, and in the process asserts itself as both a theoretical discourse and a fiction, an explicit statement and a literary endeavor ('I propose, making use of all the

liberties and licences of a novelist, to tell you the story of the two days that preceded my coming here . . .'). Thus, one way of reading *A Room of One's Own* seriously is to look for embodiment of its ideological content within its artistic expression" (p. 100). I agree with Furman that in *Three Guineas* and *A Room of One's Own*, as well as in the attempt represented by *The Pargiters*, Woolf is seeking new "artistic formulations" and successfully and [auto]biographically displaying a text of "self" that she has not presented before.

30. The phrase is Colette's. See Miller, "Women's Autobiographies in France," p. 269: "We are given in the autobiographies [of women] clues telling us where to look, or not to look, for what Colette calls the 'unsaid things.'"

31. Rhys, *Smile Please*, pp. 20–21.

32. Hoffmann, "The Sand-Man," p. 185.

33. See Eisenstein and Jardine, eds., *The Future of Difference*, pp. 1–70. Also see Chodorow, *The Reproduction of Mothering*; and Gardiner, "On Female Identity and Writing by Women," pp. 347–61. Gardiner's essay includes specific discussion of Rhys.

34. Rhys, *Smile Please*, p. 64.

35. Bowen, *Drawn from Life*, p. 167.

36. Alvarez, "The Best Living English Novelist," p. 7.

37. Naipaul, "Without a Dog's Chance," p. 31.

38. Mellown, "Characters and Themes," p. 464.

39. Naipaul, "Without a Dog's Chance," p. 31.

40. Alvarez, "The Best Living English Novelist," p. 7.

41. See Olney, ed., *Autobiography*, pp. 17–18.

42. Vreeland, "Jean Rhys," p. 220.

43. Athill, Foreword to *Smile Please*, pp. 6–7.

44. Naipaul, "Without a Dog's Chance," pp. 30–31.

45. Ibid., p. 31.

46. Mellown, "Characters and Themes," p. 470.

47. Ibid., p. 467; my emphasis.

48. See Nebeker, *Jean Rhys: Woman in Passage*, Chapter 3, "Voyage in the Dark," especially pp. 39, 43–46. Also see James, *Jean Rhys*, p. 34.

49. See Rhys, *Smile Please*, pp. 103–5. Nebeker also notes this biographical, and autobiographical, incident; see note 48, above.

50. Vreeland, "Jean Rhys," p. 223.

CHAPTER 5

1. Alvarez, "The Best Living English Novelist," p. 7.

2. Wyndham, Introduction to *Wide Sargasso Sea*, p. 6.

3. Rhys, *Voyage in the Dark*, p. 84. All further page references in the text are to this edition.

4. Rhys, *Smile Please*, p. 20.

5. Rhys, *Wide Sargasso Sea*, pp. 76–77. All further page references in the text are to this edition.

6. See Ellmann's discussion of the novel's possibilities in women's hands. Her discussion is not thoroughly optimistic, but she touches on the problematical aspects of the "under-life" and the "sub-conversation" that women are advantageously positioned to present (*Thinking about Women*, pp. 221–29).

7. Gauthier, "Is There Such a Thing as Women's Writing?," p. 163.

8. Ibid., p. 164.

9. Rhys, *Smile Please*, p. 143.

10. Ibid., p. 127.

CHAPTER 6

1. Rhys, *Smile Please*, pp. 104–5. Subsequent page references are incorporated into the text; unless otherwise noted, parenthetical page references in this chapter are to *Smile Please*.

2. Vreeland, "Jean Rhys," p. 223.

3. Ibid., p. 224.

4. Ford, "Preface to a Selection of Stories," p. 148.

5. Vreeland, "Jean Rhys," p. 225.

6. Plante, "Jean Rhys: A Remembrance," p. 267.

7. Ibid., p. 266.

8. Rhys, *Smile Please*, p. 133. Plante's is a journalistic biography, a first-person account that self-dramatizes and becomes, in part, his own autobiography. Rhys's remarks are overtly autobiographical.

9. Vreeland, "Jean Rhys," p. 229.

10. Ibid., p. 232.

11. Pritchett, "Displaced Person," p. 8.

12. Abel, "Women and Schizophrenia," p. 157.

13. Ibid., p. 158.

14. Ibid.

15. Ibid., p. 163.

16. Ibid., p. 176; ellipses in original.

17. Rhys, *After Leaving Mr Mackenzie*, pp. 100–101. Subsequent page references in the text are to this edition.

CHAPTER 7

1. Rhys's short stories are collected in *Tigers Are Better Looking*, which includes a selection from *The Left Bank*; and *Sleep It Off, Lady*. Athill's foreword (pp. 7–8) gives a brief account of the circumstances of the radio production. Vreeland, "Jean Rhys," p. 234; first ellipses in original; second ellipses, mine.

2. Vreeland, "Jean Rhys," pp. 234–35.

3. Woolf, *A Room of One's Own*, pp. 79–80.

4. Brontë, *Jane Eyre*, pp. 95–96.

5. "The eye (so active always in fiction) gives its own interpretation of impressions that the mind has been receiving in different terms . . . so that all the time [as we read] . . . we have been aware of check and stimulus, of spectral architecture built up behind the animation of variety and scene" (Woolf, "Phases of Fiction," p. 117).

6. Kristeva, "Women's Time," p. 31.

7. The "dream book," as Rhys called *Wide Sargasso Sea* in a letter to Francis Wyndham (*The Letters of Jean Rhys*, p. 214), was variously titled "Dream" (p. 208) and "Le revenant" (p. 213). "It [*Wide Sargasso Sea*] should have been *all* a dream I know with start and finish present day" (p. 216). Concerning finishing the novel, Rhys wrote to Diana Athill, "So the book must be finished, and that must be what I think about it really. I don't dream about it anymore" (p. 301).

8. Gilbert and Gubar, *The Madwoman in the Attic*, p. 85.

9. Brown, *Shakespeare's Plays in Performance*, pp. 52–53.

10. Ibid., p. 53.

11. Freud, *Interpretation of Dreams*, pp. 311–312.

12. Ibid., p. 312.

13. Ibid., passim.

14. Brown, *Shakespeare's Plays in Performance*, p. 53.

15. Ibid., p. 55.

16. Freud, *Interpretation of Dreams*, p. 349.

17. With the exception of the black men, the local islanders, who (except for the "Young Bull," who is a stranger like Rochester) serve in a position auxiliary to the women. They are not men who represent or use the power offered by the system through which Rochester and the colored man, Daniel Cosway, for example, define themselves.

18. Williams, "The Flamboyant Tree," p. 39.

19. Ibid.

20. See Rabinowitz ("Assertion and Assumption," pp. 408–19) for another view of the way in which these "gray areas" may offer "the firmest reality in a novel" (p. 416).

21. Gauthier, "Is There Such a Thing as Women's Writing?," p. 162, emphasis in original; Nebeker, *Jean Rhys*, p. 169.

22. Nebeker, *Jean Rhys*, p. 135.

23. For a differently focused discussion of identity and the mother-text in *Wide Sargasso Sea*, see Scharfman, "Mirroring and Mothering."

24. Gardiner, "On Female Identity and Writing by Women," p. 348.

25. Freud, *Dora*, p. 81. Freud's footnote here tells us, "In answer to an inquiry Dora told me that there had never really been a fire at their house."

26. Rhys *may* have read this analysis of Freud's. Staley writes, ". . . in the 1920's . . . Rhys found a book on psychoanalysis, but to her the man who wrote it was surely wrong. She hoped then that someday a man would write about women fairly—an unfulfilled hope which provided her with another impulse to write" (p. 4). Staley does not give us the specific source of this information, however. Concerning Rhys's reading habits in general, see Nebeker, *Jean Rhys*, p. 204; Plante, "Jean Rhys," pp. 277–78; and Vreeland, "Jean Rhys," p. 236; for the time during which she was writing *Wide Sargasso Sea*, see Nebeker, *Jean Rhys*, p. 127. Also see *The Letters of Jean Rhys*. In addition, the Jean Rhys collection at the University of Tulsa includes a large collection of letters, manuscripts, and autobiographical material; the Humanities Research Center at the University of Texas at Austin holds some additional material, primarily a small collection of letters.

27. In this discussion I inevitably simplify much that is valid and useful in the complex of Freud's perceptions and analytical practice. Similarly, much of Dora's case is not discussed. However, a generalized application of this sort can perhaps be of some comprehensive use. Two excellent collections of essays offer detailed readings of Dora's case and of Freud's analysis: *In Dora's Case: Freud—Hysteria—Feminism*, ed. Bernheimer and Kahane, and *The (M)other Tongue: Essays in Feminist Psychoanalytic Interpretation*, ed. Garner, Kahane, and Sprengnether. See also Showalter, *The Female Malady*, pp. 158–61.

28. Freud, *Dora*, pp. 86–87.

29. Rhys, *Smile Please*, pp. 132–33.

30. Freud, *Dora*, pp. 87–88; emphasis in original.

31. Ibid., p. 88.

32. Freud, *Dora*, pp. 140–42. Because of his professional interest in her case, Freud felt, I think, a genuine regret at Dora's stopping of the treatment. But some of her "revengefulness" apparently hit home, and his remarks, some of them perhaps inadvertent, show us something of the man, rather than the analyst. We should keep in mind that Freud may have offered the proof of his "humanity" to us deliberately.

33. Ibid., p. 142.

34. Rich, "Compulsory Heterosexuality," pp. 631–60, especially p. 648.

CHAPTER 8

1. Some commentators, Cummins and Thorpe among them, view this aspect of characterization in the novel as a positive reinforcement of Rhys's "sympathetic" rendering of Rochester. It *is* a mark of sympathy for the character. However, in my reading of the novel, it does not suggest a positive view of him vis-à-vis Antoinette; their positions are not equalized or neutralized by virtue of the sympathy that Rhys extends to Rochester (see Thorpe, " 'The Other Side,' " p. 103). Characterological readings inadvertently displaying a masculinist bias are often at work in commentary on Rhys.

2. Cf. Foucault, *The History of Sexuality*, pp. 104, 121, 146–47.

3. Kamuf, "Writing Like a Woman," p. 289.

4. Quoted ibid.

5. Ibid.

6. Ibid., p. 298; emphasis in original.

7. Cummins, "Point of View," pp. 370–71; Staley, *Jean Rhys*, p. 100; Thorpe, " 'The Other Side,' " p. 103.

8. Kamuf, "Writing Like a Woman," p. 289.

9. Cixous, "Castration or Decapitation?," p. 53; emphasis in original. Cixous's theoretical work has been especially compelling for American readers. However, so far she has not applied her theory and general analysis to a specific textual examination of an individual woman's fictional work. In explicating the ways in which a "womantext" reveals itself, she has looked to male texts, describing the feminine in the work of Jean Genet, for example, or, more recently, using Lewis Carroll's *Through the Looking-Glass* as the basis for her discussion (pp. 231–51). Her own novels—*Vivre l'orange*, for example—attempt to demonstrate her theory, but in my reading they seem primarily to demonstrate the aspect of her thinking that is the least helpful in a general application of her overall theory. This aspect shows itself in "Castration or Decapitation?" in Cixous's final emphasis on the "tactility" and deliberate "archaism" in the feminine text (p. 54). The metaphorization of a woman's body, even if the maneuver is in a woman's hands, is for me the least useful of Cixous's suggestions and descriptions, as it would appear to be for others (see Miller, "Women's Autobiography in France," p. 271, for example). Finally, Cixous's theory itself becomes diffuse if it rests solely on general description, no matter how acute, and on masculine examples of fictional revelations of the "feminine."

10. Kristeva, "Women's Time," p. 16.

11. Kamuf, from the title to her essay, "Writing Like a Woman," p. 89.

12. Staley, *Jean Rhys*, p. 100.

13. Cummins, "Point of View," pp. 370–71.

14. Kamuf, "Writing Like a Woman," p. 289.

15. Freud, "Uncanny," pp. 220–21; emphasis in original.

16. Ibid., p. 221.

17. Ibid., pp. 224–25.

18. Ibid., pp. 225–26.

19. Ibid., p. 226.

20. Kristeva, "Women's Time," p. 15; emphasis in original.

21. Strouse, *Alice James*, p. 120.

22. Ibid., p. 118.

23. The *hortus conclusus*, the enclosed garden, is also Narcissus's place. Rochester, like the dreamer-lover in the *Romance of the Rose*, finds himself looking not only into (and "through") the "eyes" of the lady in that secret place, a place where earlier he had stayed "for hours, unwilling to leave" (*Wide Sargasso Sea*, p. 73), but finally—and primarily—what he sees is his own image; and, like Narcissus, he loses what he thinks he has found. The allegory here, like that of the *Romance*, comes to center itself on the impediments, the "thorns and briars," of the garden and its possibilities. The man, the Narcissus-figure, loses himself finally for love of his *own* image, unlike Antoinette who finds her self in response to an other, the mirror image of her alter-ego. In finding and seeing "the lady's eyes" in the secret place, the man also realizes he cannot sustain the vision. And the place of vision and reflection itself becomes the locus of a redoubled image and reflection of himself and his world. "Her" eyes become his and the moment of seeing becomes the occasion for a return to the strictures and constraints of his world, the "real" world, as it opposes the dream of the garden.

24. Thorpe, "'The Other Side,'" p. 103.

25. As Luengo points out, the Gothic and neo-Gothic influence on Rhys's presentation is not thoroughly remarked ("*Wide Sargasso Sea* and the Gothic Mode," p. 232). See also Ramchand's discussion of what has been termed "Caribbean Gothic" in "Terrified Consciousness," pp. 224–25, and Helman, "Charlotte Brontë's New Gothic," pp. 165–80.

26. Rochester never fully accedes to the "Symbolic" (to use Lacanian terminology) represented by the Name of the Father. (See Laplanche and Pontalis, *The Language of Psychoanalysis*, pp. 239–40. Also see p. 210 for the concept of the "Imaginary" and pp. 250–52 for a description of the "Mirror-phase," which "is said to constitute the matrix and first outline of what is to become the ego.") One could, in other particulars as well (e.g., the lack, the "blanks" in Rochester's mind that can never be "filled up"), make an elaborate allegory or scenario using the Lacanian scheme. The man, "Rochester," "fits" as exemplarily into the Freudian as into the neo-Freudian construct; Rhys's rendering and observation of the man are that acute.

27. Cf. Hartman, "The Voice of the Shuttle: Language from the Point of

View of Literature," and his use of what Sophocles calls "the voice of the shuttle": Philomela's weaving of the "tell-tale account of her violation [by Tereseus] into a tapestry (or robe)" (p. 337). The misreading of the phrase from Hartman's masculinist perspective is implicit from the outset. (See Culler's remarks on the attitude of Hartman's work [*On Deconstruction*, p. 44].) Hartman writes: "The power of the phrase lies in its elision of middle terms and overspecification of end terms" (p. 338). My point here is to emphasize the extent to which Hartman's reading of "the voice of the shuttle" is at odds with Rhys's use of the technique represented by the idea of the shuttle. Rhys's rendering of the woman's "sentence" completed in *Wide Sargasso Sea* refutes the "elision of middle terms" and the "overspecification of end terms," a "tension" that her text resolves.

28. Like Brontë, Rhys has scattered literary allusions throughout her text, although Rhys's use of the masculine father-texts, both major (e.g., Shakespeare) and minor, in the culminating passages of "Rochester's" narrative, is precise and strategic. The more general reasons for the many literary allusions and references found in both, and in each case, offer an area of speculation interesting in itself. How unconsciously dependent, we might wonder, were either of the women in *some* of their allusions? How dependent may they have been on the authority conferred by the allusions, in contrast to what is merely writerly recall and inclusion, cultural texturing, and the like? These questions arise as corollaries to their obviously deliberate and iconoclastic use of such allusions.

29. Cf. *Hamlet* III.iii.73–95.

Now might I do it pat, now he is praying;
And now I'll do't. And so 'a goes to heaven,
And so am I reveng'd. That would be scann'd.
A villain kills my father; and for that,
I, his sole son, do this same villain send
To heaven.

. . . .

. . . his soul may be as damn'd and black
As hell, whereto it goes. *My mother stays.* (my emphasis)

30. Gilbert and Gubar, *The Madwoman in the Attic*, p. 354.

31. Rochester, "A Song," p. 51.

32. Shakespeare, *Henry IV, Part One*, II.i.30–33.

33. Ramchand, "Terrified Consciousness," pp. 224–25.

POSTSCRIPT

1. *Pace*, John Gardner. See *On Moral Fiction*.
2. Burke, *A Grammar of Motives*, p. 15.
3. Kristeva, "Women's Time," p. 31.
4. Ibid.
5. Ibid. Cf. her earlier remarks, pp. 15–16; and see her distinction between the terms *semiotic* and *symbolic* in "From One Identity to Another," pp. 133–34.
6. Kristeva, "Women's Time," pp. 34–35.
7. Burke, *A Grammar of Motives*, p. xv. The three "doctrines" with which Burke is centrally concerned in his use of the term "Grammar" are not surprising, given the context with which we are concerned: they are the areas that concern what Christophine calls "Letter of the Law," and certainly the other two categories with which Burke involves his discussion—the Rhetoric and the Symbolic—"hover about the edges" of his "central theme, the Grammar" with its illustrations from "theological, metaphysical, and juridical doctrines" (p. xviii).
8. Culler, *On Deconstruction*, p. 22; also p. 29 and passim.
9. Brontë, *Villette*, p. 234.

BIBLIOGRAPHY

Abel, Elizabeth, ed. *Critical Inquiry* 8 (1981): 179–206. Issued in book form as *Writing and Sexual Difference*. Chicago: University of Chicago Press, 1982.

———. "Women and Schizophrenia: The Fiction of Jean Rhys." *Contemporary Literature* 20 (1979): 155–77.

Adams, Robert M. "Ecstasy." *New York Review of Books*, 24 September 1981, pp. 57–58.

Alvarez, Albert. "The Best Living English Novelist." *New York Times Book Review*, 17 March 1974, pp. 6–7.

Angier, Carole. *Jean Rhys*. New York: Penguin Books, 1985.

Arnold, June. Transcript of panel discussion presented at the Modern Language Association seminar, "Lesbians and Literature" (1975); reprinted in *Sinister Wisdom* 1, no. 2 (1976): 20–33.

Athill, Diana. Foreword to *Smile Please: An Unfinished Autobiography* by Jean Rhys. New York: Harper and Row, 1979.

Auerbach, Nina. *Woman and the Demon: The Life of a Victorian Myth*. Cambridge, Mass.: Harvard University Press, 1982.

Austin, J. L. *How to Do Things with Words*. 2d ed. Edited by J. O. Urmson and Marina Sbisa. Cambridge, Mass.: Harvard University Press, 1975.

Bamber, Linda. "Jean Rhys." *Partisan Review* 49 (1982): 93–100.

Baym, Nina. *Woman's Fiction: A Guide to Novels by and about Women in America, 1820–1870*. Ithaca: Cornell University Press, 1978.

Benjamin, Walter. *Illuminations*. Translated by Harry Zohn. New York: Schocken Books, 1969.

Benstock, Shari. *Women of the Left Bank: Paris, 1900–1940*. Austin: University of Texas Press, 1986.

Bernheimer, Charles, and Claire Kahane, eds. *In Dora's Case: Freud—Hysteria—Feminism*. New York: Columbia University Press, 1985.

Bitzer, Lloyd. "The Rhetorical Situation." *Philosophy and Rhetoric* 1 (1968): 1–14.

Blake, Susan L. "Black Folklore in the Works of Ralph Ellison." *PMLA* 94 (1979): 121–36.

Bloom, Harold. *The Anxiety of Influence: A Theory of Poetry*. New York: Oxford University Press, 1973.

Booth, Wayne C. *The Rhetoric of Fiction*. Chicago: University of Chicago Press, 1961.

Bowen, Stella. *Drawn from Life*. Enlarged ed. Maidstone, Kent: George Mann, 1974.

Bridgman, Richard. *Gertrude Stein in Pieces*. New York: Oxford University Press, 1970.

Brontë, Charlotte. *Jane Eyre*. New York: W. W. Norton, 1971.

———. *Villette*. London and New York: J. M. Dent & Sons, Ltd./Dutton, 1957.

Brown, John Russell. *Shakespeare's Plays in Performance*. New York: St. Martin's Press, 1967.

Bruss, Elizabeth W. *The Autobiographical Act: The Changing Situation of a Literary Genre*. Baltimore: Johns Hopkins University Press, 1976.

Burke, Carolyn G. "Report from Paris: Women's Writing and the Women's Movement." *Signs* 3 (1978): 843–55.

Burke, Kenneth. *A Grammar of Motives*. Berkeley: University of California Press, 1969.

Chaucer, Geoffrey. "Troilus and Criseyde," *The Complete Poetry and Prose of Geoffrey Chaucer*. Edited by John H. Fisher. New York: Holt, Rinehart & Winston, 1977.

Chodorow, Nancy. *The Reproduction of Mothering: Psychoanalysis and the Sociology of Gender*. Berkeley: University of California Press, 1978.

Cixous, Hélène. "Castration or Decapitation?" *Signs* 7 (1981): 41–55.

———. "Introduction to Lewis Carroll's *Through the Looking-Glass* and *The Hunting of the Snark*." *New Literary History* 13 (1982): 231–51.

———. "The Laugh of the Medusa." Translated by Keith Cohen and Paula Cohen. *Signs* 1 (1976): 875–93.

Cixous, Hélène, and Catherine Clément. *La jeune née*. Paris: Union Générale d'Editions, 1975. Issued in translation as *The Newly Born Woman* (tr. Betsy Wing). Minneapolis: University of Minnesota Press, 1986.

Critical Inquiry 7 (1980), "On Narrative," 1–236.

Culler, Jonathan. *On Deconstruction: Theory and Criticism after Structuralism*. Ithaca: Cornell University Press, 1982.

Cummins, Marsha Z. "Point of View in the Novels of Jean Rhys: The Effect of a Double Focus." Paper presented at Modern Language Association session (1981), "Jean Rhys: A Commemorative Colloquium"; the revised essay appears in *World Literature Written in English* 24 (1984): 359–73.

Daly, Mary. *Beyond God the Father: Toward a Philosophy of Women's Liberation*. Boston: Beacon Press, 1977.

de Lauretis, Teresa. *Alice Doesn't: Feminism, Semiotics, Cinema*. Bloomington: Indiana University Press, 1984.

Deleuze, Gilles, and Felix Guattari. *Anti-Oedipus: Capitalism and Schizophrenia*. Translated by Robert Hurley et al. New York: Viking, 1972.

Derrida, Jacques. "The Purveyor of Truth." Translated by Willis Domingo et al. *Yale French Studies* 52 (1975): 31–113.

DuPlessis, Rachel Blau. *Writing beyond the Ending: Narrative Strategies of Twentieth-Century Women Writers.* Bloomington: Indiana University Press, 1985.

Eisenstein, Hester, and Alice Jardine, eds. *The Future of Difference.* Boston: G. K. Hall & Company, 1980.

Eisenstein, Zillah R. *The Radical Future of Liberal Feminism.* New York: Longman, 1981.

Ellmann, Mary. *Thinking about Women.* London: Virago, 1979.

Fetterley, Judith. *The Resisting Reader: A Feminist Approach to American Fiction.* Bloomington: Indiana University Press, 1978.

Flynn, Elizabeth A., and Patrocinio P. Schweickart, eds. *Gender and Reading: Essays on Readers, Texts, and Contexts.* Baltimore: Johns Hopkins University Press, 1986.

Ford, Ford Madox. "Preface to a Selection of Stories from '*The Left Bank.*'" Pp. 147–50 in Jean Rhys, *Tigers Are Better Looking.* New York: Harper & Row, 1974.

Foucault, Michel. *The History of Sexuality: Volume One: An Introduction.* Translated by Robert Hurley. New York: Vintage Books, 1980.

Freedman, Ralph. *The Lyrical Novel: Studies in Herman Hesse, André Gide, and Virginia Woolf.* Princeton: Princeton University Press, 1963.

Freud, Sigmund. "Female Sexuality." Translated by Joan Riviere. Pp. 194–211 in *Sexuality and the Psychology of Love.* New York: Macmillan/Collier Books, 1963.

———. "Fragment of an Analysis of a Case of Hysteria." Pp. 21–144 in *Dora: An Analysis of a Case of Hysteria,* edited by Philip Rieff. New York: Macmillan/Collier Books, 1973.

———. *The Interpretation of Dreams.* Translated by James Strachey. New York: Avon Books, 1965.

———. "Some Psychological Consequences of the Anatomical Distinction Between the Sexes." Translated by James Strachey. Pp. 183–93 in *Sexuality and the Psychology of Love.* New York: Macmillan/Collier Books, 1963.

———. "The 'Uncanny.'" Translated by James Strachey. Vol. 17, pp. 219–52 in *The Complete Psychological Works of Sigmund Freud.* Standard Ed. (London: Hogarth Press, 1953–.)

Furman, Nelly. "*A Room of One's Own*: Reading and Absence." In *Women's Language and Style,* edited by Douglas Butturf and Edmund L. Epstein, pp. 99–105. Akron, Ohio: Language & Style Books, 1978.

———. "Textual Criticism." Pp. 45–54 in *Women and Language in Literature and Society,* edited by Sally McConnell-Ginet, Ruth Borker, and Nelly Furman. New York: Praeger Publishers, 1980.

Gallop, Jane. *The Daughter's Seduction: Feminism and Psychoanalysis.* New York:

Cornell University Press, 1982.

———. "*Writing and Sexual Difference*: The Difference Within." *Critical Inquiry* 8 (1982): 797–804.

Gardiner, Judith Kegan. "On Female Identity and Writing by Women." *Critical Inquiry* 8 (1981): 347–61.

———. "*Good Morning, Midnight*: Good Night, Modernism." *Boundary* 2 11, nos. 1 and 2 (1983): 223–51.

Gardner, John. *On Moral Fiction*. New York: Basic Books, 1978.

Garner, Shirley Nelson, Claire Kahane, and Madelon Sprengnether. *The (M)other Tongue: Essays in Feminist Psychoanalytic Interpretation*. Ithaca: Cornell University Press, 1985.

Gauthier, Xavière. "Is There Such a Thing as Women's Writing?" Translated by Marilyn A. August. Pp. 161–64 in *New French Feminisms*, edited by Elaine Marks and Isabelle de Courtivron. Amherst: University of Massachusetts Press, 1980.

Gielgud, John. "Interview," *The Dick Cavett Show*. PBS, Fall 1981.

Gilbert, Sandra M., and Susan Gubar. *The Madwoman in the Attic: The Woman Writer and the Nineteenth-Century Imagination*. New Haven: Yale University Press, 1979.

Givner, Joan. "Charlotte Brontë, Emily Brontë and Jean Rhys: What Rhys's Letters Show about that Relationship." Paper presented at Modern Language Association session (1981), "Jean Rhys: A Commemorative Colloquium."

Glaspell, Susan Keating. "A Jury of Her Peers." Pp. 370–85 in *Images of Women in Literature*, edited by Mary Anne Ferguson. Boston: Houghton Mifflin, 1973.

———. *Trifles*. Pp. 423–33 in *Images of Women in Literature*, edited by Mary Anne Ferguson. 2d. ed. Boston: Houghton Mifflin, 1977.

Grahn, Judy. *The Work of a Common Woman*. New York: St. Martin's Press, 1978.

Gubar, Susan. "'The Blank Page' and the Issues of Female Creativity." *Critical Inquiry* 8 (1981): 243–63.

Hartman, Geoffrey. "The Voice of the Shuttle: Language from the Point of View of Literature." Pp. 337–55 in *Beyond Formalism, Literary Essays 1958–1970*. New Haven: Yale University Press, 1970.

Heath, Stephen. "Difference." *Screen* 19 (1978): 51–183.

Helman, Robert B. "Charlotte Brontë's New Gothic." Pp. 165–80 in *The Victorian Novel: Modern Essays in Criticism*, edited by Ian Watt. New York: Oxford University Press, 1971.

Hernadi, Paul. "The Erotics of Retrospection: Historytelling, Audience Response, and the Strategies of Desire." *New Literary History* 12 (1981): 243–52.

Hoffmann, E. T. A. "The Sand-Man." Pp. 183–214 in *The Best Tales of Hoffmann*, edited by E. F. Bleiler. New York: Dover Publications, 1967.

Howe, Florence, and Ellen Bass. *No More Masks! An Anthology of Poems by Women*. Garden City, N.Y.: Anchor Press/Doubleday, 1973.

Irigaray, Luce. *Ce sexe qui n'en pas un*. Paris: Editions de Minuit, 1977.

———. "When Our Lips Speak Together." Translated by Carolyn Burke. *Signs* 6 (1980): 69–79.

———. *This Sex Which Is Not One*. Translated by Catherine Porter. Ithaca: Cornell University Press, 1985.

Iser, Wolfgang. *The Implied Reader: Patterns of Communication in Prose Fiction from Bunyan to Beckett*. Baltimore: Johns Hopkins University Press, 1974.

James, Louis. *Jean Rhys*. London: Longman, 1978.

James, Selma. *The Ladies and the Mammies: Jane Austen and Jean Rhys*. Bristol: Falling Wall Press, 1983.

Jehlen, Myra. "Archimedes and the Paradox of Feminist Criticism." *Signs* 6 (1981): 575–601.

———. "*The House of Mirth* and *Portrait of a Lady*: Two Accounts of the Same Story." Paper presented at Modern Language Association session (1980), "Literary Influence: Gender to Gender."

Jelinek, Estelle C., ed. *Women's Autobiography: Essays in Criticism*. Bloomington: Indiana University Press, 1980.

Kamuf, Peggy. "Writing Like a Woman." Pp. 284–99 in *Women and Language in Literature and Society*, edited by Sally McConnell-Ginet, Ruth Borker, and Nelly Furman. New York: Praeger Publishers, 1980.

Kinneavy, James L. "The Relation of the Whole to the Part in Interpretation Theory and in the Composing Process." Pp. 1–23 in *Linguistics, Stylistics, and the Teaching of Composition*, edited by Donald McQuade. Akron: Language and Style Books, 1979.

———. *A Theory of Discourse*. New York: W. W. Norton, 1980.

Koedt, Anne, Ellen Levine, and Anita Rapone. *Radical Feminism*. New York: Quadrangle/New York Times Book Company, 1973.

Kolodny, Annette. "Dancing through the Minefield: Some Observations on the Theory, Practice, and Politics of a Feminist Literary Criticism." *Feminist Studies* 6 (1980): 1–25.

———. "A Map for Rereading: Or, Gender and the Interpretation of Literary Texts." *New Literary History* 11 (1980): 451–68.

———. "Some Notes on Defining a 'Feminist Criticism.'" *Critical Inquiry* 2 (1975): 75–92.

———, et al. "An Exchange on Feminist Criticism: On 'Dancing through the Minefield.'" *Feminist Studies* 8 (1982): 629–75.

Kristeva, Julia. "From One Identity to Another." Pp. 124–47 in *Desire in Language: A Semiotic Approach to Literature and Art*, edited by Leon S.

Roudiez, translated by Thomas Gora et al. New York: Columbia University Press, 1980.

———. "Women's Time." *Signs* 7 (1981): 13–35.

Lacan, Jacques. "Seminar on *The Purloined Letter*." Translated by Jeffrey Mehlman. *Yale French Studies* 48 (1972): 38–72. (Originally written in 1956 as the opening text of *Écrits*.)

Laplanche, J., and J. B. Pontalis. *The Language of Psychoanalysis*. Translated by Donald Nicholson-Smith. New York: W. W. Norton, 1973.

Lessing, Doris. "Introduction" to *The Golden Notebook*. New York: Bantam Books, 1973.

Luengo, Anthony. "*Wide Sargasso Sea* and the Gothic Mode." *World Literature Written in English* 15 (1976): 229–45.

Macherey, Pierre. *A Theory of Literary Production*. Translated by Geoffrey Wall. London: Routledge & Kegan Paul, 1978.

Marcus, Jane. "Art and Anger." *Feminist Studies* 4 (1978): 69–98.

———. "Storming the Toolshed." *Signs* 7 (1982): 623–40.

———. "Thinking Back through Our Mothers." Pp. 1–30 in *New Feminist Essays on Virginia Woolf*, edited by Jane Marcus. Lincoln: University of Nebraska Press, 1981.

Marks, Elaine. "Women and Literature in France." *Signs* 3 (1978): 832–42.

Marks, Elaine, and Isabelle de Courtivron, eds. *New French Feminisms*. Amherst: University of Massachusetts Press, 1980.

Mellown, Elgin W. "Character and Themes in the Novels of Jean Rhys." *Contemporary Literature* 12 (1972): 458–75.

Miles, David H. "Portrait of the Marxist as a Young Hegelian: Lukàcs' Theory of the Novel." *PMLA* 94 (1979): 22–35.

Miller, Nancy K. "Emphasis Added: Plots and Plausibilities in Women's Fiction." *PMLA* 96 (1981): 36–48.

———. "Women's Autobiography in France: For a Dialectics of Identification." Pp. 258–73 in *Women and Language in Literature and Society*, edited by Sally McConnell-Ginet, Ruth Borker, and Nelly Furman. New York: Praeger Publishers, 1980.

Millett, Kate. *Sexual Politics*. New York: Ballantine Books, 1970.

Moers, Ellen. *Literary Women: The Great Writers*. New York: Doubleday, 1976.

Morgan, William. "Feminism and Literary Study: A Reply to Annette Kolodny." *Critical Inquiry* 2 (1976): 807–16.

Naipaul, V. S. "Without a Dog's Chance." *New York Review of Books*, 18 May 1972, pp. 29–31.

Nebeker, Helen. *Jean Rhys: Woman in Passage*. Montreal: Eden Press, 1981.

New Literary History 13 (1982), "Narrative Analysis and Interpretation," 179–378.

Olney, James, ed. *Autobiography: Essays Theoretical and Critical*. Princeton: Princeton University Press, 1980.

Olsen, Tillie. *Silences*. New York: Delacorte Press/Seymour Lawrence, 1978.

Ong, Walter J. "The Writer's Audience Is Always a Fiction." *PMLA* 90 (1975): 9–21.

Plante, David. "Jean Rhys: A Remembrance." *Paris Review* 76 (1979): 238–84.

Pratt, Annis. *Archetypal Patterns in Women's Fiction*. Bloomington: Indiana University Press, 1981.

Pratt, Mary Louise. *Toward a Speech Act Theory of Literary Discourse*. Bloomington: Indiana University Press, 1977.

Pritchett, V. S. "Displaced Person." *New York Review of Books*, 14 August 1980, pp. 8–10.

Rabinowitz, Peter J. "Assertion and Assumption: Fictional Patterns and the External World." *PMLA* 96 (1981): 408–19.

Ramchand, Kenneth. "Terrified Consciousness." Pp. 223–36 in *The West Indian Novel and Its Background*. London: Faber and Faber, 1970.

Rhys, Jean. *After Leaving Mr Mackenzie*. London: Penguin Books, 1971.

––––––. *The Letters of Jean Rhys*. Edited by Francis Wyndham and Diana Melly. New York: Viking, 1984.

––––––. *Good Morning, Midnight*. London: Penguin Books, 1967.

––––––. *Quartet*. London: Penguin Books, 1973.

––––––. *Sleep It Off, Lady*. London: André Deutsch, 1976.

––––––. *Smile Please: An Unfinished Autobiography*. New York: Harper & Row, 1979.

––––––. *Tigers Are Better Looking*. London: André Deutsch, 1974.

––––––. *Voyage in the Dark*. London: Penguin Books, 1967.

––––––. *Wide Sargasso Sea*. London: Penguin Books, 1968.

Rich, Adrienne. "The Burning of Paper Instead of Children." Pp. 15–18 in *The Will to Change: Poems 1968–1977*. New York: W. W. Norton, 1971.

––––––. "Compulsory Heterosexuality and Lesbian Experience." *Signs* 5 (1980): 631–60.

––––––. "XXI," "Twenty-One Love Poems." Pp. 35–36 in *The Dream of a Common Language: Poems 1974–1977*. New York: W. W. Norton, 1978.

––––––. "When We Dead Awaken: Writing as Re-vision." Pp. 33–49 in *On Lies, Secrets, and Silence: Selected Prose 1966–1978*. New York: W. W. Norton, 1979.

Rigney, Barbara Hill. *Madness and Sexual Politics in the Feminist Novel: Studies in Brontë, Woolf, Lessing, and Atwood*. Madison: University of Wisconsin Press, 1978.

Rochester, John Wilmot, 2d Earl of. "Song." P. 51 in *The Complete Poems of*

John Wilmot, Earl of Rochester, edited by David M. Vieth. New Haven: Yale University Press, 1968.

Russ, Joanna. *The Female Man*. New York: Bantam Books, 1975.

———. "What Can a Heroine Do? Or, Why Women Can't Write." Pp. 3–20 in *Images of Women in Fiction: Feminist Perspectives*, edited by Susan Koppelman Cornillon. Bowling Green: Bowling Green University Popular Press, 1972.

Scharfman, Ronnie. "Mirroring and Mothering in Simone Schwartz-Bart's *Pluie et vent sur Télumée Miracle* and Jean Rhys's *Wide Sargasso Sea*." *Yale French Studies* 62 (1981): 88–106.

Scholes, Robert, and Robert Kellogg. *The Nature of Narrative*. Oxford: Oxford University Press, 1966.

Searle, John R. *Speech Acts: An Essay in the Philosophy of Language*. Cambridge: Cambridge University Press, 1969.

Showalter, Elaine. *The Female Malady: Women, Madness, and English Culture, 1830–1980*. New York: Pantheon Books, 1985.

———. "Feminist Criticism in the Wilderness." *Critical Inquiry* 8 (1981): 179–205.

———. *A Literature of Their Own: British Women Novelists from Brontë to Lessing*. Princeton: Princeton University Press, 1977.

Spacks, Patricia Meyer. *The Female Imagination*. New York: Avon Books, 1975.

Spivak, Gayatri Chakravorty. "Displacement and the Discourse of Woman." Pp. 169–95 in *Displacement: Derrida and After*, edited by Mark Krupnick. Bloomington: Indiana University Press, 1983.

———. "Finding Feminist Readings: Dante-Yeats." *Social Text* 3 (1980): 73–87.

Staley, Thomas. *Jean Rhys: A Critical Study*. London: Macmillan, 1979.

Stone, Lawrence. *The Family, Sex and Marriage in England, 1500–1800*. London: Weidenfeld and Nicholson, 1977.

Strouse, Jean. *Alice James: A Biography*. Boston: Houghton Mifflin, 1980.

Suleiman, Susan R., and Inge Crosman, eds. *The Reader in the Text: Essays on Audience and Interpretation*. Princeton: Princeton University Press, 1980.

Thorpe, Michael. "'The Other Side': *Wide Sargasso Sea* and *Jane Eyre*." *Ariel* 8 (1977): 99–127.

Tompkins, Jane P., ed. *Reader-Response Criticism: From Formalism to Post-Structuralism*. Baltimore: Johns Hopkins University Press, 1980.

Vreeland, Elizabeth. "Jean Rhys: The Art of Fiction LXIV." *Paris Review* 76 (1979): 219–37.

Wadlington, Warwick. *Reading Faulknerian Tragedy*. Ithaca: Cornell University Press, 1987.

Wharton, Edith. *The House of Mirth*. New York: Signet Books, 1964.

Williams, Angela. "The Flamboyant Tree: The World of the Jean Rhys Heroine." *Planet*, August 1976, pp. 35–41.

Wilson, W. Daniel. "Readers in Texts." *PMLA* 96 (1981): 848–63.

Wittig, Monique. *Les Guérillères*. Translated by David Le Vay. New York: Avon Books, 1973.

_____. *The Lesbian Body*. Translated by David Le Vay. New York: Avon Books, 1976.

Woolf, Virginia. *The Letters of Virginia Woolf. Volume 5:1932–35*. Edited by Nigel Nicholson and Joanne Trautmann. New York: Harcourt Brace Jovanovich, 1979.

_____. "Phases of Fiction." Pp. 93–145 in *Granite and Rainbow*. New York: Harcourt Brace Jovanovich, 1958.

_____. *A Room of One's Own*. New York: Harcourt, Brace & World, 1957.

Wyndham, Francis. Introduction to *Wide Sargasso Sea*. London: Penguin Books, 1968. Reprinted from *Art and Literature*, No. 1.

Yeazell, Ruth Bernard. *The Death and Letters of Alice James*. Berkeley and Los Angeles: University of California Press, 1981.

INDEX